Professional Men

Also by W. J. Reader

MEN AND MACHINES
(with Charles Wilson)

PROFESSIONAL MEN

The Rise of the Professional Classes
in Nineteenth-Century England

W. J. READER

Basic Books, Inc., *Publishers*
New York

Printed in Great Britain

CONTENTS

PREFACE

In 1933 Sir Alexander Carr-Saunders and P. A. Wilson, in the preface to *The Professions*, remarked how little attention had been paid to the history of the English professions, in spite of their great and growing importance. More than thirty years later, the field is still sparingly cultivated, which is why I have ventured into it. As the title indicates, I have made no attempt at a full comparison with the nineteenth-century professional classes abroad, though some of the more important aspects of the matter are touched upon in Chapters 7 and 12.

I should like to thank Professor C. H. Wilson for seeking to remove some of the book's weaknesses; any that remain are my fault, not his. Professor Bernard Crick has also been kind enough to comment on the typescript. I am indebted to Mr K. M. Reader for access to published and unpublished material in the archives of the Civil Service Commission, and to Lord Weir for permission to draw on private papers. My wife has directed my attention to sources of information on her own profession – medicine.

Mrs W. V. C. Maffett and Mrs W. Meek have both allowed me to impose on them to the extent of reading the book more than once at various stages, and Mrs Meek has undertaken a number of wearisome calculations. In recording my thanks to her I must point out that I am far from wishing to impute to her any responsibility for any misuse I may have made of her work.

W. J. R.

Highgate, February 1966

Chapter 1

DIVINITY, PHYSIC AND LAW

'THE importance of the professions and the professional classes can hardly be overrated, they form the head of the great English middle class, maintain its tone of independence, keep up to the mark its standard of morality, and direct its intelligence.'[1] These words were written in 1857 by H. Byerley Thomson (1822–67) who, after University College London and Jesus College Cambridge, had himself taken to the profession of the law, and who lived to become a legal author of some eminence. He was about thirty-five in 1857 and he may perhaps be taken as representative of the professional men of his day. As such, he felt himself a member of the middle class, yet conscious of distinctions within that class, and the particular marks of professional standing which he stressed were independence, morality and intelligence. His remarks give a good general indication of what this book is about.

It is not a history of the professions. It does not attempt to define a profession in general terms, preferring rather to let the definition emerge rather hazily – as it does in real life – from the discussion of particular cases. It is a study of the English middle classes in the nineteenth century, at a time when they had, and knew that they had, more power and influence in the national life than ever before: a time when Richard Cobden could say to the House of Commons: 'If you talk of your aristocracy and your traditions, and compel me to talk of the middle and industrious classes, I say it is to them that the glory of this country is owing.'[2] And it is especially a study of the English middle classes at three of their characteristic activities: earning a living, raising the moral tone of society, and social climbing. They did all these things with great energy and earnestness, and each reacted on the others to

1

produce a conception of the professions which, with its subtle blend of self-interest and public spirit, is perfectly intelligible to us today.

It is intelligible because the professions as we know them are very much a Victorian creation, brought into being to serve the needs of an industrial society. But, like so much else in Victorian England, they took on some of the outward forms of older and very different institutions. If we want to get to the root of what the Victorians were doing when they set about constructing – quite self-consciously – their image of what a profession, a professional man and professional conduct ought to be, we have to begin by looking at some aspects of English society as it was before the great nineteenth-century transformations set in. And we have to bear in mind that on the one hand much had begun to change before Victoria's time, but on the other hand many attitudes and institutions characteristic of the eighteenth century survived well into the middle of the nineteenth. All of which is only to say that people do not as a rule conduct their affairs neatly, logically or with a due sense of period, and this applies to the development of the professions as much as to anything else in history. With these qualifications stated, therefore, let us look at the eighteenth-century origins of Victorian professional life.

In the eighteenth century English society still drew most of its wealth pretty directly from the land. It always had done so and most people thought it always would: no other possibility presented itself. Most of the land was firmly in private ownership, and the possession of land was at the root of the most important political, legal and social assumptions. Not, however, the possession of land by an individual. The holder of an estate for the time being was fundamentally looked upon more or less as a life tenant, managing the estate for the benefit of his descendants and of his family generally, as much as for himself, and the legal system was well adapted to see that he did so.[3] It could not always avert the consequences of selfishness or folly, but the intention behind it was clear, and the landed family rather than the individual landed gentleman was the central unit of eighteenth-century society.

This had an important effect on the way the gentry looked upon the matter of getting a living. Since the prestige of the gentry was immense, it also affected the way the matter of getting a living was looked upon in the country at large, particularly among those classes who fancied their chances of becoming gentry themselves. Nor were their chances all that poor. The framework of society was rigid, but movement within it was fairly free if you were able, fortunate, and, no doubt, ruthless. The folksong which traces 'the little ploughboy Who whistled o'er the lea' to a seat in the House of Lords is no doubt a fiction, but there is nothing fictitious about Bubb Dodington (1691–1762), who from very obscure origins became Lord Melcombe, or about Sir Matthew Wood (1768–1843), the Tiverton serge-maker's son who became Lord Mayor of London, or about a number of other Georgian worthies. It was by no means idle fancy which prompted the ambitious merchant, apothecary or attorney to model his attitudes on the attitudes of those above him.

In the matter of getting a living, the essential point about landed property was that it broke the direct connection between work and income which governed the life of the ordinary middle-class man. It gave him independence, that first necessity of gentlemanly life. Income, in fact, from the point of view of a landed family, was a matter of social standing. A member of such a family ought to have 'a competence' – that is, enough money to live like a gentleman – and he expected to find it, directly or indirectly, through his family connections.

The direct claim arose from the fact that a landed estate was not primarily regarded as a commercial undertaking. Many landowners were shrewd men of business. They had to be in order to survive, especially in the eighteenth century, when many of the smaller estates disappeared. But profit was not, or was assumed not to be, the main object. The estate was there to support a family, and to enable it to take its due position in society. For that more was needed than money: in particular a local connection – ancient if possible – as a foundation for influence and authority.

If this was what an estate was for, it meant that the family in possession, for its own credit, must provide for its members according to their sex and standing, which gave each of them a claim, greater or less, directly on the revenues of the estate. Among the women it meant proper provision for daughters on marriage and often, in the case of spinsters or widows, maintenance for life after the fashion of Squire Western's sister in *Tom Jones*. Among the men, with whom we are mainly concerned, the claim diminished from that of the eldest son downwards through his younger brothers, and might extend in attenuated form to more distant relations. So far as the sons of the house were concerned, the eldest would inherit the estate, and with it a burden of obligations to other members of the family, varying in formality from enforceable legal contracts such as those which guaranteed a dowager's jointure to *ex gratia* tips and subsidies. The younger sons would expect education and, at the outset of their careers, more or less prolonged and heavy financing, depending on what their father could or would afford. All this expense was in one way or another a charge on the estate, either on its income or, by way of mortgage, on its capital.

Expensive backing – which might go on for years – was almost indispensable as the foundation of a career, for salaried employment in the modern sense, either in government or private employ, was by no means readily come by. How to find the money to get a start, therefore, was the perennial problem of the young man and his parents, and it will crop up again and again in this book. In the eighteenth century, when wealth was so heavily concentrated among the land-owners, it could be found much more readily and plentifully by the gentry than by any other class.

There was more to it than that. Belonging to a landed family, or being connected with one, gave not only direct access to private fortunes. It gave something which might be even more important: access to patronage, which meant access to the revenues of Church and State. With 'interest' you might hope to be comfortably independent almost as soon as you were grown up: without, you might be poverty-stricken until you died. And patronage was linked very closely with property and political power.

Until well into the nineteenth century patronage was one of the central facts of life, especially for those who had no independent source of income and had to find means to earn their living. You might not like patronage, unless it was on your side, but you had to accept that it existed, that it was respectable, that it was the only known method of selection for a great many official and unofficial appointments, and that it would generally be exercised for personal, political, or family advantage. That is not to say that patrons would pay no attention to the character or abilities of their nominees. No doubt many of them took these things seriously, especially in cases where their own interest or credit stood to be affected by their nominees' success or failure. But they took the other things into account as well, and they were expected to. Indeed many people would have held that a patron who preferred an able candidate, simply on grounds of his ability, to one of his relations or dependents was behaving improperly, provided that within his own circle he could find someone reasonably competent to take the post.

As late as 1851 Sir James Stephen, an experienced public official, mentioned the difficulty of finding people to serve as Ministers, because of the large private fortune they needed to support the expense, and went on: 'the range of choice will become still more narrow ... if the remuneration of these great offices be further reduced, by depriving the holders of them of all their most valuable patronage ... I never yet served under a Secretary of State who did not, at least, appear to attach a very high interest indeed to the power of giving such places to dependents and friends.'[4] Patronage was part of the national life – almost of the Constitution – and although the more blatant use of it for corrupt purposes was continually deplored and occasionally checked, it was not until the 1850s that people began seriously to take steps to get rid of it.

An eighteenth-century gentleman did not give out that he was looking for a 'job', though his enemies or unsuccessful rivals might suggest that he was seeking one, for the word had over-tones of corrupt patronage and dishonourable conduct. According to Johnson it meant 'petty, piddling work', or a 'low, mean, lucrative, busy affair' (the juxtaposition of adjectives is interest-ing). What the man without a private fortune sought was 'a provision' or 'a competence', and in finding one he would be helped, in what every unprejudiced observer would consider a perfectly justifiable manner, if his friends (which in this context generally meant his family) could bring 'interest' to bear on his behalf.

The sort of thing that could then happen may be plentifully illustrated from, among other sources, the *Dictionary of National Biography*. Lord Kenyon (1732–1802), Master of the Rolls, lived for some years as a young lawyer, on £80 a year from his father, but by the time he himself had sons to provide for he had made his fortune and had official patronage at his disposal, so as his two eldest boys attained their majority he made one *custos brevium* and the other filazer of King's Bench: both appointments were 'valuable sinecures'.

Another successful lawyer who did well for himself and then for his family was Joseph Phillimore (1775–1855). He went into Parliament and from 1822 to 1828 he was on the Board of Control for India. One of his sons was a clerk to the Board from 1827 to 1832: another from 1832 to 1835. This second son, who became Sir Robert Phillimore, was a friend of Gladstone from Oxford onwards and, like his father, a prominent lawyer in admiralty and ecclesiastical courts. Greville Phillimore, the third son, took orders and was presented eventually to the valuable Crown living of Ewelme, not far from Oxford. No doubt this was an extremely able family: no doubt, also, family 'interest' was of great value to them in their careers.

With or without patronage, the range of occupations open to a young man of the upper classes, before the industrial age, was narrow. Trade, in the ordinary contemporary meaning of the word, was beneath him: partly because commercial morality was not high and its associations were all rather grubby, partly for the simple reason that it did not pay enough. 'Trade' was what the blacksmith did, or the carpenter, or the tailor, or any other skilled craftsman, and there certainly was not a gentlemanly competence in that. 'Trade', also, was retail shopkeeping: again, not likely to be highly profitable, though no doubt there were exceptions.

The only trade likely to attract the gentry, except in desperation, was the trade of a really large merchant, and to get a place in that, by marriage or otherwise, they were often willing to sink their social prejudices. Large merchants, after all, were indistinguishable from gentry, especially after a generation or two. But there were not many of them, they had their own families to think of, and really desirable openings were few. Manufacturing industry in the modern sense barely existed in the eighteenth century, outside the large breweries and perhaps a few engineering establishments. A manufacturer was someone who made things by hand – a trades-man – not a factory owner. There was nothing for a young gentleman in that direction.

Science and technology might provide an agreeable means of spending money: hardly of earning it. They were learned diver-sions for country gentlemen: hardly more. 'Perhaps it may be thought,' wrote R. L. Edgeworth in 1808, in his book on pro-fessional education, 'that much skill in mechanics would be necessary to enable a country gentleman to judge of the merits of

6

new machines, and to explain their principles to illiterate un-
informed neighbours and tenants; but in fact, the knowledge
necessary for this purpose is so easy, and comprised in so small a
compass, that a few hours well employed are sufficient for the
purpose.' A little further on he suggests that metalwork may be
'an agreeable occupation and amusement in the country' because
'a carpenter or cabinet-maker is to be hired everywhere; but for
optical and astronomical instruments, timekeepers, and various
other works, accurate workmen cannot be easily procured: and
as these employments require invention, as well as execution, they
are peculiarly suited to a gentleman.' And he concludes by sug-
gesting some knowledge of astronomy 'which is indeed peculiarly
suited to a country life'; mineralogy ('at least such a tincture of it
as would prevent his being imposed upon by the finders of mines
and minerals') and chemistry which 'every day promises more and
more to be serviceable to agriculture.'[5] But none of these pursuits
is put forward as a possible basis for a gentleman's livelihood. The
view of science as a fit hobby for well-bred amateurs, but nothing
more, persisted long in England.

The natural occupations of the gentry, from which most of their
notions of proper behaviour were derived, and for which their
upbringing and education were especially supposed to fit them,
were government and war. Government, in the eighteenth century, meant service as a Minister of the Crown, as a Member of
Parliament, as a local magistrate; and in this connection it must be
remembered that the word 'magistrate' was not yet restricted to its
modern meaning of an amateur judge. It had a much wider
significance, and the magistrates in quarter sessions were responsible for all aspects of local administration, not the administration
of justice only.

Most of these occupations were unpaid, in the sense that there
was no fixed salary attached to them. The notion, however, that
they were to be undertaken purely in a spirit of public service,
without thought of reward, although not unknown, was not really
a part of the eighteenth-century outlook. Sir Robert Walpole
made an immense fortune out of being Prime Minister. Members
of Parliament accepted sinecures and places in rather the same
spirit as MPs today accept a salary – there was, after all, no other
way of paying them and they could not all afford to serve at their
own expense, though those who could were inclined to make a

great virtue of it. Ministers in charge of public funds invested them, until they were needed, for their own profit, and the elder Pitt may well have been considered something of a prig for ostentatiously refusing to do so. The Law Officers of the Crown regularly made fortunes out of fees. At the local level, probably, there was less to be made (though 'trading justices' were not unknown), but by and large the business of government was not an unprofitable one – if you could get into it.

But the most gentlemanly occupation of all, really, was fighting, particularly on land. Warfare, like government, had founded many a family fortune, and in the eighteenth century the industry had only recently been nationalized: a strong flavour of private enterprise remained. Thus at sea honest sailors had only quite recently been clearly distinguishable from pirates (had not Sir Henry Morgan been a royal official, to say nothing of Sir Francis Drake?), and the line was still fairly easily crossed, especially by privateers in time of war. Even in the Royal Navy, prize money was still the lure. Soldiers had been earlier and rather more reliably differentiated from brigands, but officers still regarded their commissions and colonels their regiments pretty much as their private property and a source of gain (especially the colonels of regiments). Moreover in wartime, on land no less than at sea, there was still the ancient bribe of loot, though not on the spectacular scale of Anson and his Spanish galleons.

The trouble with the Army, in time of peace, was that it was less likely to provide a competence than to tempt a young man to squander his way into debt. An officer bought his commission, and the money he or his parents paid was looked upon as an investment in a life annuity at rather a poor rate of interest. Nobody supposed that a young officer's pay would take him off his family's hands. These are matters we shall go into later (Chapter 4 below). Meanwhile, it may be sufficient to observe that many people in the eighteenth century thought the peacetime officer's life idle and quarrelsome: not good for the moral fibre of the young. Fortunately wars were very frequent.

Navy commissions were not bought, but interest was essential to get one and highly desirable if you hoped for quick promotion. Moreover, admirals were apt to be political animals and that aspect of affairs needed careful watching. But the pay, even low down, was just enough to live on, and from captain upwards there was

8

quite a good chance of making money. The *Journal* of Augustus Hervey (1724–79) gives an insight into the life of a well-connected naval officer (he belonged to the family of the Earls of Bristol, and eventually became third Earl himself) between the years 1746 and 1759. As a captain in and about the Mediterranean he followed the usual practice of carrying treasure and charging 1 per cent on the value of the cargo for doing so. Captains who undercut were not at all popular. Hervey charged the full rate and did very well out of it, and in peacetime he used his ship very much as a private yacht. In wartime a fortunate or well-contrived posting – 'interest' again – to a station where rich merchantmen might be captured could yield a very large fortune indeed: enough to found a noble family. Even warships were worth having after the Government had sensibly altered the prize-money regulations to make them so, in order to induce sea-officers not to neglect them.[6] Conditions of life were rough, but they appalled the eighteenth-century mind less than ours and the compensation might be substantial.

For anyone who wanted to get rich very quickly indeed, and was prepared to face the high probability of dying in the attempt, there was the East India Company's civil or military service, if he could get a Director to nominate him. The risks were enormous – the rewards in proportion. Professor Parkinson has suggested that between 1760 and 1834 about one cadet in four sent to India lived to return to England: a chance of survival which compares very badly with the chance of being killed in the army in France in the Great War. But the one who returned, unlike the returning Great War soldier, would be wealthy: perhaps very wealthy indeed. Lord Lake and his son – no doubt an exceptional case, but it shows what could be done – were reliably said to have made £300,000 between them in six years.[7]

East India patronage was for the few. For the generality of those who had a claim to be considered gentlemen the occupations conventionally considered most suitable, apart from government and the armed services, were the 'liberal professions', and of these there were only three: divinity, physic, and law.

'Profession', by itself, was a word that could be used of any 'calling, vocation, known employment' (Johnson), and it frequently turns up in the phrase 'mechanical professions', meaning the trades of skilled workmen. The force of much that later came to be absorbed into the word 'profession' was carried in the adjective 'liberal', which meant that the essential qualification for entry into any of these three occupations, which were sometimes also called the 'learned' professions, was a liberal education: that is, the education of a gentleman, not of a trader or an artisan.

Liberal education, as the term was usually understood in the eighteenth century (and long afterwards), was based firmly upon the classics: that is, upon Greek and Latin literature, and on mathematics, meaning chiefly the systems of geometrical reasoning associated particularly with the name of Euclid. The more thoughtful defenders of the system, such as William Whewell in 1845, did not put it forward as 'a complete scheme of human knowledge', and Whewell himself was very conscious of the immense advances in knowledge that were being made in his own day. What was claimed, by him and others, was that the study of ancient authors trained literary taste and the use of language, and that the study of mathematics trained the powers of reasoning. It was also claimed, as Whewell put it, that the classics 'have supplied the subject of sympathy among civilized nations ever since civilization began; at least the civilization with which the European world is concerned', and that classical studies therefore 'connect a man's mind with the general mind of the human race.' If the question of practical or vocational training was raised, the answer was that the mental gymnastics required to master the classics and mathematics would so train a man's mind that in later life he would be able to tackle any subject he might require. Technical training might be good enough for the narrow purposes of a craftsman or trader, but for a gentleman who might have to deal with wide issues of government and policy, it was much more important to grasp general principles of intellectual activity: his education should teach him how to learn.[8]

This was by no means a contemptible theory, especially for a society which might expect the general body of knowledge to remain fairly small and unchanging, and to be manageable by any well-trained mind. Its dangers, in a swiftly developing industrial society increasingly reliant on knowledge and habits of thought undreamt of in classical times, will become clear in the later chapters of this book. Meanwhile it is necessary to point out that theories rarely work out perfectly in practice and that the social overtones of the liberal education, explicitly designed as it was for the upper classes, made many people pursue it for reasons which had nothing much to do with education. It might not of itself make you a gentleman, but without it a gentleman you could hardly hope to be.

This was true of what it left out as much as of what it included, and if you took your social standing seriously there were subjects best not meddled in too deeply: not, at any rate, as Edgeworth implies, much beyond the stage of elegant recreation. This was unfortunate for those who had no turn of mind for the classics but had other aptitudes less educationally and, therefore, socially acceptable. As Addison remarked of Will Wimble, 'younger Brother to a Baronet', whose abilities, practical rather than academic, had been neglected because they were socially rather discreditable: 'The same Temper of Mind and Application to Affairs might have recommended him to the publick Esteem, and have raised his Fortune in another Station of Life. What Good to his Country or himself might not a Trader or Merchant have done with such useful tho' ordinary Qualifications?'[9] And indeed the social glamour of the classical training, quite apart from educational or vocational considerations, was to colour the Englishman's view of his schooling – still more, of his son's schooling – right through the nineteenth century and beyond, with profound results on the national life. And it particularly influenced the classes with which we are most concerned: the classes which produced professional men.

Against liberal education and its prestige, professional education made a poor showing. No doubt it was desirable that a clergyman, a physician, or a barrister should have the knowledge and skill appropriate to his calling, and in the latter two he could hardly hope to prosper without it. But nobody made any very serious efforts to systematize the means of acquiring it, and nobody thought it necessary to make any strict enquiry into a young man's knowledge of divinity, physic, or law before he took up the practice of those professions. It was, after all, assumed that a gentleman who had had a liberal education could learn the rest fairly easily when the need arose. Qualification by written examination, today often quoted as one of the marks of professional standing, was in no profession enforced until long after the end of the eighteenth century.

The mother of all the learned professions was the Church. Before the Puseyites began to spread their exalted notions of priestly dignity; before open scepticism, on the other hand, became widespread and respectable, it was far less a profession set apart. It was the natural occupation for men of bookish tastes – even, perhaps, of a scientific turn of mind – who had no private fortune. The Church dominated the universities and the endowed schools, and the normal route to fellowships, professorships and headmasterships lay through holy orders. The ordinary clergyman was a country parson, but he could easily be a schoolmaster as well. James Mayo, Vicar of Avebury, Wiltshire, towards the end of the eighteenth century, was many years headmaster of Queen Elizabeth's Grammar School at Wimborne, fifty miles away in Dorset – apparently a notable piece of clerical commuting, though no doubt he had a curate and perhaps an under-master. Outside the schools, a private tutor in a noble household might hope for very lucrative preferment if he behaved himself: why not a bishopric, even? And the parson had plenty of time, as the long roll of clerical authors shows.

A parson need not be a scholar. Many men of no intellectual pretensions at all who sought a decent unexciting livelihood, and whose consciences did not strain at a general acceptance of the doctrines of the Church of England, found the prospect of holy orders very agreeable. For a few the Church was a compelling vocation: for a few at the other end of the scale of sincerity it looked like a road to riches and power. For most it offered a leisured life in the country, lived in very much the same way as the parson's lay neighbours of his own social standing. 'Parsons then [1815] enjoyed a little hunting, shooting and fishing without being railed at,' wrote Sir Roderick Murchison, and went on: 'I thought that I might slide into that sort of comfortable domestic life.'[10] He had been a captain of dragoons, but the prospect of peacetime soldiering did not please him and a demand for classical scholarship put him off the Church. He became a geologist, and in 1855 succeeded Sir Henry De la Bèche as head of the Royal School of Mines.

The Church in the eighteenth century had none of the proud or agonizing separateness of later times. Many people, no doubt, would have agreed with Edgeworth: 'To put a young man of dull understanding, or of unfixed principles, into the church, would be folly or wickedness: but those who are convinced, that education can form the habits and principles, and successfully cultivate the understanding, will feel little apprehension, that a youth, judiciously educated, should fail to do honour to that sacred profession, for which he has been early destined.'[11]

If the Ministry of the Church of England, then, was seen not as a priesthood but as a rational occupation for a gentleman, preferably of bookish tastes, then considerations could be applied to it which could be applied to any other profession. This, in fact, was frequently done by authors of books and articles on it until well into the nineteenth century.[12] What, they enquired, were the expenses of education and starting? What was the return on this investment likely to be? What were the chances of a tolerable livelihood, of promotion, of worldly distinction? How did these things compare with what was offered by the law, medicine, the Army or any other gentlemanly occupation?

'Prudence,' says Edgeworth, 'should prevent [parents] from choosing the clerical profession for a son, unless they are fully able not only to defray the very considerable expenses of his education, but to add to his income, perhaps for many years, what may be sufficient to render him at least independent whilst he continues to be a curate.' This is a plain warning, which Edgeworth goes on to elaborate, that a clerical career was even more dependent than most on patronage. It was worse even than the armed services, for in them, at least in wartime, death and distinguished service might between them make lack of 'interest' less of a barrier to unprivileged ambition. But the Church could hardly be expected to provide the equivalent, in disposing of professional rivals, of 'a bloody war and a sickly season', which it is said that Army officers used to drink to.

If a clergyman's family property included the gift of a living, all was well, and no one would expect that living to go outside the family while there was a candidate within it. There is in Mells Church, Somerset, a memorial to a lady who was daughter to the parson and sister-in-law to the squire. Her husband, in his turn, became Rector of Mells, which shows how these things might be arranged. Or sometimes you could buy the right of presentation to a living. James Bransby, in the eighteenth century, bought a living for his son-in-law, who in turn passed it on to his son. So there were two clergymen provided for, in successive generations, and all competition effectively kept out.[13]

For the Fellow of a college, like James Woodforde the diarist, there would in time be a college living: he had but to wait his time, unmarried. It might be a longish wait. Woodforde himself became a Fellow of New College Oxford in 1761, about two years before he took his BA degree. He got the living of Weston Longeville, Norfolk, in 1774, and went to live there in 1776.[14] The living, when he got it, was a good one, and while he waited he had the income from his fellowship and from various college offices.

As a general rule the safest guarantee of a benefice, as of many other appointments clerical and lay, was parliamentary influence. Edgeworth, with a touch of irony, calls it

'beneficial, as it tempts parents of good families and fortunes to educate younger sons for the church ... who ... may, by their manners and rank, raise the whole profession in the esteem and respect of the public. Church benefices may thus be considered a fund for the provision of the younger sons of our gentry and nobles; and in this point of view, it cannot surely be a matter of complaint to any of the higher and middle classes in the community, that the clergy enjoy a large portion of the riches of the state.'[15]

Without 'interest' the clergyman's prospects were very poor, since intellectual or other qualifications were very frail reeds to rely upon. These considerations applied with increasing force all the way up the ladder to the Bench of Bishops who, having seats in the House of Lords, were political figures in their own right. Their hopes of translation from poor sees to rich ones depended entirely on the goodwill of the Government and they were expected to behave accordingly.[16]

The friendless clergyman was little, if any, better off than the working man. He might find himself, for life, a starveling curate on £30 a year or so, or the despised hanger-on of some great man, and in either case he might be turned out of his place at a moment's notice for any reason or none, save that his patron wished it so. If he managed to get a living he would at least have security, but nothing more, for there were many livings, especially in the north and in Wales, which were much too poor to attract anyone who had the remotest prospect of anything better. It was often impossible to find university men to fill them. Bishops were forced back to ordaining 'literates' who may or may not have been good Christians but were most unlikely to be educated men: a serious matter in an age when the parson might have to attend to many things in his parish which people in later times could do for themselves or could find specialized professional advice for.[17] The poverty-stricken clergyman was a perennial scandal, particularly on account of the pathetic and discreditable shifts he might be driven to in his search for a livelihood.

But the clergyman of the Established Church, poor though he might be, was everywhere considered a gentleman, fit for at least token recognition by the best society of his neighbourhood, and commonly for a good deal more. This could not be said of any dissenting minister. He gained no social prestige at all, but rather the reverse, from his occupation, because the Dissenters, as the word implies, had only a precarious legal existence. They were 'tolerated', not 'established', and the social standing to be derived from any occupation was closely related to its position in the State.

In this respect the Church of England was unassailable. It was an essential constituent of the State, co-terminous with the civil power and in some people's view superior to it, though that opinion was less fashionable in the eighteenth century than it became in the nineteenth. The clergyman was therefore an official of the Establishment, properly so-called, just as the Army officer or the judge was, and it was from this aspect of his occupation, rather than from his aspect as a minister of the Gospel, that he drew his social standing, in so far as he drew it from his occupation at all, and not from his family background. It will appear in Chapter 10 that the social standing of other professions also has frequently been judged, in part, by their constitutional importance, and that the distribution of honours by the Crown – particularly peerages – has been narrowly watched as an index of it.

The clergyman was also respected, no doubt, for his learning, and Thomson considered that improved education had raised the Church 'from the degrading place it socially occupied in the reigns of the Stuarts'. A modern writer has been inclined to place at least as much importance on the rise in the value of incomes from land, on which the clergy chiefly depended.[18] However that may be, education was certainly an important element in a clergyman's professional standing, and it was another thing which came to be regarded as important in judging professional standing generally. From the point of view of the socially ambitious, the great virtue of education was that it could be acquired, whereas a string of ancestors could not, and for that reason the placing of a son in the Church was often a sign of a family's rise in the social scale, as George Eliot makes clear in more than one of her novels.[19] As the number of professions multiplied, the opportunities for this sort of thing, without the necessity of taking orders, multiplied also.

Alongside the eighteenth-century clergy in social estimation stood a few of the eighteenth-century doctors. We say 'a few' because reputable medical men were by custom considered to be divided into three orders: physicians, surgeons, and apothecaries. Of these, in the eighteenth century, only physicians had a clear title to rank among the learned professions. The others, whom we shall consider in the next chapter, had by no means separated themselves from 'trade', in the sense of skilled handicraft (surgeons) and retail selling (apothecaries).

Physicians, strictly speaking, were Fellows and licentiates of the Royal College of Physicians of London (1518) or members of similar colleges set up in Dublin and Edinburgh in the seventeenth century. Holders of degrees in physic from the universities might also qualify for the title, though not necessarily by depth of professional knowledge, as we shall see. The government of the profession, so far as England was concerned, lay entirely with the Fellows of the Royal College, and the licences they granted conferred the right to practice within their jurisdiction (London and seven miles roundabout) but nothing more – no say, that is, in the running of the affairs of the College. The College, by the end of the eighteenth century, had a brilliant but distant past, a torpid present and, many people hoped, no future.

It was a very small body. Between 1771 and 1833, both years inclusive, 168 Fellows were admitted, and the number of licentiates about equalled the number of Fellows. Its general character may be judged from its policy for admitting Fellows. It habitually, and as many people held, illegally, refused to admit anyone who was not a graduate of Oxford or Cambridge, although neither university, for many years, gave any medical education at all. A side effect of this policy was that it kept out anyone who was not a member of the Church of England: an exclusion bitterly resented by Dissenters.

In 1834 a Select Committee of the House of Commons investigated the state of medical education. It was not friendly to the Physicians (nor to their sister institution, the Royal College of

Surgeons, which we consider in the next chapter), and it did its best to build up a case against them. Even allowing for this bias, the evidence which the Committee routed out is as convincing now as it was then, when it had a considerable effect on public opinion. The Chairman was Henry Warburton and the members included Lord Howick, son of Lord Grey of the Reform Bill, Henry Halford, whose father was President of the Royal College of Physicians, Daniel O'Connell, Thomas Spring-Rice, Joseph Hume, Lord Oxmantown, and Sir Robert Peel.

The Physicians' prejudice in favour of Oxford and Cambridge was very thoroughly probed. Sir Henry Halford, the Physicians' President, was driven to admit 'a certain preference of those members [of the universities of Oxford and Cambridge]; for they ... have undergone a moral and intellectual trial ... to which they are not subjected at the foreign universities [in which he included the Scottish universities].' The moral trial consisted of residence in college: the intellectual, of the conventional classical training. 'I think,' said Sir Henry, 'a knowledge of both languages, a knowledge of mathematics, are absolutely necessary with reference to the dignity and respectability of the profession.'

Here he touched on a point of great importance to the Physicians: their standing as gentlemen. So much emphasis did they place on it, in fact, that they rather spoilt their case. Evidently their social standing was by no means so secure as they would have liked. Their concern for it had a solid economic justification. They did not practice among the poor, because the fees they charged were much too high. It was as important, therefore, to their pockets as to their pride that they should be able to mingle with the upper classes. A gentlemanly bearing was part of a physician's professional qualifications: as Pelham Warren put it, 'I consider that that class of society look up to a physician as a superior person, and expect superior manners from him.'

The social standing of physicians was attributed by William Macmichael, another witness, 'in the first place' to 'the circumstance of many physicians in this country being educated at the English universities. There they have the same education as those who fill the highest stations; they are brought up with those persons, and afterwards become physicians. I think the distinguished post which they hold, elevates the whole profession; that all physicians partake of the dignity which their education and their good conduct give.' This touchiness about social standing, so evident among the physicians of 1834, was to be characteristic of the whole medical profession during the nineteenth century and is not, perhaps, entirely absent from doctors' discontents today.

The exclusiveness of the Royal College infuriated doctors who, because they had not been to Oxford or Cambridge, stood no chance, however professionally eminent they might become, of ever being more than licentiates. These men's liberal education might be deficient, but they had usually been professionally trained in medical schools of high repute abroad or in Scotland. At Oxford and Cambridge, the intending physician took his degree in Arts, then went away to study medicine in any way he chose, then came back and took a medical degree. There was no examination because, as John Kydd, Regius Professor of Physic at Oxford, engagingly explained to the Select Committee: 'as it was naturally understood by the university that a person who had given so much time previously to his general education, did not lightly enter upon the study of any particular branch, it was considered that, in lieu of a formal examination, the professor of medicine, or whoever in his place presented to a degree, might satisfy himself that the candidate was well grounded in it; and upon his testimony, the university granted the degree'. At Cambridge until about 1825, when an examination came to be insisted upon, they seem to have taken much the same view. They contented themselves with purely formal exercises before a degree was conferred.

The degrees so granted carried the right to practise throughout England, as well as opening the door to a Fellowship of the Royal College of Physicians. No wonder the licentiates were bitter. No wonder they fought to get into the College, usually by litigation but once, in 1767, by force of arms. In 1834 they still felt themselves, as John Yelloly put it, 'in a sort of vassalage.'

The Physicians prided themselves on being learned men, but not especially on their medical learning. This may have been because there was little to be medically learned about. 'The amount of medical knowledge adequate for work was at that time still very small,' says a modern medical historian. 'It consisted essentially of the art of treatment by drugs and the writing of complicated prescriptions.'[20] Evidence given by several witnesses before the Select Committee of 1834 bears Dr Newman's judgement out. The College's examination for the Fellowship was entirely oral and might take about two hours for three or four candidates. It was conducted entirely in Latin. 'There is no English talked at the Board', said Sir Henry Halford, and both he and others made it plain that classical scholarship and its traditional accompaniments were the accomplishments above all others which he and other physicians of his time really valued.

It is fairly clear that the physician's chief professional asset was an impressive manner, bolstered by experience and guarded by elaborate etiquette, of which one of the cardinal rules was to make certain that the patient knew of no difference of opinion that might arise in consultation. No doubt that was good for the patient's peace of mind, but was that the only consideration? 'I was dining at the Duke of Richmond's one day last winter,' wrote the physician Thomas Young about 1800, 'and there came in two notes, one from Sir W. Farquhar, and the other from Dr Hunter, in answer to an enquiry whether or no His Grace might venture to eat fruit pies or strawberries. I trembled for the honour of the profession, and could not conceal my apprehensions from the company: luckily, however, they agreed tolerably well, the only difference of opinion being on the subject of the pie-crust.'[21]

A physician's success might be long in coming, if indeed it ever came. Sir Henry Halford had an income over £10,000 a year for many years, but during his first six years in practice his income varied between £164 (1793) and £511 (1797).[22] All those who gave advice on the choice of a profession indicated that an intending physician needed a private income or support from his friends to see him through his training and the early years of practice: the more so since he could not hope to attract patients unless he could make an outward show of prosperity, or at least of decent gentlemanly circumstances.

Professional success in the end depended on personal qualities rather than on patronage, and for that reason the profession of physic may have offered slightly more hope of advancement to the uninfluential than the Church or the Army. It is also probably the reason why few men from great families seem to have taken up physic. They could use the backing of their relations much more advantageously in other fields.

In particular, parliamentary connections were of far less consequence to the rising physician than, say, to the ambitious parson, officer, or lawyer. What were useful were connections within the profession, which were widespread. Thus Thomas Young (1773–1829) was the son of Quaker parents of Milverton in Somerset – not, on the face of it, a promising background for an intending physician. But he was a brilliant boy and he was taken up by his great-uncle Richard Brocklesby, who was already a successful London physician, and was introduced by him to the circle of the Duke of Richmond.[23] His nephew, in turn, became physician to the Nawab of Bengal: no doubt a paying, if precarious, appointment. Another nephew was a surgeon in Sackville Street.[24] If we glance at another medical family, we find that J. A. Wilson, a distinguished Victorian physician (1795–1883), was the son of a surgeon of considerable reputation, grandson of a Wellingborough doctor, and nephew to two 'distinguished accoucheurs in London', Dr John Clarke and Sir Charles Mansfield Clarke. His mother's sister married Dr Stone, physician to the Charterhouse, and his cousin T. A. Stone inherited much of the practice of the Clarkes.[25] Despite the aloofness of the physicians, it is apparent that members of the same family often went into different branches of the medical profession and contributed to each other's prosperity by doing so. We shall notice much the same phenomenon among the lawyers.

Family connections, together with the influence of the Royal Colleges, and to some extent parliamentary considerations, dominated the coveted appointments to London hospitals which could be the basis of wide and fashionable practice. These appointments were usually in the hands of the governing bodies of the hospitals, and a serious candidate would find he had to canvass the voters exactly as he would if he were standing for Parliament, and there might be 150 or so of them. Young, commenting on his election as one of the physicians to St George's Hospital in 1811, describes the sort of influences that came into play: 'Local interest and the protracted efforts of a whole family made the Cabells very naturally confident ... parliamentary influence and the natural wish to serve a man who is likely to be Lord Chancellor, made Sir S. Romilly's nephew very formidable; and for myself the event speaks.' In this election 146 votes were cast. The relative professional competence of the candidates does not seem to have carried much weight.[26]

By the beginning of the nineteenth century the professional pre-eminence of the physicians was being strongly challenged.

Most of the new thought on medical matters, including new thought on professional organization and training, was growing among the despised surgeons and apothecaries. But for the present they were still very much the lower branch of the profession – the 'general practitioners', a term, not of honour, that came into use round about this time. The physicians were fighting a determined defensive action, not at all to their own credit or ultimate advantage.

The third of the liberal professions, the law, was also divided. There was an upper branch – the Bar, and a lower branch – the attorneys and solicitors. Only the Bar was considered to have any claim to superior social standing, and there is little doubt that the barrister's claim was derived primarily from the fundamental importance of the law in the constitution, just as the clergyman's claim was derived from the constitutional importance of the Church. Some of the greatest officers of the State were lawyers, just as the bishops, on the side of the Church, were also great public figures. Until Tudor times, indeed, the two professions had been in some degree united, in so far as churchmen had been canon lawyers and the Lord Chancellor had normally been a great prelate.

The Common Law Bar, however, had a long history of lay independence, running well back into the Middle Ages, and it may perhaps be considered as the first of the lay professions to stand anywhere near the Church in public esteem. Its origins were obscure and its organization was correspondingly ill-defined, regulated by ancient custom rather than by precise written statutes, which of course was enormously convenient for the lawyers, if for no one else. They were grouped, as they still are, in four ancient unincorporated private clubs, responsible to no outside authority and of an indefinite but privileged legal standing. These clubs – the Inns of Court – determined and determine absolutely who should be allowed to practise as a barrister in England.

The Inns of Court were supposed to be, among other things, places of legal education, but in fact the manner in which an intending barrister set about learning law was left very much to himself. He could go to the university, though by the end of the eighteenth century comparatively few did, because the English universities were neglecting legal studies as much as all other branches of professional education. Nevertheless for those who could afford time and money there was the somewhat debatable advantage of the conventional liberal education. There were also the more solid attractions of forming useful connections and of possibly getting a Fellowship to endow the hungry start of a career at the Bar. Charles Abbott (1762–1832), the Canterbury wig-maker's son who became Lord Tenterden, Chief Justice of King's Bench, did very well in both ways. He was a Fellow and tutor of Christ Church, Oxford, and one of his pupils was the son of a judge, who advised him to take up the law.[27] The usual method of learning to be a barrister was a mixture of apprenticeship and private reading, which we shall consider in its place, and virtually the only formal requirement, apart from the payment of fees, was to appear at one's Inn often enough to eat a stipulated number of dinners, which was not so eccentric as it sounds since, in theory at least, it was a method by which all the members of the profession, senior and junior, could get to know each other.

Many were called to the Bar who had no intention of practising. A country gentleman found legal knowledge useful both in the administration of his property and in the work of local govern-ment, and there were others, particularly in the nineteenth century, who became barristers in the hope of picking up official appointments for which a legal qualification was necessary, as well as patronage. Those who did intend to practise found their in-tention difficult to realize: the briefless barrister was an all too familiar figure. Patronage could hardly help them because, as many writers pointed out, no one was likely to entrust his in-terests, his property, perhaps his liberty or his life, to anyone who was recommended on grounds of friendship alone. There was really no substitute for professional ability (which did not neces-sarily mean a deep knowledge of law), but it could be powerfully aided, just as in the case of the physicians, by family connections within the profession, especially if they included attorneys.

Since patronage was comparatively unimportant, the Bar offered an opportunity to those who had little to rely on but their wits and energy, and some eminent lawyers, like Lord Tenterden, came from comparatively humble origins, or at any rate from origins where neither money nor interest was plentiful. Scots were called to the English Bar in considerable numbers. Some, like Boswell, cut no particular figure at it. Others, like Lord Mansfield, rose to the heights.

The heights, for the few who could get there, were very high and very lucrative indeed, providing both places of great honour in the State and the opportunity of very large fees. Lord Kenyon (1732–1802), according to the *Dictionary of National Biography*, 'made £80,000 in 16 years; his fees for opinions on cases alone were in 1780, 2,578 guineas, in 1781, 2,936 guineas; and in 1782, 3,020 guineas ... his gains, which were large, and his savings, which were larger, he invested in land in Wales, often buying estates on indifferent titles; for, as he said, 'if he bought property he would find law to keep it till twenty years' occupation gave him a title better than deeds.' No wonder the country gentry found it advisable to know the law.

Between the great men like this and the barristers who never got a brief there was little in the way of comfortable, undistinguished livelihood. This is not to say that there were no barristers who made a living without making a fortune: of course there were. But they were comparatively few, and a career of this sort was much more easily made in the 'lower branch', among the attorneys, whom we shall consider in detail in the next chapter. During the eighteenth century the division of labour between them and the barristers was setting hard into something like its modern form – very largely, it would seem, at the attorneys' insistence. No doubt that is the main reason why the uneasy relationship between the two branches of the law has rumbled on right up to the present day, rather than disappearing, as the distinctions between the doctors did, under the insistent attacks of those on the lower side of the division.

The three 'liberal professions' of the eighteenth century were the nucleus about which the professional class of the nineteenth century was to form. We have seen that they were united by the bond of classical education: that their broad and ill-defined functions covered much that later would crystallize out into new, specialized, occupations: that each, ultimately, derived much of its standing from its connection with the established order in the State, and that for this reason the parsons and the lawyers had a much more certain claim to social recognition than the doctors.

It was this connection with the State, as well as their reputation for polite learning, which made the professions generally acceptable as occupations fit for gentlemen, and for that reason especially attractive to the rising middle class. They were also, of course, profitable. Two of the liberal professions had lower branches which the middle classes already occupied in force. Why, it might reasonably be argued, should they not be equal in status with the upper branches? Why should a surgeon be socially inferior to a physician: an attorney to a barrister? There were, in fact, some quite compelling reasons. These the members of the lower branches were well aware of and, as their ambitions grew, they struggled to eliminate them.

Chapter 2

THE LOWER BRANCHES

DR JOHNSON is reported to have said that he didn't care to speak ill of any man behind his back, but he believed the gentleman was an attorney.[1] In this, as in many of his remarks, Johnson was giving more or less memorable expression to one of the common prejudices of his time. The eighteenth-century attorney was one of those stock figures of ridicule and contempt which every age seems to stand in need of: a convenient scapegoat, and at the same time giving just enough cause for offence to colour prejudice with a decent show of reason. So deeply did attorneys feel this public odium that in 1874, by Act of Parliament, they assumed the title of solicitors.[2]

Solicitors had previously been Chancery officials, whereas attorneys had practised at common law. The names differed more than the functions, and they were all fundamentally agents for litigants. Their business was to guide their clients' affairs through the legal maze, making sure that all proper technicalities were observed and adversaries' errors duly taken advantage of. Their position was privileged, in so far as they were 'officers of the court', and the court would not recognize anyone not on the rolls, but their standing in the legal world was low. They were absolutely under the dominion of the judges and they had none of the independence of the barristers, who were liable only to the discipline of their equals organized in the ancient and honourable societies of the Inns of Court.

It followed that the higher knowledge of the law, theoretically, was not a matter for the attorney, but for learned counsel, whose opinion had to be sought and bought whenever it seemed needful. Advocacy was not for the attorney either, but only for the barrister, and the great prizes of the law were utterly beyond him. No attorney could become a judge: still less, Lord Chancellor. Nor, despite the names of the appointments, could he become either Attorney-General or Solicitor-General. And there were a good many other official positions, requiring a legal qualification, which only a barrister might hold.[3]

The attorney might not aspire to the heights of a barrister's career, and even some of the middle ranges of the law were denied to him. Nevertheless, his livelihood was much more secure than a barrister's, especially if a due division of labour was observed. The strength of the attorney's position was that he was the ordinary man's point of contact with the law. If you wanted to assert your rights, or even to know them, the first man you turned to was not learned counsel, but whoever in your particular neighbourhood happened to be practising as an attorney. And if the attorney had his way, you never would get to learned counsel except with the attorney's assistance. This was reasonable, in so far as you would need specialized advice and the attorney would know where best to find it. It also gave the attorneys great power as gate-keepers, and by 1800 they had managed to establish it as a rule of professional etiquette, observed both by themselves and the barristers. The general practitioners of medicine, somewhat similarly placed, have never asserted themselves quite so strongly, though they have done their best. In the eighteenth century the law was mainly concerned with property, especially landed property, and it was by the land, in one way or another, that the attorney might most reasonably expect to make his living. Every sale, every purchase, every settlement of landed property required his services: likewise every dispute, either to compose or prosecute. And there were the wills. His clients need not all be individuals or families. Eighteenth-century life had a large place for corporations, municipal and otherwise. Corporations owned property: they needed attorneys. Moreover they never died and only rarely went out of existence, so that once an attorney was established in a corporation's service he might expect that his children and his children's children after him would be similarly established. In March 1811 Edward Archer Wilde was appointed solicitor to the Royal College of Surgeons and the connection then set up, first with his family and after a hundred years with his firm, has never since been broken.[4]

From purely legal matters it was not difficult to move to the wider business of estate management. From estate management it was a short step to the management of elections. In the waking of industry, from the middle of the eighteenth century onwards, property-owners became more and more concerned with such things as mining rights, the building of canals, the setting up of turnpike trusts. They might even, though rarely, go directly into industry themselves, as the Leveson-Gower family did at Lilleshall in the Shropshire iron district. On the commercial side of the law there were contracts, partnerships, patents and so on, though the importance of these things was more for the nineteenth century than the eighteenth.

This was how the attorney came to be known as 'my man of business'. To take full advantage of his opportunities he needed more than knowledge of the law – that might be a fairly small part of his equipment. He needed shrewdness in money matters, in agriculture, in politics, and indeed in almost every aspect of practical life. Inside the eighteenth-century attorney half a dozen later professional men – the accountant, the land agent, the company secretary, and others – were struggling to get out.

Such might be the activities of respectable attorneys.

There were also the unrespectable, living perhaps by collecting petty debts bought at a discount, or on the gleanings of the criminal law. There was William Wreathocke, attorney and high-wayman, condemned to death in 1735, reprieved, transported, returned, and eventually struck off the roll in 1756. He may have been concerned in an action in which one highwayman sued another, in terms suitably disguised, for his share of their swag. The disguise was penetrated, both parties were hanged, and the solicitors for the plaintiff were attached and fined. One of them was later transported. Then there was Frazer, whose articled clerk turned out to be a turnkey of the King's Bench Prison. Frazer was taken to court by outraged colleagues and 'the Court were all very clear that these articles were merely collusive; that the whole was a contrivance between Frazer and the Turnkey to secure the business arising from the Prisoners; that the exercise of the office of a Turnkey in a Prison was . . . a very improper education for the profession of an Attorney; and that these Articles ought to be cancelled.'[5]

It was men like Wreathocke, Frazer and Landen Jones, an

attorney who was pilloried in 1744, who got attorneys their bad name, and it became evident to reputable members of the profession that they would never get their claims to higher standing taken seriously unless they actively discountenanced and deterred disgraceful practices. In or before 1739, therefore, they took a step which has since been followed by most occupational groups seeking to raise themselves to professional status. They founded a voluntary professional association: the Society of Gentlemen Practisers in the Courts of Law and Equity, commonly called the Law Society, and one of its principal objects was to clean up attorneys' practice. It was also designed to further attorneys' interests, particularly in their relations with the Bar and other branches of the legal industry; to check unqualified practice; and to promote professional education.

Law societies were also founded in Bristol (1770), Yorkshire (1786), Somerset (1796), and Sunderland (1800).[6] They illustrate the strength of the attorneys in the provinces: a contrast to the barristers who, apart from their practice at assizes, were rarely met with outside London. In this, as in other ways, the lower branch of the law resembled the lower branches of medicine, in so far as physicians were most numerous and influential in London, but surgeons and apothecaries were widely spread. The provinces evidently could not support much specialized practice in either profession, but there was a lively demand for general practitioners.

The Law Society (which was not the direct ancestor of the present body of that name: see p. 54 below) had a firm foundation to work from, in the shape of an Act of 1729 (2 Geo. II, c. 23) which had attempted to improve the professional qualifications of attorneys by requiring five years' apprenticeship and an examination by the judges before they were sworn in. The examination seems never to have been anything but the merest formality. The apprenticeship clause was important, for it gave statutory force to a method of training which increasingly became and still remains the central feature of English professional education. With the persistent neglect of professional education by the public schools and universities, until very recent times indeed, some form of apprenticeship was virtually the only way of learning a profession. It was something which the professions inherited, along with other characteristics, from below – from the skilled trades – rather than from above, from the world of liberal education.

Even with this Act to rely on, it was by no means easy for the Law Society to get rid of unqualified practice. In eighteenth-century England book-learning was middling rare and a school-master or any other fairly literate person might quite readily take on legal business for his neighbours. It might even be done by the parson as part of his pastoral labours. No one was likely to complain except the professional attorneys.

The Law Society did its best to make the attorneys' complaint effective. During the 1760's, for instance, it took action against John Jackson of Sleaford, schoolmaster, who had been butler and clerk to Sir John Therold of Cranwell, Bart (the variety of Jackson's employments is in itself interesting, and shows how fluid and unspecialized professional functions then were, to say nothing of its implications in the matter of social standing). At about the same time, the Society also pursued Thomas Pilgrim, a farmer and grazier. Jackson and Pilgrim had both practised as attorneys, and both claimed to have been properly articled, but the Society suspected, no doubt with reason, that their claims were rather flimsy. Towards the end of the century this kind of activity, which had been spasmodic, settled into a routine. The Society regularly scrutinized applications for admission to the rolls and opposed some of them, sometimes successfully.[7]

The Society was determined not only that attorneys should be qualified but that qualified attorneys should behave themselves. If they did not, it took measures to have them struck off. Landen Jones, after the pillory episode, still practised as a solicitor in Chancery, but the Society pursued him until he was struck off. In 1748 it was agitating for legislation 'for preventing broken tradesmen and other loose and disorderly persons from soliciting, carrying on, or defending causes . . . by means of some Attornies or Agents who encouraged such practices', and in 1752 it resolved to prosecute, at its own expense, 'any Attornies guilty of illegal practices'.[8] This included practice from prison, made illegal by an Act of 1749. The Society set out to suppress it. Prison could more easily happen to an honest citizen then than now, because of the nature of the bankruptcy laws, but clearly the Society was right in thinking it hardly likely to enhance the good name of the profession.

The Society energetically defended the attorneys' flanks. It reacted vigorously against anyone, whether barristers, officials of the Court of Chancery (the Six Clerks), clerks in Parliament, or the Scriveners Company, who appeared to be taking work that belonged to attorneys. The barristers, in particular, were firmly shut out from conveyancing work as the century went on, and direct dealings between barrister and client, as we have seen, were pretty effectively prevented by 1800.

Against the Scriveners there was a major battle and a glorious victory. The Scriveners, a Livery Company of the City of London, had the monopoly of preparing formal documents within the City, which had led them to business activities very like some of those carried on by attorneys. It was a dying trade, dating from the Middle Ages, but the members of the Company sought to revive their fortunes by forcing attorneys in practice in the City to take up the freedom of the Company and pay for the privilege. The Law Society took up the challenge and from 1749 to 1760 campaigned through all the convolutions of eighteenth-century law. The end was a complete defeat of the Scriveners' ancient privilege and a triumph for the 'new men' of the day.

The Society's five counsel waived their fees: a concession no doubt judicious as well as generous. The Society, not to be outdone in magnanimity, voted them plate, nicely graded in value and in floweriness of Latin inscription according to counsel's seniority. One man, Norton, got a cup worth fifty guineas with twelve lines of Latin on it. The two most junior got cups worth fifteen guineas and seven lines each. '*Jurisconsulto peritissimo*' dwindled into '*jurisconsulto perito.*'[9]

The Society's whole attitude towards the Bar was a blend of deference and self-assertion. In 1766 Mr Serjeant Davy said to a jury: 'You gentlemen who are on the outside of the curtain do not see the tricks and management within; we that are on the inside see the whole, and I will take it upon me to say, that out of the many mistakes that happen in the management of causes, nineteen out of twenty happen by the ignorance of attorneys.' When they heard what Davy had said, the members of the Law Society resolved that 'any Counsel at the Bar making use of such like reflections upon the attorneys in general, ought not to be employed as Counsel by any member of the Society.'

Davy had to eat his words, though he took several months over the meal. 'I . . . declare', he eventually wrote, 'that I never meant to cast the least reflection on the profession in general, or on any gentleman concerned in it; but on the contrary, I have always held the attorneys and solicitors in the most esteem and gratitude ... I hope it will not be deemed improper that I thus address the Society through the medium of a friend. If I knew of a more respectful method of application I would gladly embrace it.' Some years later Davy had evidently been fully forgiven, for he was acting on behalf of the Society. He declined to take a fee.[10]

There seems to be no doubt that by the end of the eighteenth century the attorneys had very much raised their standing. The old gibes were still made, but they had lost some of their sting. The profession had come to act with a mixture of regard for the public interest and regard for itself which was quite different from a decent tradesman's probity and from the self-assured loftiness of older professions, yet which had something of both in it. The more spectacular rapscallions, and the more squalid, were hounded down. At the same time the rights of the profession, as the profession understood them, were firmly asserted and, in general, accepted. Moreover with the quickening of the economy there was more worth-while work for a respectable attorney to do. He was on the threshold: very soon he would be over it.

The eighteenth century saw also a rise in the standing of the lower branches of the medical profession. Surgeons and apothecaries both bettered themselves, though by the end of the century they still had a long way to go. Compared with the lawyers, acrimony between the various branches of the profession was greater. Barristers and attorneys seem to have been fairly amicable about sharing professional duties, dignities and spoils. Doctors were far more quarrelsome, and perhaps some of the results are with us yet, particularly in the touchiness of GPs. And matters were made worse by the number of corporate bodies more or less closely interested in medicine – the Royal College of Physicians, the Company (later the Royal College) of Surgeons, the Society of Apothecaries, the universities, and so on – to say nothing of the Irish and Scottish medical authorities. Nothing like this luxuriant proliferation of vested interests existed in any other profession, and the difficulty of getting agreement between them was demonstrated time and again.

The attorneys found unqualified practice a nuisance. It was even worse for the doctors, largely because the state of medical knowledge compared very badly with the state of legal knowledge. An ignorant attorney was fairly easily found out, as soon as he ran up against anyone who really knew the law. An ignorant quack could get away with murder, or at any rate manslaughter, and often did, simply because no one could say with certainty that the quack knew too little, or that what he knew was dangerous.

Medicine moreover was – and is – readily susceptible to the taint of magic, folklore, and humbug. Add to this the fact that most of the population could not afford qualified advice, such as it was, and that they were illiterate, credulous, easily imposed upon, and you have a situation made for quackery. And not amongst the poor only. Sir Astley Cooper discussed the problem with the Select Committee on Medical Education in 1834. 'Below the druggists,' he agreed, 'and far more ignorant than they are, come the worm and water-doctors, bone-setters and others, whose name is Legion', and another witness observed how 'you daily see the rich, as well as the poor, entrusting their lives to wholly uneducated pretenders.'[11]

Above this welter of ignorance, as the eighteenth century came to an end, some surgeons and apothecaries were gradually thrusting their heads, and it was to practitioners of their orders, rather than to the arrogant and expensive physicians, that most people below the level of affluence went for medical attention. It was among them, too, and particularly among the surgeons, that most of the advances in knowledge were being made. The surgeons were not hampered by veneration of the classics, and they cut people up to see what really went on inside.

Neither the surgeons nor the apothecaries were yet clearly distinguishable from skilled tradesmen. Throughout the eighteenth century they were still organized, so far as they were organized at all in England, in livery companies of the City of London. The apothecaries had parted company with the grocers in 1617 and the surgeons had divorced the barbers in 1745, but neither had founded learned bodies. Nor, indeed, would it have been generally considered reasonable that they should do so. The surgeon was a craftsman: the apothecary, a shopkeeper. Neither, in these circumstances, could be a gentleman – not, at any rate, until he had become rich and famous, as some of the late eighteenth-century surgeons did. The first surgeon to be knighted for professional eminence, it is said, was Sir Caesar Hawkins in 1778, and at about the same time John Hunter was advancing the prestige of surgery by applying scientific method to it.[12]

Surgery without anaesthesia, after all, was a rough and bloody business, unlikely to attract anyone of refined taste and adequate fortune. Moreover, there was no settled course of professional education – or of education of any kind – and no legal requirement to be formally qualified. But success could bring position and considerable wealth, and then there would be the chance that you could breed your sons up to something really gentlemanly. They might become physicians, and father's influence would help them on their way. If they, too, became surgeons, they could follow a really ambitious course of training and, again, an established family connection would be useful.

So we find that surgeons were usually men of little fortune – younger sons, sons of ruined men, orphans. A good many were Scots. There was Joseph Hume, for instance. His father was master of a coasting vessel trading from Montrose. His mother, left an ill-provided widow, set up a retail crockery shop and apprenticed Joseph in 1790, at the age of thirteen, to a master-surgeon-apothecary in Edinburgh. Six years later he acquired what seems to have been a somewhat shaky qualification and then his fortune was made, in a thoroughly eighteenth-century way, by getting an appointment through the interest of David Scott, MP for Forfar, as assistant-surgeon of an Indiaman. From that point he prospered – 'labour was to him a pastime, especially if any rupees could be gained by it' – his career became steadily less medical, and we need follow it no further.[13]

An East Anglian surgeon called Joseph Ayre had rather similar origins. His father, a younger son, 'worked his way to a moderate independence as a shipowner' at Lynn, but then he died, leaving a widow with eight children, of whom Ayre was the youngest. At fourteen, in 1795, he went to sea, but came ashore again as a merchant's clerk. The merchant failed, and Ayre 'determined to invest . . . his little capital in his medical education.' He became a pupil of Cline and Astley Cooper, both eminent surgeons, qualified and, settled in Hull, where he became an alderman. He died in 1860.[14]

Some surgeons had rather more distinguished ancestry. Richard Cremer (1770–1860) belonged to an old Norfolk family. They lost most of their money and he took to surgery.[15] Sir Astley Cooper's father was a well-to-do clergyman, but it is clear from his biography (by his nephew) that his boyhood was turbulent and unstudious, and there is a hint of desperation in the way he was finally packed off as a pupil to his uncle, a London surgeon. He rose to eminence, affluence, and to the head of his profession.[16]

It is not necessary to believe that surgeons were all the children of misfortune, but it seems fairly clear that their social origins, as a rule, were not above the middle class unless, like Cremer, they came of a more exalted family which had fallen on evil days. Newman, in his *Evolution of Medical Education* (p. 16), considers that the social origins of surgeons and physicians, speaking generally, were much the same. That may well be true, but it seems clear that surgery was a much less eligible occupation than physic, and one that needed a far less expensive training (there was no university education to be paid for), so that it was often seen as a means of repairing shattered fortunes or of making a position for oneself in the world, rather than a calling honourable or desirable for its own sake.

The basis of the surgeon's training was a combination of apprenticeship with courses in anatomy and surgery, and 'walking the wards'. In the eighteenth century the requirements were imprecise and the Company of Surgeons did very little in the way of professional education, though they ran examinations for the diploma which, by the standards of the late eighteenth century, were well conducted.[17] In 1800, under rather curious circumstances, the Royal College of Surgeons replaced the Company, whose officials were held to have caused it to be dissolved by acting beyond their powers (among other things, the Court of Examiners had given orders to sell the Company's Hall without consulting the Court of Assistants, as they were bound in law to do). The College, however, in its early years, was not notably more stringent in its requirements for qualification than the Company. Up to 1813 it would often accept four years in a druggist's shop as part of the six years' apprenticeship formally required, and besides that it demanded only proof of attendance on one course of lectures on anatomy and another on surgery. In 1813 it added a requirement for a certificate of attendance on the surgical practice of a hospital. From 1815 onwards the example of the Apothecaries' requirements began to have some effect but that we shall come to later.[18]

For anyone who took his medical education seriously the only thing to do was to go to Edinburgh or the Continent: perhaps to both, as Sir Astley Cooper and most other eminent surgeons did, and as Sir Astley recommended for anyone who was aiming really high.[19] But that was beyond the resources of the majority, and a lurid light is thrown on the lower depths of surgical training by evidence given by the President of the Royal College of Surgeons, G. J. Guthrie, to the Select Committee of 1834. Of army surgeons in the Peninsula, where he himself had served, he said:

'The only certificates at the time required were one course of anatomy and another of surgery; and it was found that even this was so much more than the public could meet, that his Majesty's Government were obliged to give warrants to persons, finding that they had not enough men who could obtain this simple qualification; and some of those men who came out to us in Spain, committed such destruction in consequence of their ignorance, as to render it most deplorable; and I now place this fact on record, in order to prevent a circumstance of this kind occurring again.'[20]

Even in normal times the qualifications required for appointment as a surgeon in the Army or Navy were lower than were needed for the ordinary diploma of the College, but after three years' service a military or naval surgeon could go into civil practice on the same terms as other members of the College, which no doubt accounts for the fact that a great many surgeons of the early nineteenth century found it convenient to devote some part of their early career to the service of their country.

The surgeon, like other professional men, took time to work up his earning power. The earnings of Sir Astley Cooper's early years, with excellent backing and introductions, were:

1792 £ 5 5s.	1795 £ 96	1798 £ 400
1793 £26	1796 £100	1799 £ 610
1794 £64	1797 £200	1800 £1,100

The jump to £1,100, in 1800, marks Cooper's appointment as Surgeon of Guy's Hospital, after an energetic canvass and a prudent change of political opinions (he had been suspected of Jacobinism). That made his position more secure, if not yet affluent, but in 1815, with the Prince Regent among his patients, he had an income of £21,000, said to be the largest income of any medical man in the country.[21]

The surgeon's conventional fee in the eighteenth century was a guinea for a consultation. It rose with eminence, naturally, and on the other hand it might be less, or nothing. Cooper would treat the poor at his house, early in the morning, for nothing, for the sake of the experience, and he was generous towards impoverished ex-officers after the Napoleonic Wars. And some patients were mean. One, early in Cooper's career, gave him half a guinea, saying: 'I gave Mr Cline a guinea, but, as you were his apprentice, I suppose half-a-guinea will do for you.' There is a story of Abernethy, paid a similar fee, searching on the floor, as he said, 'for the other half.'

The beginner had no defence against this kind of treatment, and even at the height of a surgeon's career his fees had a curious air of tipping about them. In 1813 Cooper operated for the stone on a man called Hyatt, a wealthy West India merchant. As he was leaving the room after his last visit, Hyatt threw a nightcap at him. It had a cheque for a thousand guineas in it. Cooper liked being paid by cheque, for he said no one ever drew one for less than five guineas, whereas he might only get two in cash. He had a large income from practitioners and patients in the country, who generally sent one-pound notes by post. This nettled him, because in his consulting-room he would probably have got a guinea, but he consoled himself with the reflection that he quite often received five-pound notes.[22] The story of these proceedings throws a curious light on the medical ethics of the day. It looks very much as if Cooper, who was very sensitive about his professional standing, saw no harm in conducting a postal practice, in which he could not possibly examine the patients he was treating.

Money matters are discussed with great frankness by Sir Astley's biographer, and they help to throw light on that very delicate subject: the professional man's attitude to his fees. These anecdotes of a distinguished surgeon are presumably typical, and certainly they are not related as if there was anything odd about them. Yet they have a curiously undignified air. How much better, surely, if the whole thing had been on a regular basis, instead of being dealt with in this coy, half-jocular, hole-and-corner manner.

Barristers and physicians carried the matter even further. They made a virtue of the fact that etiquette forbade them to sue for fees due to them. Quite why they were so proud of this curious quirk is not clear, for it certainly did not mean that they were indifferent to money, nor that they would overlook a failure to pay. The whole subject of payment, however, seems to have caused professional men acute embarrassment, making them take refuge in elaborate concealment, fiction, and artifice. The root of the matter appears to lie in the feeling that it was not fitting for one gentleman to pay another for services rendered, particularly if the money passed directly. Hence the device of paying a barrister's fee to the attorney, not to the barrister himself. Hence, also, the convention that in many professional dealings the matter of the fee was never openly talked about, which could be very convenient, since it precluded the client or patient from arguing about whatever sum his adviser might eventually indicate as a fitting honorarium.

The matter of payment came close home to the question of social status, which is largely, no doubt, why it was treated so gingerly. The fact that army surgeons in the Napoleonic Wars were granted warrants rather than commissions shows how the gentry regarded the ordinary run of surgeons at that time, and even so eminent a practitioner as Sir Astley Cooper was sufficiently uncertain of his position in society to make him talk about it a good deal. What, in fact, he really was certain of was that it was not as high as he thought it ought to be.

If one thing more than another held the surgeons down, it was probably their connection with body-snatching. It arose from their entirely laudable desire to be properly educated in their profession, to place it on a sound scientific basis, and thereby to raise its standing in society. But until 1833 they had to face the fact that there was no legal way of getting 'subjects' except, under an Act of 1828, the bodies of executed criminals. The result was a flourishing minor industry, or skilled trade, which seems to have reached its height late in the eighteenth century or early in the nineteenth, to meet the demand of the medical schools and of men like Cline, Astley Cooper and Abernethy who were working to improve the state of anatomical knowledge.[23]

The body-snatchers were swift, skilful, and not without a craftsman's pride. They were also enterprising. A man called Butler, once a porter at St Thomas's Hospital in London and an articulator of skeletons, went to Spain during the Napoleonic

Wars with the object of drawing the teeth of soldiers killed in battle. He had to be careful how he did it, because there was a good chance of getting killed either by a stray French bullet or by the outraged comrades of the dead men. But it was paying, because there was a brisk demand for teeth from dentists. Butler prospered and became a dentist himself, in Liverpool. At that, however, he failed, and he tried to rob the Edinburgh mail. He was caught and condemned to death. In gaol he was bored and asked the Governor for something to do. He was given the bones of a horse, which he articulated. While he was at work the gaol was visited by two Austrian archdukes, Lewis and John, who interested themselves in his case. They managed to get him pardoned, on condition that he left the country. He went, and was heard of no more.[24]

With men like this – some worse – respectable surgeons had to deal if they wished to improve their professional knowledge or run schools of anatomy. The body-snatchers were bold and impudent. They charged monopoly prices, carried on blackmail, and induced their clients to busy themselves in getting them out of gaol when necessary. 'The very Government itself ... had to sustain some degree of odium, from the necessity which induced its members to shut their eyes to the transactions of the Resurrectionists, for, without their passive permission ... England in a short time would have stood lowest among European nations as to the conditions of her Medical science.'[25]

Burke and Hare in Edinburgh, and Bishop and Williams in London, went so far as to provide their own 'subjects', but in general there was no need for the body-snatcher to commit murder. England in the early nineteenth century was unruly, unpoliced, and it was easy enough to bribe or overawe sextons and others who looked after cemeteries. Then he could trust to his own swift skill to be in, out, and away leaving scarcely a trace behind him; certainly nothing so crude as an obviously disturbed grave. But he had to be careful of the local people, who took strong exception to body-snatching and would mob anyone they suspected of being concerned in it, including dissecting surgeons.

Properly conducted, the trade was marvellously efficient. Sir Astley Cooper once told a Select Committee: 'the law does not prevent our obtaining the body of an individual if we think proper; for there is no person, let his situation in life be what it may, whom, if I were disposed to dissect, I could not obtain . . . nobody is secured by the law; it only adds to the price of the subject.'[26]

The Anatomy Act of 1833 killed the trade. It permitted the use of unclaimed workhouse bodies, provided that an inspector, appointed under the Act, had seen a death certificate and knew the circumstances of death. If he was satisfied, dissection could go ahead, but only in schools of anatomy licensed under the Act and not, as in times past, also in the surgeons' houses. 'Although', wrote Astley Cooper's nephew in 1843, '. . . there is still a difficulty in obtaining a sufficient supply of Subjects, it is equally certain that the modern system has much raised the characters of those who are studying anatomy, as well as the science itself, in the estimation of the public.'[27]

The physicians watched the surgeons pretty narrowly, especially as the surgeons' prestige rose in the latter part of the eighteenth century. In theory there was a clear-cut division between surgery and physic. The one was a crude affair of the knife: the other a recondite art. In fact, no clear distinction was possible. Prescribing was supposed to lie at the heart of physic and to be the physician's special prerogative, but the surgeon would certainly prescribe if he needed to. Whether the physician would ever descend to surgery was less certain, but he might from time to time lance a boil. Many of the witnesses before the Select Committee of 1834 were ready to admit, or anxious to proclaim, that the supposed division of labour was nonsense. 'There is no distinction', said Dr John Sims, a disgruntled licentiate of the Royal College of Physicians, '. . . with the sole exception of the physician being understood to apply himself to internal diseases only; and the sooner that is done away with, the better.'[28]

That was a dreadful thing to say, in the view of most Fellows of the Royal College of Physicians. They cherished the distinction and took every opportunity to block any proposal which might blur it, which meant, in general, that they blocked every proposal for reform or up-to-dateness. In particular they required any candidate for their Fellowship to disfranchise himself from any college of surgeons or company of apothecaries. When Sir Henry Halford was asked why he replied, 'Because we think it would diminish somewhat the high respectability of men of education, who stand on the same ground as members of the English

Universities.'[29] This was an attitude which might commend itself to some trade unionists, but it was hardly calculated to foster close and friendly co-operation in the furtherance either of medical science or of the reorganization of the profession.

The apothecaries were the third of the recognized 'orders' of medical practitioners. The physicians regarded them with even greater contempt than the surgeons, and even the surgeons would not admit to their Fellowship anyone who practised pharmacy. The physicians' contempt had a tincture of alarm because the apothecaries, shopkeepers as they were, presumed to prescribe for people who came into their shops, and also for patients whom they visited. In 1703 the physicians tried to crush this presumption by legal action, but the House of Lords held that the apothecaries were within their legal rights, which thereafter became a standing grievance with the physicians.

Nevertheless, the physicians could always point to the fact that the apothecaries lived not by charging for attendance and advice, like proper professional men, but by selling drugs, like the trades-men they were. This gave them a direct interest in the quantity of drugs they sold and cut across developing notions of professional ethics. The practice was still going on in 1834 and most witnesses before the Select Committee agreed that it ought to cease – that apothecaries should charge for attendance and leave the drug trade to the chemists and druggists. The trouble was that the apothe-caries' customary fee, which seemed to be limited in some shadowy way by law, was half-a-crown, and that did not yield enough to live on. Even if the fee could be raised, it was doubtful whether many of the apothecaries' patients, generally among the poorer sort of people, would be able to afford it. If the apothecary tried to get out of his difficulty by charging more to some patients than others, he might be in a different sort of trouble. Why should the well-to-do pay extra?

The apothecaries, too, had their pride. They rated themselves above the chemists and druggists, though quite how the distinc-tion was established and kept up it would be difficult to say. It seems to have rested on the fact that apothecaries went out and visited patients, whereas chemists and druggists were shop-bound. From behind their counters they might, as they still do, prescribe for minor ailments, but the question of charging for attendance and advice, and so of gaining full professional status, could scarcely arise. Nevertheless the chemists and druggists fought hard against the line which was slowly being drawn, cutting them off from the medical profession, and in 1834 it was not yet quite hard and fast, though very nearly so. After a few more years – in 1841 – the pharmacists tacitly admitted defeat by setting up their own professional body, the Pharmaceutical Society. The apothecaries had left their shops and become doctors. The druggists had stayed in them and become pharmaceutical chemists.

But the apothecaries – the despised apothecaries – were the first professional body to establish a system of qualification and registration on modern lines. This is a matter which properly belongs to the next chapter, since it deserves much more than incidental notice. Here it will be sufficient to observe that the passing of the Apothecaries Act, in 1815, marked the emergence of the nineteenth-century general practitioner, in the sense of a practitioner holding recognized qualifications in medicine and surgery, since from that time forward it became customary for anyone who wanted to go into reputable general practice to 'pass the Hall', which meant getting the Society of Apothecaries' licence, and to get the diploma of membership of the Royal College of Surgeons. Between 1824 and 1834 the Surgeons granted 3,902 diplomas and the Apothecaries 3,872 certificates, 'showing', as a witness said to the Select Committee, 'that general practitioners do pass both examinations, and substantially are qualified to practise surgery as well as medicine.'[30] Until the conjoint board was set up in the 1880s the letters after the name of the ordinary local doctor were usually MRCS, LSA, with perhaps a Scottish or Irish designation as well.[31]

Let us now look at the professional education of general practitioners as it was about 1834, after the haphazardness of the eighteenth century had been taken in hand, but before nineteenth-century reforms had really begun to bite. We shall then be well placed to understand the energy which the Victorians put into setting up systems of professional qualification by written examination.

G. J. Guthrie, describing the education of an ordinary country doctor, began with 'the lowest grade of professional education, that of the chemist and druggist.' A boy of fifteen or sixteen 'with little or no education' would spend about five or six years at it, 'and then considers himself to be quite fit, perhaps, to be a chemist and druggist, as much so as his master.' A boy intending to be a doctor would count four years in a druggist's shop, when perhaps he had spent a good deal of time sweeping it out and running errands, as four years of his professional training. He would then begin 'that course of study, which is enjoined by the Company of Apothecaries and the College of Surgeons, which would need two years more.

'He is thus', concluded Guthrie, 'educated as a professional man, as a surgeon and apothecary, with the lowest possible degree of means, that can be given to any such person. He has, probably, had no preliminary education; it is very likely that, in some instances, he may be little more than able to read and write; and, as to the dead languages, in a great number of instances, he knows nothing about the matter. Now this is an exceedingly defective mode of education.'

Nor was this the worst.

'Supposing that he is not qualified, or cannot qualify himself, to become a member of the Apothecaries' Company, or of the College of Surgeons, he goes back to his native town, sets up a shop, and practises, in defiance of both, as chemist, druggist, surgeon, apothecary, and man-midwife. If the Apothecaries' Company are informed that he is acting as an apothecary, they may take the necessary steps to punish him, and probably make him take down the title of apothecary; but as the College of Surgeons possesses no such power, he keeps up his titles of surgeon and man-midwife, in open defiance of all the authorities of the country.'[32]

This was the state of general practice in the fourth decade of the nineteenth century, when witnesses before the Select Committee were pretty generally agreed that it had recently been very much improved. As to how many GPs there were in the early nineteenth century, it is impossible to have any very precise idea, since the census authorities did not enumerate the professions separately until 1841. John Nussey, however, of the Society of Apothecaries, in 1834 quoted a figure of about twelve thousand in England and Wales in 1812–13, against fewer than fifteen hundred physicians even allowing the widest interpretation of that term. 'Inasmuch', Nussey told the Select Committee, 'as the mass of the community cannot afford to call in the physician, the general practitioners are the most important branch in relation to the community. They may live and practice to very great advantage, where physicians cannot live at all.'[33]

If, then, we look at the lower branches of law and medicine in the early part of the nineteenth century, we find them active, self-conscious, struggling to better themselves. We find them acutely anxious for full professional status, and yet by no means fully differentiated from skilled trades. We find that they had realized that the way to get what they wanted was to establish, among other things, a regular system of professional education, with a recognized body of knowledge and acceptable standards of quali-fication, preferably enforceable at law. These things were not yet fully developed, either in the lower or the higher branches, and neither was the elaborate code of conduct which the professions were later to set so much store by. Both professional ethics, however, and the modern idea of professional qualification were emerging from the mingled principles of craft-pride, job protec-tion, division of labour, snobbery, service to clients, and genuine regard for the public interest.

Chapter 3

PAPER QUALIFICATIONS

DR JOHN SIMS, like other leading practitioners of the early nineteenth century, learnt his medicine at Edinburgh, and he was an MD of Edinburgh University. He practised, however, in London, and in 1819 he was examined for the Licence of the Royal College of Physicians. The proceedings were entirely oral, and first of all he was asked to construe a small portion of the works of either Celsus or Sydenham. Both were much respected medical authors, one of whom had been active in the first century and the other in the seventeenth. Both wrote in Latin, although Sydenham was English.

Then there was an examination in physiology which lasted about twenty minutes. Pathology came next and took up about a quarter of an hour. Therapeutics, the third subject, dealt with 'the application of remedies to disease . . . and it involved descriptive pharmacy and materia medica'. There was no examination in surgery, midwifery, or the diseases of women and children.

Sims told the Select Committee on Medical Education, for whose benefit he was describing the examinations, that he did not consider them strict: 'I think the examination . . . might prove he [the candidate] knew something of medicine, but it would fail to prove he knew much.' Certainly very few candidates failed. Between 1823 and 1833, including both years, 126 licentiates were admitted and seven were rejected.[1]

The examination for the Fellowship does not seem to have been much stiffer. Sir Henry Halford said in 1834 that it covered 'two dead languages; . . . anatomy, physiology, pathology, and the practice of physic.' That might seem middling formidable, but the president and censors of the College could take three or four

44

candidates through all these subjects in a couple of hours. It was all oral, all in Latin. Hardly anyone ever failed. From 1771 to 1833 the College admitted 168 Fellows and rejected four.[2]

But the physicians' examinations were fairly stiff by the standards of divinity and law. As for divinity, the Prayer Book required a bishop to satisfy himself, before he ordained a deacon, that the candidate was 'learned in the Latin Tongue, and sufficiently instructed in holy Scripture', but Bishops, who examined by deputy, were not usually severe. In 1822 George Spencer, intending ordination, asked the Bishop of Peterborough's examining chaplain what books he ought to read. 'It is impossible', replied the chaplain, 'that I should ever entertain any idea of ever subjecting a gentleman with whose talents and good qualities I am so well acquainted . . . to any examination except as a matter of form, for which a verse in the Greek Testament and an Article of the Church of England returned into Latin will be amply sufficient.'[3] Spencer was the son of a lord, which was no doubt one of his 'talents and good qualities', but there is no reason to believe that the chaplain would have been harsher with a commoner.

At the Inns of Court, as we shall see, there was no pretence of examining intending barristers. The 'call' depended on eating the right number of dinners and paying the right fees.

Evidently, then, until well into the nineteenth century the ancient liberal professions had found no use for written examinations and little use for examinations of any sort. Yet they had their own notions about the proper qualifications for professional standing. They were adapted, on the whole, to an earlier state of society, but it is necessary to keep them in mind in considering the agitation for qualifications of the modern sort which arose as time went on and circumstances changed.

First, as we have seen, it was taken for granted that anyone entering a liberal profession would have had a liberal education, and it was this which bound together the society of learned men, not only within the professions, not only in England, but throughout the polite world. Moreover it was fair to suppose that anyone who had mastered the classical languages and perhaps sharpened his wits on mathematics could also master, if he chose to be a clergyman, theology: if a physician, the writings of Hippocrates, Celsus, Sydenham, and Harvey: if a barrister, the voluminous authorities of the English law. It seems to have been generally considered that law required most in the way of specialized study: divinity least.

Next, before the population explosion of the nineteenth century it could safely be assumed that there would not be very many men of liberal education, nor many members of any one profession. There were several thousand clergymen, it is true, but the physicians, strictly defined (that is, taking members and licentiates of the Royal College only), did not run to more than four hundred or so, though common usage might expand the figure two or three times.[4]. As to barristers, there were 821 in 1814.[5]

With numbers like these it was perfectly possible for many members of a profession to know each other, either personally or by repute; the more so since the members of two professions – physic and law – were heavily concentrated in London. It was also reasonable to expect a high degree of personal knowledge of candidates for admission, since the class from which alone they could be drawn was itself pretty small. These are no doubt the reasons, mainly, why the ancient procedures of professional admission relied on personal knowledge of candidates' characters and abilities much more than on formal examination. No one, after all, has yet found an adequate substitute for personal knowledge, gained over a term of years.

In the Church, accordingly, an ordaining bishop, as well as examining ordinands' knowledge of Latin and Scripture, was expected to know 'either by himself, or by sufficient testimony' that every candidate was 'a man of virtuous conversation, and without crime.' The barristers, in order to make sure they got to know their students before they were called, required them to come to dinner at the Inn a certain number of times during twelve law terms, covering three years, and there was nothing inherently absurd in the requirement. It could be reduced to a meaningless formality and no doubt often was, but the basic idea that a man can be judged by his behaviour in small groups of his equals and his seniors has by no means disappeared from modern methods of selection. The physicians also liked to know their men, and they were even more leisurely. They required every new Fellow to have spent two years at a university and then ten years as a licentiate 'to have his conduct observed.'[6]

In deciding whom they should admit, and generally in matters of discipline, the older professions made their own rules. They were sometimes taken to law by people who thought they had a right to be called to the Bar, when the Inn concerned disagreed, or by disgruntled licentiates of the Royal College of Physicians, but the plaintiffs did not usually have much practical success even if they won. The governing bodies of the older professions were formidable opponents, heavily entrenched behind generations of custom and usage, and even if they could not establish the legal rectitude of any point they wished to defend, they could usually preserve it by deliberate inactivity. They doggedly defended their ancient independence.

Broadly speaking, then, what the older professions seem to have conceived of themselves as doing, when they let in new members, was admitting educated gentlemen to small, self-governing groups of their social equals, to whom they would be personally known and by whom their fitness would be judged. The idea of testing specialized qualifications was not unknown, but it is hardly surprising that it had been allowed to dwindle to a formality or to die out altogether. In the two competitive professions, physic and law, the incompetent, the unlucky and the under-financed were shaken out after admission. It was widely recognized that this was rough justice, to say the least of it, but it was argued that the situation would not be improved by a different system of admission. A man might satisfy examiners: not necessarily either patients or clients. As to the clergy, their competition was for patronage, and again examination results would not be wholly relevant, particularly where family interests were concerned. Nevertheless scholarship was generally regarded as befitting a parson, and as the universities woke up in the early nineteenth century very severe academic competition broke out among the small group able enough to entertain the idea of taking part in it, with rich preferment as the prize. But for the ordinary run of country clergymen, that was well above their heads. A pass degree and a family living were more commonly attainable than a double first and a bishopric.

It was not, therefore, in the higher branches of the professions, among the ancient three, that the demand arose for qualifications of the modern type. It came from the lower branches, where conditions were very different.

We have already observed (above p. 43) that the surgeon, the

47

apothecary, the attorney did not belong to the world of the gentry but to that of the skilled craftsman, the tradesman, and the shopkeeper: the 'middling sort of people', in eighteenth century phraseology. This meant that there could be no presumption of a liberal education. A middle-class boy might start at the local grammar school alongside the son of the squire, but whereas the young gentleman might go on to the university, a private tutor, perhaps the grand tour, no such things were likely for the tradesman's son. Unless he was of the type to get an exhibition or a scholarship, the natural thing for him to do would be to leave young and be bound apprentice. Matthew Wood, for instance, who became Lord Mayor of London, left Blundell's free grammar school at Tiverton to help his father, who was a serge-maker, and then, at the age of fourteen (1782), became an apprentice to a cousin who was a chemist and druggist at Exeter.[7]

Whether such a boy was apprenticed to an attorney, an apothecary, a surgeon, or to some other tradesman – perhaps a skilled artisan – would depend on opportunity, family connections, and parents' means more than on the relative social standing of these various occupations. Some apprentices preferred to be known as articled clerks or pupils. Some parents paid premiums running up to 250 guineas. All this made no difference to the principle, which was the same as if the apprentices were bound to stonemasons. They turned their minds away from 'polite literature', which had probably gone no further than the third declension, and turned to specialized knowledge with a direct application to the business of earning a living. This was the only meaning which people below the gentry, generally speaking, could afford to attach to the word 'education', and it long remained so.

Then there were far more people in the 'lower branches' than in the upper, and in the early nineteenth century their numbers were growing. In 1824 there were 5,205 members of the Royal College of Surgeons and in 1833, 8,125. Having regard to the custom among general practitioners of qualifying both with the Surgeons and with the Apothecaries, that is probably a fair indication of the rising numbers of doctors in the country, though something – how much it is impossible to say – ought no doubt to be added for men who took Scotch or Irish qualifications instead of English ones. As to attorneys, it was said in 1854 that the number annually admitted fell from about five hundred a year before examinations were started in 1836 to an average of 391 between 1837 and 1852, but a writer in 1850 thought the total number might have doubled in the previous forty years. Precision is impossible, either in estimates of increase or of total numbers, but what does seem to be clear is that at a time when members of the 'liberal professions' (except clergymen) were counted in hundreds, there were already thousands in the lower branches. [8]

As well as being more numerous, practitioners in the lower branches were more scattered than those in the higher. They were provincial, as we have seen, rather than metropolitan. For both reasons it was difficult for them to know each other personally and to protect themselves against unqualified practice. They needed something in the way of formal qualifications impartially assessed, universally recognized, ubiquitously enforced, and their essentially practical view of education, no doubt, made them the readier to take to the idea of specialized studies and examinations.

Moreover, they wanted status. A leading surgeon like Sir Astley Cooper knew himself to be not a whit less 'learned' in the professional sense than Sir Henry Halford or any other Fellow of the Royal College of Physicians. He might, indeed, be a great deal more so, being less concerned with his reputation for classical scholarship. Nor was there any inherent reason why an attorney, after five years' articles, should be less learned in the law than a barrister. He might know more, and often did. But unless it could be made clear to the world that one species of doctor or lawyer was at least equal to another in point of professional attainments, it was unlikely that they would ever be admitted to anything like equality of social standing.

Along with this demand went another, similar and closely associated: the demand for self-government, or at least for a say in the running of professional affairs, particularly when ancient governing bodies claimed authority over the lower branches. From one point of view nothing could be more natural. The governing bodies represented the rightful ruling classes in the State; the lower branches, the ruled. The justice of this arrangement, however, was not always plain to the attorney who knew more law than the barrister he briefed, nor to the surgeon who had trained himself more thoroughly in medicine than the physician who snubbed him. Astley Cooper believed strongly that

scientific knowledge was the only proper basis for the professional standing he claimed, with its associated social standing. It
is consistent with this outlook that in 1792 he should have gone to
Paris to see what was happening, and that he should have become
known for a democrat at a time when most upper-class Englishmen thought of democracy as a brand of treason.[9]

For a variety of reasons, therefore, in the first thirty or forty
years of the nineteenth century there were a good many able and
determined men setting out to organize professional education as
it had never been organized before. They belonged to the same
energetic, ambitious, serious-minded middle class which at the
same time was demanding reform elsewhere in the national life,
not least in morals and in politics. The same sort of men, sometimes the same men, were at the same time trying to free the slaves,
get votes for ten-pound householders, make the upper classes
respectable, and force the poor into the workhouses if they did
not fancy the prospect of destitution outside.

Demands for professional reform came both from attorneys
and from GPs, but the GPs were considerably the noisier and
angrier. They were also the first to score a really resounding
triumph, with the passing of the Apothecaries Act in 1815. The
movement which led to the Act, which is described by Dr Newman in *The Evolution of Medical Education*, seems to have started
about 1804, and it was directed mainly, as so much professional
activity was, at suppressing unqualified practice. About this time,
and presumably independently of each other, the Royal College
of Physicians and a provincial GPs organization – the Lincolnshire Benevolent Medical Society – began to consider measures
to restrain unqualified practitioners. The Lincolnshire society had
as Patron, Sir Joseph Banks, PRS, and the leading spirit in it,
Dr Edward Harrison, was diplomatic enough to set up friendly
relations with the Master of the Royal College of Surgeons as
well as with the President of the Royal College of Physicians, so
that a body called 'The Associated Faculty' came into existence
to press for the legislation required.

With so many vested interests concerned – the characteristic
weakness of nineteenth-century medical reform movements –
progress was bound to be slow. Moreover, cordiality between the
'orders' did not survive mainly because the College of Physicians,
predictably, did not greatly relish co-operating on anything like

equal terms with their professional inferiors, especially the Apothecaries, over whom they considered that they had indefeasible, if indefinite, rights of control. The Surgeons, though less arrogant, do not seem to have been very actively helpful, and on at least one occasion their opposition caused a bill to be withdrawn. From another direction altogether, the chemists and druggists opposed the movement because they suspected – rightly – that it would depress their standing, or at least prevent them from raising it.

The fight to get an Act therefore developed into a struggle between the general practitioners, with strong provincial backing, and the two Royal Colleges (especially the Physicians), which were essentially London institutions, and in this it set the pattern for a great deal of medical controversy for many years to come. In 1812, at a meeting of apothecaries called principally to oppose a tax on glass bottles, 'The Association of Surgeons and Surgeon-Apothecaries' and the 'General Committee of Apothecaries' were formed to carry the reform movement forward.

The Apothecaries Act which finally passed into law in 1815 was the last of a series of measures which had come to grief, successively, on one or other of the obstacles placed by various professional bodies in their path. This was also a pattern of events which was to repeat itself, especially in the wrangles leading up to the Medical Act of 1858. It did not prevent the Apothecaries' Act from being a remarkable measure, giving statutory form to some quite new ideas about professional status.

The Act gave the Society of Apothecaries power to determine the education required for entry into their profession, to examine for proficiency, and on the results of examinations to grant or withhold licences which alone would authorize their holders to call themselves apothecaries. Moreover, the Act gave the Society power to prevent unqualified persons from calling themselves apothecaries anywhere in England or Wales. These powers were quite unprecedented at the time. Both Royal Colleges were examining bodies, but the Surgeons had no power to prevent anyone from calling himself a surgeon, qualified or not, and even the august Physicians' authority, founded on a Royal Charter, only extended to London and the district seven miles about.

The Act set up a model for nineteenth-century professional organization. It showed that other professions besides the ancient three might be self-governing and that the ancient three had no prescriptive right to overriding control of their 'lower branches'. It gave statutory force to the notion of formal professional education under the control of a professional body and tested by strict examination. It reinforced the whole structure with the licensing power given to the Society of Apothecaries, in which again the standing and independence of the professional body was emphasized. Licensing was not made a function of the State, but it was backed with the State's authority.

The Act did not forbid unqualified practice, though it did put obstacles in the path of it, and in this also it set a pattern for later legislation. If people wanted to go to quacks, it was felt, they should be free to do so; it was not for the State to interfere. The most the State would do was to empower the Society of Apothecaries to bring to public notice practitioners who, in the Society's opinion, were fit to call themselves apothecaries, and to prevent those whom the Society considered unfit from using the title. It was then for the individual to decide whom he would employ – a typical expression of the nineteenth-century belief in the importance of individual liberty.

The Apothecaries went briskly about their new business. The Act required the Master, Wardens and Court of Assistants to set up a Court of Examiners of at least twelve members, and by 19 July 1815, a week after the Act was passed, they had done so. The Court proceeded to make regulations for the first course of professional education to be prescribed in detail by an examining body in England in modern times. The regulations required a competent knowledge of Latin; certificates of attendance at lectures on anatomy and physiology, medicine, chemistry, and materia medica; six months' hospital attendance; five years' apprenticeship.

From the start the Apothecaries' examinations were serious attempts to test knowledge, never mere formal interviews. Their system imposed a discipline on professional studies impossible when an examining body required only answers to a few perfunctory questions and certificates of attendance at lectures. The discipline may not have been severe by later standards. John Nussey, Master of the Apothecaries, was rather defensive in evidence to the Select Committee of 1834. He spoke of 'herbalizing expeditions' to the country in the summer, organized by the

Society, but he added that there were 'refreshments twice a year only: we allow that at the first two meetings.' The Committee seem to have suspected that the whole thing was a series of picnics, and they may have been right.[10] Nevertheless, in the years from 1815 to 1834, presumably as the examiners grew more skilful and confident, the proportion of candidates whom they rejected rose from five or six per cent to fifteen or more, and in 1830–31 it shot up to 104 out of 465, but that was exceptional. Over the whole period, 7,028 candidates were examined and 795 rejected.

By 1834 the Apothecaries' system had considerable prestige and even the Physicians admitted that it had done good. There seems to be no doubt that it reacted sharply on the Surgeons, who also set about tightening up their educational requirements and their examinations. They examined roughly the same number of candidates as the Apothecaries – most of them, as we have seen (above p. 41), the same men – and rejected rather fewer. Between 1823 and 1833 they granted their diploma of membership to 4,305 candidates and refused it to 326.[11]

From all this forward-looking activity the Physicians stood aloof in immense and touchy dignity. The essence of their attitude was their determination to preserve the separateness of the professional orders. The essence of the reformers' attitude was a determination to destroy it, since all doctors relied, or ought to rely, on the same body of basic knowledge. The Physicians were ill-advised to be so obstructive. The reformers' cast of thought was new and living: their own, old and dying.

The attorneys followed the doctors, a good deal more decorously, along the road towards the examination hall. Perhaps because their occupation bred a habit of discretion and an instinct for compromise, they were less turbulent in their methods and less far-reaching in their aims, at any rate in so far as they were prepared, without much grumbling, to go on putting up with the overriding authority of the 'higher branch'. They did not seek independence from the ultimate control of the judges, nor did they seek to assert that an attorney should have the opportunity to become an advocate or a judge himself.

The old Law Society of the eighteenth century, towards the end of its life, considered various more or less ambitious proposals aimed at better professional education. About 1807 there was a suggestion for an articled clerks' society 'for the purpose of discussing legal questions'. At much the same time a scheme was put forward for setting up a College of Attorneys and Solicitors, rather on the lines of the Royal College of Surgeons. It would have run examinations for admission to the rolls. Neither idea came to anything, and some time after 1810 the Society of Gentlemen Practisers quietly died.

In 1825 a new professional association was set up: 'The Society of Attorneys, Solicitors, Proctors and others not being Barristers, practising in the Courts of Law and Equity in the United Kingdom'. This preposterous title – almost a legal document in itself – soon came down to 'The Incorporated Law Society' and then to 'The Law Society', and the body was granted a Royal Charter in 1831 which was surrendered and replaced, in 1845, by a new one. In that document one of the Law Society's objects was proclaimed to be 'promoting professional improvement and facilitating the acquisition of professional knowledge.'[12]

The first public manifestation was a series of lectures, twice a week, which began in November 1833. Twenty years later it was said that attendance, though not compulsory, had been good,[13] but obviously it would have been unwise to rely on the unstimulated ardour of articled clerks; a properly organized system of examination was required. The Law Society, unwilling to act as an examining body itself, memorialized the judges on the subject in May 1835. In Trinity Term 1836, under the judges' authority and with help from the Law Society, which was represented on the examining board, the first serious qualifying exams for any branch of the legal profession were held.

By 1854 four solicitors and a Master of one of the Courts of Common Law were acting as examiners in each term, and Chancery had its own examining board. The examination was in writing and the procedure, still somewhat unfamiliar to the legal mind of the day, was explained to Commissioners enquiring into the arrangements for legal education at the Inns of Court.

'Fifteen questions', said W. S. Cookson, an attorney, 'are prepared and printed. The candidates, on the day of the Examination, are all assembled together in the Hall of the [Law Society's] Institution, and the questions are then submitted to them, and their answers, which are written, are carefully examined by the *push for status is from lower branches, not entrenched – a / educ, which higher or less ignored*

Examiners, and such men as have shown themselves sufficiently acquainted with the different subjects are certified to be proper men to be admitted Attornies.'[14]

As soon as qualifying examinations started, there was a drop in the number of attorneys admitted to the rolls. 'I think', said Cookson, 'that about that time an apprehension began to prevail that the reforms then in contemplation in the practice of the Law would materially diminish the number of Solicitors, and that many gentlemen were thereby deterred from incurring the expense of placing their sons in the Profession.'[15] The inescapable necessity, newly instituted, of having to produce proof of adequate professional knowledge may also have had something to do with it.

Cookson went to some pains to point out to the Commissioners – all eminent members of Bench and Bar: not one of them an attorney – that the Law Society, at the expense of its members, was doing much more for legal education than the Inns of Court. The Law Society's Institution, in Chancery Lane, London, had cost about £90,000 and there was all the recurring expenditure on lectures, examinations, and so on. He indicated sharply that the least the Inns of Court could do was to make their students take examinations too, and he put in a strong claim (which went unheeded) for the attorneys to share in the revenues of the Inns of Court and Chancery.[16]

Here he came close home to the reason why the Commission had been set up, which was simply that since time out of mind the Inns had done nothing at all for legal education, although that was supposed to be one of the main purposes of their existence. The evidence given before the Commission illustrates clearly the division of opinion, still very lively in the fifties, between the new professional men and the old. One side regarded properly organized professional education, tested by severe examinations, as the only acceptable guarantee of a would-be practitioner's competence. The other preferred to rely on the ancient tests of liberal education and personal knowledge before admission and of competition after.

Trollope cf. T-N report

The Treasurers of the various Inns, between them, put the conservative case. Sir Fitzroy Kelly, QC, MP, of Lincoln's Inn, in the course of denying the need for examinations to stimulate industry, said: 'I think that anyone of liberal education and good character who has an opportunity of acquiring the knowledge requisite for a Barrister, will do so if he really means to practise as a Barrister', and the Treasurer of the Inner Temple, William Whateley, QC, carried the argument for liberal education a little further: 'I believe that it is of great importance to the Profession to make it a gentleman's profession, and to make its foundation a liberal education.' And the whole matter was disposed of by C. H. Whitehurst, QC, Treasurer of the Middle Temple: 'I do not think that Examination is really of any use. I think the advantage of dining in the Hall, is associating together. The question of men associating together, I think, is of very great importance.' And a little later on: 'If he [the new barrister] is not qualified, he will get no business, and if he is qualified, he will get business ... Some of the very best and first Advocates at the English Bar, were no Lawyers, they were very ignorant of Law ... The Profession must be looked at, not as a mere profession of jurisconsult, to advise. The Inns of Court are rather considered as places where people are educated to be Advocates.'[17] And with that, in White-hurst's view, a system of qualifying examinations had nothing to do.

In conformity with this cast of mind, such tests of legal knowledge as the Inns had once imposed had ceased to have any reality. 'I may observe', said Whateley, 'that in Lincoln's Inn, the Exercises have dwindled away. When I was a Student, I used to be marched up to the Barristers' table, with a paper in my hand, and I said, "I hold the widow – ", the Barrister made a bow, and I went away ... and that was the remnant of performing the Exercises.'[18]

This was a state of affairs which the newer type of professional man, including some barristers, considered deplorable, and the Inns had not been able to withstand the pressure of new thought entirely. In 1833 two lectureships had been set up at the Inner Temple, but they failed for lack of support in 1835. The idea was revived in 1847, when lectureships were set up at the Inner and Middle Temple and at Gray's Inn, and in 1851 the Council of Legal Education, representing all four Inns, came into existence. This body set up a system of qualifying examinations in 1852, but what they really thought of it may be judged from the fact that it was voluntary. You could still become a barrister by the ancient procedure of eating dinners, though attendance on lectures became compulsory instead of voluntary, as it had always been before.

By the time the Commission sat, J. G. Phillimore, QC, MP (1808–65) was Reader of Constitutional Law and Legal History at the Middle Temple and H. J. S. Maine (1822–88), later Sir Henry Maine, was Reader in Jurisprudence and Civil Law. There were also readers in other legal subjects. They were all quite clear that the only way to get a satisfactory system of legal education was to reinforce it with compulsory exams. 'I believe it', said Maine, 'to be the only means of absolutely ensuring industry', and he was supported by the Reader in Equity, W. Lloyd Birkbeck, and the Reader in Conveyancing, Reginald Walpole, as well as by Phillimore, who took the opportunity to compare the English Bar very unfavourably with the French and to remark: 'In France, under a despotism, the Bench was often independent; in England, with free institutions, it has often been servile.' What Maine wanted to see, and he had a considerable body of opinion behind him, was the conversion of the Inns of Court into a legal university. As Robert Lowe said in evidence: '. . . the Inns of Court are as at present constituted a University in a state of decay.' Why let the decay continue?[19] The Commissioners themselves came out on the side of the reformers. 'As regards intellectual qualifications and the professional knowledge of a Barrister', they said in their report, 'we are of opinion that there is not such security as the community is entitled to require', and they went on '. . . there ought to be a test both of the general and the Professional knowledge of every candidate for the Bar . . . The Clergyman, the Physician, the Surgeon, the Apothecary, as well as the Attorney or Solicitor, are all required to pass an Examination before they are permitted to practise . . . In every other country in Europe an educational test is applied to Advocates . . . In Scotland, the Faculty of Advocates have so recently as last year required a Test both of General and Professional knowledge.'[20] But the defensive, not to say obstructive, strength of the ancient professional bodies, as we have already had occasion to remark, was very great. The Inns of Court did not make examinations compulsory until 1872, and they escaped altogether becoming a legal university, which would presumably have meant abolishing the demarcation between barristers and the 'lower branch'.

Not that the attorneys seem to have minded that very much.

Their resentment against the Bar was rather muffled. They liked to indicate how injured they felt, on suitable occasions such as the sitting of the Commission had provided, but they were doing quite well with things as they were and they did not really want to get rid of the division of labour which they themselves had done so much to set up. The Commissioners put the case for a unified legal profession to the attorneys' witnesses, but they shied away from it. 'I believe', said Cookson, 'that if all were at liberty to practise in both branches ... they would naturally and inevitably separate themselves. Those who were qualified to act as advocates, would go into Court, and would be employed by those not so gifted, who would do much of the work now transacted by Solicitors.' He would have none of the American idea of law firms in which partners of equal professional status shared the various functions. He did not even want the Law Society to have the power of striking off. He preferred to leave it where it was – with the judges – saying: 'I think it is desirable that so important and serious a question as that of depriving a professional man of his livelihood, should be submitted to the highest authorities.'[21]

The Inns of Court, then, stood to the attorneys in rather the same relationship as the Royal Colleges to the general practitioners of medicine. They had a privileged position and wide powers, and they were of a very conservative cast of mind. But the attorneys' solution of their problem was to go ahead with their own plans for professional improvement and leave the barristers' privileges unchallenged, thus preserving the ancient two-fold division in the profession of the law. And the barristers, in return, did nothing to hinder the attorneys' activities within their own branch, though they resisted suggestions that they should reform themselves. The doctors followed a very different line, and to them we must now return.

Chapter 4

MID-CENTURY CONSOLIDATION

THE Select Committee on Medical Education of 1834 provided a
public platform for those who wished to reform the medical
profession, just as the Inns of Court Commission, twenty years
later, provided one for reforming lawyers. And this was inten-
tional, in the earlier case as in the later. The Chairman of the
Select Committee, Henry Warburton, was a friend of Thomas
Wakley, the Editor of *The Lancet*, whose views on his own
profession, and especially the College of Surgeons, were violently
hostile to the ancient doctrine of the three orders. Accordingly
witnesses were given every chance to put the case for a unified
profession and the conservatives who gave evidence were very
searchingly examined.[1]

Professional education lay at the root of the matter, for the core
of the reformers' case was that a great deal of medical knowledge
was essential to all doctors, no matter whether they eventually
practised mainly as physicians or mainly as surgeons, and hence
all practitioners should be trained in the main branches of their
art – medicine, surgery, and midwifery. Sir Astley Cooper told
the Committee that he would like to see a prospective surgeon do
seven years' training, at home and abroad, ending with examinations by the Physicians, the Apothecaries, and the Surgeons. And
the Surgeons' examination ought to last three days.[2]

This point of view had for many years found many ways of
expression, particularly in efforts to build up a sound body of
general medical knowledge by collaboration between the orders.
In 1805, for instance, a group of eminent physicians and surgeons
had set up the Royal Medico-Chirurgical Society, and four years
later, when the first *Transactions* were published, the preface said

that the society had two main objects – to read communications presented to it, and to exchange practical knowledge 'in the way of easy conversation.' 'In furthering this important object', the preface went on, 'the union of gentlemen in both branches of the profession affords a greater facility of obtaining accurate information on many points of practice, than could have been derived from a Society, composed of either Physicians or Surgeons alone.' In twenty-nine years (1805–34) the Society published 406 papers in seventeen volumes: over the same period, the Royal College of Physicians published seventy-three in three. Yet the general acrimony surrounding such an apparently sensible and uncontentious institution may be gauged from the fact that the society itself was born of a split in an older society – the Medical Society of London – and that in 1811 an application for a charter was opposed by the Royal College of Physicians in its corporate capacity, in spite of being supported by Sir Henry Halford and two other Fellows.[3]

The Royal College of Physicians, in fact, was the focus of the opposition to any movement to blur the distinctions between the orders. The College's attitude was investigated very thoroughly by the Committee, and the core of it was exposed when Pelham Warren, MD, was asked what he thought of the idea of 'reducing the three branches of the profession, medicine, pharmacy and surgery, to one faculty.' 'It would be the downfall of all three', he replied, '. . . it would reduce those which are professions now to a mere trade, and would be very fatal to the character of the whole medical profession, and very injurious to the public.'[4]

Whatever the Physicians thought about it, general medical education had to be provided somehow, especially after the passing of the Apothecaries Act. The ancient universities would not, and in any case they hardly could, for neither was in a town large enough to provide really good teaching hospitals. London, on the other hand, was very large and the hospitals had long been centres of medical training. It was natural, therefore, that the newly founded colleges of London University should take up medicine as an academic subject, and both University College and King's College provided themselves with hospitals.

Among those who took the lead in founding University College Hospital was John Elliotson (1791–1868), whose career illustrates the opportunities, peculiarities, and drawbacks of the old-style physician's education. He was a Londoner, the son of a chemist and druggist – not, it will be noticed, particularly highly born – and he seems to have had his early schooling from the Rector of St Saviour's, Southwark. Having decided on medicine, he went first to Edinburgh, then to St Thomas's Hospital and Guy's, both in London, and took the Licence of the Royal College of Physicians.

He then decided to become a Fellow: 'a Fellow', as he himself said, 'being considered a higher sort of person than a licentiate.' For that, a degree from Oxford or Cambridge was necessary, so he went as a fellow-commoner to Jesus College Cambridge, where he read 'pretty hard . . . about eight hours a day,' but not at medicine. No medical studies were required for a medical degree and no medical lectures were given 'excepting some popular lectures by Sir Busick Harwood on physiology, in which he used to show the process of incubation by having one-and-twenty eggs of different ages, so as to see them crack; and the most pleasing and popular points he thus illustrated.' He took his doctorate in 1821. It is only fair, perhaps, to add that by 1825 it was necessary to take a written examination for the Cambridge degree of MB. It was a paper on anatomy, physiology, pathology, and pharmacy, and it took three hours.

As a physician Elliotson was highly successful but eccentric. His eccentricity, remarked on by the *Dictionary of National Biography*, first took the form (in 1826) of getting rid of knee-breeches and silk stockings, 'then the orthodox dress of physicians', and he was also one of the first to wear a beard in nineteenth-century England. Later, and more seriously, he took to mesmerism, which caused such scandal professionally that in 1838 he had to resign the Chair of the Practice of Medicine which he held at London University. Even after he had ceased to be a professor, however, his practice flourished. He is said to have been the first physician to use a stethoscope, but that is no doubt a claim which could be challenged.[5]

Elliotson's career shows the use which was made by English doctors of the Scottish medical schools, of the London teaching hospitals, and, for purely decorative purposes, of the ancient universities. These were all public institutions, but medical education was also a prosperous branch of private enterprise. A surgeon could take apprentices and a well-known one, such as Cline or Abernethy, could charge high premiums. In return, apart from the training which he would give, it was pretty well understood that he would launch his pupils profitably into the profession.

Many schools of anatomy, in London and outside, were owned and run by surgeons. They might be more or less closely attached to hospitals or they might be entirely independent, but there was no question that they were commercial undertakings as well as teaching institutions. James Wilson's school, in Great Windmill Street London, was very well known. The nature of anatomists' teaching material inhibited warm-weather activity, and medical education was principally carried on in the autumn and winter.

Lists of anatomy schools licensed under the Anatomy Act of 1833 show them widely distributed over the country, emphasizing the importance of country doctors and doctors in provincial towns in the development of professional organization and attitudes. The Royal College of Surgeons, in the twenties, gave great offence by its reluctance to recognize provincial medical schools for the purposes of its diploma, thus providing a good deal of ammunition for Thomas Wakley. He was campaigning for the control of the College by its members, most of whom were in the provinces. Under the Charter of 1800, control lay with the Council and Court of Examiners, self-perpetuating bodies, firmly based on London, whose members held office for life.[6]

Those who held the College's diploma, on the other hand, were mostly men who had spent a few years in Edinburgh or London, or both, when they were young, had 'passed the Hall' as well as the Surgeons' examination, and perhaps taken some other qualification as well, and had then gone to the provinces for their life's career. There, very probably, they would become men of substance and of local importance, at the centre of that kind of middle-class society which George Eliot knew so well. One can form an idea of the kind of men they were by reading their obituaries in *The Lancet*.

John Haddy James (1788–1869) was born in Exeter. His father, a retired Bristol merchant, was 'in reduced circumstances' but his mother was ambitious. He took the Surgeons' diploma in 1811, then became Assistant Surgeon to the 1st Life Guards, with whom he served in the Waterloo campaign. He left the army in 1816 and joined the staff of the Devon and Exeter Hospital, on which he remained until 1858. From this secure base he blossomed professionally, privately, and as a citizen. He was a strong supporter of provincial medical training and helped to found the Provincial Medical and Surgical Association, later the British Medical Association. He was a town councillor, sheriff, and mayor. He had eleven children by the first of two wives, and the lady had money, which no doubt was what enabled him to indulge interests in his cider orchards, his wine cellar, art, and his garden.

A younger Devon surgeon who made a rather similar place for himself in Plymouth was W. J. Isbell (1813–70), the son of a physician at Stonehouse and a member of a prominent local family. He qualified in Edinburgh and spent the rest of his life in practice in Plymouth, where he was surgeon to the Royal Western Yacht Club and for the last three years of his life a JP, as nineteenth-century provincial doctors fairly commonly were. Robert Elliott (1812–83), for instance, who made a wide reputation for himself through his interest in sanitation, was a JP at Carlisle. He was mayor in 1856 and is credited with having had a leading hand in setting up working mens' reading rooms in the town. He had been educated in Edinburgh, Paris and Heidelberg and he taught at the Newcastle School of Medicine, besides examining at Durham.

The titles of a string of publications often reflect, in obituaries, the professional eminence of these local worthies. They applied themselves particularly, as Elliott did, to cleaning up the filth of towns, and the science of public health, which is generally associated with names like Chadwick, Southwood Smith, and Sir John Simon, owes a great deal to them. Elliott was MOH at Carlisle. John Bacot, Surgeon to St George's Hospital London, was a member of the Board of Health in the fifties. Ayre, as well as being a surgeon in Hull and an alderman, became Chairman of the Sanitary Committee of the Board of Health.[7]

To doctors like these, near the head of local society and sometimes with a national reputation, the Royal Colleges did not look like worthy leaders of the profession. They looked far more like gatherings of pompous obstructionists, intent on bullying the provinces from London, preserving their own privileges – particularly their oligarchical methods of government – and keeping able men out of their rights. The Physicians fought for many years to prevent licentiates from having any say in running the

College. The Surgeons did not do away with life-membership of
their Council, nor did they widen the electorate, until the grade of
Fellow was established by the new Charter of 1843, which also
got rid of the requirement that all members of the Court of
Assistants should live within five miles of the General Post Office
in London.[8]

It is perhaps not surprising, therefore, that the body which
became the British Medical Association was founded in a country
town – Worcester – in 1832 as the Provincial Medical and Surgical Association. It was essentially a GPs organization, hostile
alike to the rigid separation of the 'orders', to the idea that one
was superior and the others inferior, and to the undue dominance
of London over the provinces. It was dedicated, as its first prospectus said, to the 'Maintenance of the Honour and Respectability of the Profession generally in the Provinces', and to that
end it busied itself, from the beginning, with matters of medical
education (the *Journal* was founded in 1840), with the doctor's
status in the community, and with the achievement of professional
aims by political means. In other words, it began straight away to
act as a medical pressure group. In doing so, it was fighting the
same battle as Thomas Wakley and *The Lancet*, but that is very far
from saying that Wakley and the Association were in alliance: by
1836 he was in violent opposition to it.[9]

There was still plenty to be done in raising the doctor's standing
in the community, despite the advances which we have already
recorded. Public authorities, especially, were particularly inclined
to play down the medical men's position if they could. At the
local level, this was very much a matter of penny-pinching and
keeping down the rates, and it came to prominence through the
meanness with which surgeons were treated under the provisions
of the Poor Law, particularly after the passing of the new Act in
1834. On the one hand, this created employment for doctors. On
the other, the whole spirit of the legislation – apart from the
natural instinct of local politicians – was to keep their rewards
as low as possible. Since it was always difficult for a doctor to
establish himself, there was never any great shortage of applicants
even for the most miserably paid posts, and, in fact, at one time
they were let out on contract to the lowest bidder. 'I have been
told', said John Nussey to the Select Committee on Medical
Education, '. . . that an individual has taken a parish for £6 a year,

including all the operations of surgery and medical attendance
... and it is wholly impossible that such attendance can be what
it ought to be, at a price so absurdly low.' Both the BMA and *The
Lancet* campaigned against the mistreatment of the Poor Law
doctor, with all its economic and social implications, but although
they forced improvements in detail the central problem, according
to the historian of the BMA, lasted 'as long as the Poor Law
itself'. Certainly it was not much relieved until the passing of the
National Health Insurance Act of 1912.[10]

More important, perhaps, as representing the upper-class view
of middle-class social aspirations, was the attitude of the naval
and military authorities towards their medical officers. Longer
than anyone else, they preserved intact the eighteenth-century
view that a surgeon was not a gentleman and could not be
permitted to associate with gentlemen on equal terms. The results
ranged from petty social persecution to a denial of honours and
decorations, which drove *The Lancet* to complain, during the
Crimean War, that 'the State has never yet done justice to our
profession.'[11] Glaring publicity, during that war, drew attention
both to the grievances and the shortcomings of army surgeons,
which were to a certain extent inter-related, and afterwards
matters began very slowly to improve.[12] Nevertheless as late as
1860 the Lord Lieutenant of Glamorgan refused to publish the
appointment of volunteer surgeons in the *London Gazette*, thus
indicating that in his view, at least, they did not rate as commissioned officers.[13]

Surgeons in the Navy were not granted commissions at all until
1843. Until that time they had warrants, and for many years
afterwards – longer, it would seem, than in the Army – they were
treated with disdain. 'The surgeons and assistant-surgeons of the
navy', said *The Lancet* in 1860, 'have so long been treated with
unworthy disregard and disrespect, and the feelings of one of the
naval lords is so well known to be hostile to their claims as
gentlemen ... that captains and commanders do not scruple to
treat their medical officers with contumely and injustice.'[14] It had
to be admitted that service at sea did not attract the best doctors –
'no young man', said *The Lancet* in 1870, 'who can see his way clear
to land service will ever voluntarily take to the sea' – and naval
surgeons had a bad name going at least as far back as Smollett's
time, but this was no justification for cheating them of their

rights and it could be argued that better treatment would attract better men.[15] But the Royal Navy was very set in its ways.

In their struggles with public authorities for what they regarded as their proper standing, and in their struggles with each other for professional reform – especially the reform of the Royal Colleges – the combative doctors of the mid-nineteenth century were carrying a banner not only on their own behalf but on behalf of the whole emergent professional class. And the culmination of their activities was the Medical Act of 1858. It was the seventeenth in a series of Bills presented to Parliament from 1840 onwards. All its predecessors were wrecked on the various hazards of disagreement within the profession, the opposition of interests outside the profession, and the changes and chances of party politics. The Act as it was finally carried, with this stormy history behind it, went a long way towards establishing the approved pattern of a Victorian profession, whether in medicine or in any other occupation that aspired to equal dignity.

The Act created the 'registered medical practitioner', a recognizable descendant of the qualified apothecary created by the Apothecaries Act of 1815. He was a man (women had scarcely yet begun to disturb the profession's peace of mind, though they were soon to do so) who had satisfied one or more of twenty-one existing licensing bodies, after examination, that he was fit to practise. No licensing bodies were abolished: no new ones were set up – that was beyond the range of practical politics – but at least the powers of all the recognized bodies were made to cover the United Kingdom instead of being confined, as many of them had been in the past, to certain parts of it. A licence granted by one of these bodies gave the holder of it an absolute right to have his name placed on the register kept by an authority (the General Council of Medical Education and Registration of the United Kingdom) created for the purpose. Once registered, the doctor had a right to practise anywhere in the United Kingdom. He also had a right to practise any branch of medicine, even though he might only be qualified in one of the recognized three – medicine, surgery, and midwifery. Moreover, although the legal validity of the various authorities' qualifications might be equal, their real value certainly was not. But any attempt to alter these matters touched on the independence of the licensing authorities and hence on areas of great sensitivity, not least on Scottish nationalism, *govt motives behind act ?*

for the Scots universities and medical corporations saw little to gain and much to lose by joint examining with English boards. Twenty unsuccessful medical bills came before Parliament between 1870 and 1881, and the principle of complete qualification did not become law until after the Royal Commission of 1882 and the Medical Act of 1886.[16]

The authority which registered a name under the Act of 1858 could also strike it off, so that the General Medical Council became a single body for disciplining the whole profession. It was not, to the doctors' disappointment, a body appointed wholly by the profession. The Crown and the universities, as well as the medical corporations, had a say, and there was no question of direct election. But nine members out of twenty-three – the largest single group – were appointed by the corporations, and until 1926 no one who was not a doctor was a member of the Council, so that its establishment and composition substantially confirmed the notion that professional men should be responsible for their own behaviour, with the power of visiting heavy displeasure on offenders.

The Act did not give registered practitioners a monopoly. To the disgust of the profession, Parliament refused to outlaw quacks. Nevertheless it put them at a grave disadvantage by refusing to let them sign statutory certificates or prescribe dangerous drugs. Their field of action was thus very much restricted. Moreover an unregistered person who performed a surgical operation would lie open to an action for assault and might face a charge of manslaughter. The citizen's right to choose anyone he liked to tinker with his health was preserved, but the quack's power to ruin it was seriously impaired, and at the same time the qualified doctor was given a better defence against unqualified competition than he had ever had before.[17]

The principles underlying the Act were not new, but they were brought together and fortified with the prestige and authority of the State: a matter of great importance not only to doctors but to all others seeking professional status. Three points in particular were important. The recognition of the necessity of proper professional education, tested by examination and rewarded by a licence conferring important privileges, was one. Another was the exercise of professional self-discipline through the powers of registration and striking-off. The third, and perhaps, later, the most sought-after of all, was the statutory recognition of the rights of the duly qualified practitioner, with severe sanctions against the unregistered. This is what every professional man and would-be professional man longs for: the closed shop with an Act of Parliament to lock the door.

One other thing the Act did: it finally shut out the chemists and druggists from the medical profession. They had seen and accepted what was coming when, in 1841, they had set up the Pharmaceutical Society and, in 1842, the School of Pharmacy, thus establishing for themselves two of what were coming to be regarded as the necessities of professional status: a professional association and a properly organized course of training. A Royal Charter followed in 1843, so that their separation from the doctors, though undesired, was not undignified, though in the nature of things they could never escape the taint of retail trade.[18]

Rather similarly, in the forties, animal medicine was formally divorced from the human sort. In 1844, after many acrimonious disputes in the previous twenty years or so, the Royal College of Veterinary Surgeons was created by charter. No one could be a member who, at that time, did not hold a licence from one of two existing veterinary colleges or who, in future, did not pass the examinations which the RCVS was authorized to hold. The profession had been developed from human surgery by the activities of such men as Edward Coleman (1765–1839), a Kent yeoman's son and a pupil of Cline, who had taken it out of the hands of blacksmiths and farriers and applied scientific principles to it, thereby greatly raising its prestige and even bringing it to the stage which would 'qualify its practitioners to hold commissions in the Army.'[19]

In the march towards full professional status, about 1850, the GPs and the attorneys were well in the lead over all other occupations. Whatever reservations the country gentry might have, there is little doubt that in the furiously growing urban society of Victorian England the lawyer and the doctor took the lead among the middle classes and could with some conviction make a claim to gentility in the High Street of Middlemarch or in the suburbs of London or Birmingham, even if not in the mess of a fashionable regiment, in the wardrooms of Her Majesty's ships, or in the drawing-rooms of great country houses.

The rise of the attorney was duly noticed by mid-century commentators. 'They are of various grades', wrote Johnston about 1850:

> 'from the low, rapacious pettifogger, who grasps at three-and-sixpenny fees, and is something between the common cur and bulldog of the law, up to the finished gentleman, who has in his hands the most important affairs, and is professionally acquainted with the most delicate secret histories of the first families of the land.'

He goes on:

> 'Perhaps in no walk of life in England are there to be found men of such exquisite discretion as these professional advisers of great families. Their legal knowledge constitutes the least part of their value. They have the nicest appreciation of the prudent, the becoming, and the practicable; and their legal lore is in many cases only made use of in giving due form and validity to arrangements which are based on circumstances and considerations that at first sight *seem* to be wholly out of the province of the lawyer . . . many of them become very important and very rich.'

Anthony Trollope, in *Doctor Thorne*, draws a contrast between Mr Umbleby, the country attorney of Barchester, still regarded as little more than an upper servant by the gentry, and Mr Gazebee, a lawyer of the type described by Johnston – 'when Mr Mortimer Gazebee visited Greshamsbury . . . he was always received *en grand seigneur* . . . being known to be a fashionable man in London, and quite a different sort of person from poor Mr Umbleby.' But by achieving the position described, the Gazebees of middle-class England no doubt made it easier for the Umblebys to assert precedence over their shopkeeping neighbours.[20]

Both the doctors and the attorneys could claim to belong to ancient liberal professions – medicine and law. Beyond that charmed circle, in the fifties, there were other occupations which contemporary opinion, with greater or less unanimity, would allow to have some sort of claim to be admitted within the pale of 'professional standing'. Of these, from the point of view of its central position in the growing industrial society, engineering was much the most important. Without the engineer, not a railway train could run, not a steamship could be built, not a shuttle could fly in a Lancashire cotton mill. Without the engineer, industrial England could not be. How, then, did he stand in English professional society?

The answer is: not very high. In a society still deeply conscious of ancient, pre-industrial traditions, the engineer could point to no very impressive social origins. Unlike the surgeon or the attorney, he could show no connection at all, however shadowy, with liberal education and the learned professions. The nearest approach to gentility among his professional forbears were the military engineers, like Vauban, who had developed the science of fortification and of siegecraft. But for the most part the machine makers of the Industrial Revolution had come from blacksmiths or from millwrights or from other skilled craftsmen: perhaps from land surveyors or builders. They came, that is to say, from the only people in a predominantly agricultural society who were likely to know much about tools, metals, or machinery, or about what was involved in the design of great public works like canals and roads.

There were exceptions. John Smeaton (1724-92) was the son of a successful provincial attorney. Charles Vignoles (1793-1875), the railway engineer, started life as an army officer. But far more typical were the numerous engineering Napiers of the nineteenth century, who descended from a blacksmith employed in the eighteenth century by the Duke of Argyll. Henry Maudslay (1771-1831), whose inventions of machine tools were crucial, worked at one time in the blacksmiths' shop at Woolwich Arsenal. George Stephenson (1781-1848) was a colliery workman, so ill-educated that he was almost illiterate. Many engineers came, if not from the bottom of society, then from a level far beneath the notice of the polite and educated world.[21]

Moreover they weakened their own position by developing their own snobberies. As in other professions, there was an upper and a lower branch. The Civil Engineers, whose Institution was founded in 1818, looked down on the Mechanicals who, it is said in retaliation, founded an Institution of their own in 1847. It is hardly surprising that Thomson, writing in 1857, took the engineers at their own valuation and remarked: 'The machine engineers are not strictly civil engineers, nor are they, in the sense of our original definition, professional men; but they are so mixed up with the operations of the other engineers, that it is impossible not to refer to them.'[22]

By reason of their origins, the engineers' associations were largely with the handicraft trades, which had two unfortunate results. First, they had little conception of a scientific approach to their problems and, in fact, they were downright suspicious of anything in the nature of theoretical knowledge. As a consequence apprenticeship remained almost the sole method of training and qualifying examinations were very late in making their appearance. The Civil Engineers did not start them until 1898. Second, in a society which assigned a very low place to manual workers they could expect little in the way of social consideration, especially since liberal education, based on the classics, was extremely disdainful of mechanical accomplishments.

It might have been thought that in England, very consciously the leader of the industrial world of the early nineteenth century, the engineer would have been accorded an honoured place in society, in spite of traditional attitudes. The outlook of many professional men, as we have seen, was radical enough. But from about the middle of the century the heavy conservative bias of English society began again to assert itself, with what results we shall later on consider. In the meantime it is enough to observe that in the fifties the engineers – the makers of industrial England – were doubtfully on the outskirts of the professional class: certainly not unreservedly admitted within.

By 1860, or thereabouts, the elements of professional standing were tolerably clear. You needed a professional association to focus opinion, work up a body of knowledge, and insist upon a decent standard of conduct. If possible, and as soon as possible, it should have a Royal Charter as a mark of recognition. The final step, if you could manage it – it was very difficult – was to persuade Parliament to pass an Act conferring something like monopoly powers on duly qualified practitioners, which meant practitioners who had followed a recognized course of training and passed recognized examinations.

Right at the centre of the professional world, therefore, was this matter of training and examination. Moreover it was penetrating the official world as well. The idea was gaining ground that if doctors and solicitors had to qualify by examination, then army officers and Civil Servants ought to, too. And some people had an even more revolutionary idea, namely, that the award of positions in the Government service should be made to depend on the results of competitive examinations rather than on the patronage of great men: a very startling notion indeed to the orthodox mid-nineteenth-century mind.

level of prof
standards &
examins. ~>
N-T report --
what's behind all
of this in ↑ m.class -

The outs want in &
to raise/uniform
code ~us patronage -
pt. of Benthamism

Chapter 5

PURCHASE AND PATRONAGE

'THE aristocracy of this country', said Cobden in 1845, 'have the army, the navy, the colonies, and a large amount of expenditure, at their disposal.'[1] He was addressing a Birmingham audience at the height of the anti-Corn Law campaign, and he was playing upon their jealousy of the country gentry. In such a cause Cobden might not have hesitated to tailor facts to fit his purpose, but this time he had no need to. What he said was substantially true. Despite the torrent of reform which had been sweeping through the land for twenty years or so, the ancient ruling classes were still where they always had been: at the centre of affairs, and still very much inclined to regard official patronage as a natural and legitimate means of supporting their relations, pleasing their supporters, blackmailing their opponents, and discharging their obligations to their dependents.

This was not an attitude likely to commend itself to the kind of people who were fighting their way up the social scale in the manner described in previous chapters, and who were looking for wider opportunities of employment for themselves and their sons. If the gentry wanted to hang on to political power, that in itself the middle classes did not very much object to, but what did annoy them was to find themselves shut out of the material rewards of power. They wanted some of the jobs for some of their boys, and they intended to break into the official world in the same way as they were breaking into the world of the professions, which also the gentry had been inclined to regard as preserves of their own. Before we consider the attack on the old system, let us look at the system which they were attacking.

Of all employments outside the direct exercise of power as a minister, service as an Army officer was the most aristocratic, being directly derived from the most ancient function of an aristocracy: to lead the rest of the people in war. The 'profession of arms' was sometimes classed alongside the 'learned professions', but the value of specialized training was held at even more of a discount. The qualities valued in an officer were the qualities valued by the country gentry: courage, physical toughness, a determination to stand up for one's rights, a touchy sense of honour. Almost the only acquired skill highly regarded was horsemanship, and that was taken for granted. The notion that an officer should be a professional soldier, qualified by technical knowledge as well as by the traditional virtues of a gentleman, was derided and looked down upon, except in the engineers and artillery, two corps which were only rather doubtfully fit for gentlemen to serve in. The disasters of the Crimea, the astonishing spectacle of the American Civil War, and the alarming triumphs of Prussia between them gradually persuaded some of the more alert British officers of the necessity of professionalism, but a great many – perhaps the majority – remained unconvinced right up to 1914. Here, as in other departments of the national life, amateurism was apt to be regarded as gentlemanly and high technical skill as rather degrading.

This was a pity, for the essence of the old Army system was healthy enough. It rested on the seventeenth-century conviction that a professional standing army was a menace to English liberty, because the officers, having nothing to depend on but their pay, would become the hirelings of despotism. The English Army officer, it was argued, ought to be a gentleman of independent means who saw fit, while it pleased him, to place his services at the disposal of the Crown. As soon as it did not please him, he would withdraw them, and at the time of the American Revolution some officers had done precisely that because they thought the Government was behaving tyrannically. Less high-principled motives sometimes operated – particularly the desire to avoid service in remote and unhealthy foreign stations – but it could be taken for granted that no officer who valued his reputation as a gentleman would resign to avoid a war.

An officer's independence, it was held, was guaranteed by the system of purchase. He bought his commission, it was his property, and he could sell it when he chose, so that he was never entirely without capital, and as he rose in rank the value of his commission rose too. From the Government's point of view there was the great advantage that no one expected it to provide a pension fund for officers.

Commissions were not bought in the artillery, engineers, or marines – largely, no doubt, because in the case of the first two anyone who was prepared to take the trouble to acquire the necessary technical knowledge was not likely to be rich enough to afford the purchase system. A cadet of the Royal Military College, Sandhurst, got his first commission for nothing, too, but before 1870 not many officers went through Sandhurst. When new vacancies were created, as they were in fairly large numbers during the Crimean War, anyone lucky enough to get nominated did not have to purchase, but quite a number were filled from the ranks. In peace, it was reckoned in 1857, about three-quarters of all first commissions were purchased.[2]

An intending officer had to be at least sixteen, and he had to get a nomination either from the Commander-in-Chief or, for Household troops (Horse and Foot Guards) from the colonel of a regiment. Then his name was placed on a list 'where it may wait for ever, unless he has interest to push it up, or it is a time of war.'[3] Assuming, however, that he had interest, in time the young man's turn would come. Someone in his chosen regiment would 'sell out', and he would be offered his first commission. The question of going in as a cadet, or on probation, it will be observed, did not arise. Just as in the older professions – the Bar, for instance, or the Church – the young man was admitted first and got his training afterwards.

The price to be paid for a commission was controlled by regulation, with severe penalties for either paying or receiving more. Thomson, in 1857, said that at regulation prices a first commission in the Household regiments, horse or foot, would cost upwards of £1,200. In the cavalry, the price would run rather over £800: in the infantry, according to regiment, £450 to £500. In spite of the regulations, more was regularly paid for desirable vacancies, and Sir Charles Trevelyan, writing against the purchase system, asserted that in two years immediately before the Crimean War about £735,000 was paid for commissions (not all first commissions) which by rights should have changed hands for £521,000. Mrs Woodham-Smith, quoting from *The Times*, says that in 1832

Lord Brudenell (later Lord Cardigan) bought the lieutenant-colonelcy of the 15th Hussars, a very smart cavalry regiment, for between £35,000 and £40,000,[4] which would have been several times the regulation price.

Promotion up to and including the rank of lieutenant-colonel was governed by the seniority of officers within their own regiments: not in the Army as a whole. When a vacancy arose it was offered in turn to all officers who were qualified to 'buy the step'. If none would buy, the vacancy would go, without payment, to the senior amongst them, and promotion of this sort represented a capital gain, since the officer came into a more valuable piece of property without paying for it.

The authorities kept certain safeguards. There were qualifying periods of service for each rank, and the C-in-C could pass over any officer whom he considered unfit for promotion. In an extreme case he could bring in an officer from another regiment. Officers themselves, for their part, could endeavour to arrange matters to suit their own interests by exchanging between regiments: for instance, to avoid Indian service when their regiments were ordered out there. This required both the sanction of the authorities and a willing party to the transaction, but it was frequently done. Wealthy officers rarely served in the tropics.

A cardinal point in the system and one which, for reasons we shall examine later, was widely held to be much in its favour, was that there was no question of promotion by merit on the regimental list. If an officer was promoted for distinguished service (which could not happen below the rank of captain), he was given an Army rank only, and his position in his regiment was not affected. He would be offered 'steps' as they arose, but if he could not afford to take them he would find himself superseded by someone who could, and if he went back to regimental duty he would go back in his regimental rank.

After three years as a lieutenant-colonel, an officer was entitled to the Army rank of colonel. After that the system of purchase ceased to apply. Generals' commissions were not governed by it, and promotion was by seniority alone.

The purchase of a commission was an investment, but an investment in social standing, not for financial gain. It did not offer a very attractive return on capital, for one of the main features of the system was that an officer was not expected to live on his pay, since that would imply that he had insufficient private means to be independent. An officer's pay was often referred to as an 'honorarium', and was regarded rather as a retaining fee for his services, which in peacetime were by no means arduous or time-consuming. An ensign in the infantry, in the middle of the century, was paid 5s. 3d. a day; a lieutenant, 6s. 6d., and there were a large number of more or less unavoidable expenses – twelve days' pay a year for the band, for instance, besides a contribution of twenty days' pay on first appointment and twenty days' difference of pay on each promotion. 'What remains of their pay', Trevelyan goes on, 'barely suffices for their mess expenses even in the most moderate regiments; and the parents of young officers, besides purchasing their commissions and furnishing their outfits, have to make them an annual allowance for subsistence.'[5]

What was more, the investment in a commission, so poorly remunerated, was very insecure, since if the officer died or was killed his commission died with him, and the value of it was lost to his heirs. The Commander-in-Chief might decide to sell a commission for their benefit, and during the Napoleonic Wars the Duke of York fairly frequently did, but it was purely an act of grace: the heirs had no right at law. What the prudent officer, or his parents, did, therefore, on going into the Army, was to take out life insurance to the value of the commission. The premium then had to be paid, and as the officer rose in the service the sum insured, and therefore the premium, rose with him, adding yet another item of expense to be set against his pay.[6]

The purchase system, like so many things in England, had arisen by accident and was not particularly old – it dated from the latter part of the seventeenth century. It was unique in Europe and, it might be thought, uniquely bad. On the whole, however, it suited the classes who habitually worked it, for they regarded it both as a guarantee of independence and as a defence against gross abuse of patronage (though patronage, as will have been observed, was an integral part of it). In 1857, during the general attack on the patronage system which we shall discuss in the next chapter, there was an official enquiry into the purchase of commissions in the army, and plenty of witnesses were found to defend it. The core of their argument was that as long as promotion was governed strictly by seniority, combined with purchase, there could be no question of a Commander-in-Chief promoting officers corruptly or by favouritism. Officers, said one of the Commissioners, were usually 'the sons ... of merchants, lawyers, physicians, clergymen, and little country gentlemen, who having £2,000 or £3,000 at their command to provide for younger sons, send them into the Army, with the assurance that no officer can be put over their heads, on account of his influence as belonging to an aristocratic family, or his connection with a member of the legislature.' Sir George Brown, a tough old General of very conservative views, who had commanded a division in the Crimea, agreed with that analysis of the situation and added: 'I think the system of promotion by purchase is the fairest thing that can be. I think it is fairer than a system without, and that it is more possible for the Commander-in-Chief to job promotion without purchase than it is with it.'[7]

Purely as a career, the Army under this system was not at all attractive to the energetic and ambitious middle classes. They could find more profitable ways of employing their capital and their talents. But they did covet the social standing which a commission conferred, and for that reason, if for no other, they resented a system which openly and deliberately debarred men without private means from holding one. The situation was summed up in the *Saturday Review* in 1856: 'It must be remembered that commissions now bear an artificial value on account of the prejudice ... which associates an "officer" and a "gentleman". Sever this association ... and we are sure that no man of more than moderate prospects and powers will compete in time of peace for so trifling a reward.'[8]

Moreover there were very good public reasons for deploring a system which deprived the country of the services of a whole class of able men: the class', in the words of one of the 1857 Commissioners, 'that our civil engineers or merchant captains come from.'[9] Sir Charles Trevelyan, in evidence, put the case very clearly. 'I myself,' he said, 'belong to a landed country family', and he went on to say that the sons of farmers – 'one of the most energetic and spirited classes in the country' – went freely into the yeomanry but never into the regular Army. 'There is no place for them there', he said, 'they have not money to purchase as officers, and they cannot go into the ranks ... without any prospect of promotion.' He went on to press the point: 'The middle class ... a class between the clergy and the legal and medical professions and the higher merchants on the one side, and the work people on the other, has no place in the British army under the present system.' And this, he pointed out, was 'the great middle class, who carry on all our great industrial and marine operations.'[10]

Nor was this all. The great virtue of the purchase system, from the public point of view, was supposed to be the independence of the officers. But that point made less appeal to a nineteenth-century reformer, looking for efficiency, than to a seventeenth-century squire who had just got rid of Cromwell's major-generals. Men like Sir Charles Trevelyan, it may be supposed, were disinclined to regard Victoria's army as a menace to the Constitution, whatever James II's may have been, and the trouble with your 'independent' officer, who had no need to rely on his pay for his living, was that there was no very strong incentive for him to take his profession seriously, especially if that meant hard study and service in unattractive places. 'The real defect of the system of purchase', said a writer in the *Saturday Review*, 'consists in its tendency to encumber the army with amateurs and to relax the ties which bind the officer to his profession.'[11]

An officer of the old type would face any kind of impossible demand on his courage, as the charge of the Light Brigade and other regrettable errors showed. What he was notoriously unwilling to do was to study warfare sufficiently to make such blunders unlikely, or to interest himself in even duller and more ungentlemanly matters like supply and transport in the field or the comfort and health of troops in barracks at home. In the sixties the Army's own medical authorities reported, without any sign of undue concern, that about 40 per cent of the men in the ranks were known to have contracted venereal disease, which is surely evidence of gross professional neglect on the part of the officers and possibly, also, a result of their snobbery towards the medical branch. From either point of view, rather a heavy price to pay for 'independence'.[12]

It was the Crimean War which showed up the defects of the British Army on a truly spectacular scale, but even before that war broke out the first dents had been made in the old system. After 1849 no one was allowed to purchase a commission without first passing an examination in English (from dictation), history, geography, arithmetic, algebra, fortification, and a language. This sounds a formidable list, but the terrors of it may have been more apparent than real. The examination was oral, unless there was any doubt about a candidate passing, in which case 'a number of questions are put to him on paper, of which he is expected to answer a certain proportion.' Even after that 'in cases where the Deputy-Governor and professors [of the Royal Military College Sandhurst] are of opinion that the candidate has had "the education of a gentleman", although he may have failed in some particular branch, their opinion is made known to the Commander-in-Chief by a special mark', which looks like a fairly clear indication that no one expected too much, intellectually, of the Commander-in-Chief's nominees (for the C-in-C's nomination was still essential, before you could enter for the examination). In 1857 the Council of Military Education, in their first report, produced a considerably more elaborate scheme for a qualifying examination and even went so far as to recognize the necessity of 'a subsequent course of military instruction, on which the Council will report hereafter.'[13]

It was the Army, of the two armed services, which caught the full blast of the reformers' wrath. They paid far less attention to the Navy, perhaps because a career as a Naval officer was not often thought seriously of outside a rather narrow circle of families and there was consequently less pressure to break the whole thing open. Moreover in England there has usually been a reluctance to criticize the Navy in anything like the uninhibited manner which the Army has to put up with. And there was no question of Naval commissions being purchased: they never had been. The system of appointment was that common to all branches of the public service: patronage. Control of it, during the nineteenth century, passed slowly from captains and admirals to the Admiralty, but it was always true that a boy had no hope of becoming a Naval officer without 'interest' at the back of him.[14]

In the eighteenth century small children had sometimes been sent to sea. In the nineteenth the lower age limit for nomination was twelve, and after 1849 an upper limit was also set – fourteen. Many people thought Naval officers were caught much too young for their own good or the good of the service; their whole outlook and education were confined much too soon, it was said, within the 'wooden walls'. Their Lordships always replied that you couldn't make a British Naval officer if you started any later, and nobody seems to have been prepared to dispute the matter seriously until well on in the twentieth century. One concession to the mid-century reformers, however, the Admiralty did make. After 1851 they required patrons' nominees to show that they could write English (usually a page from *The Spectator*) from dictation and to be acquainted with the first four rules of arithmetic, reduction, and the rule of three. If a candidate failed the examination, his nomination was to be cancelled.[15]

Until the sixties, at least, the Navy offered very unattractive career prospects. By 1815 it already had far too many officers, and peace made things much worse. Professor Lewis has shown that throughout the first half of the century, once the wars were over, the great majority of Naval officers – some two-thirds of the lieutenants up to nine-tenths or so of the admirals and captains – were permanently on half-pay. Yet nominations were continually sought after, presumably because even half-pay (which was in fact considerably more than half the pay of the rank) represented something like a 'competence', though a beggarly one, and the chances of more lucrative employment at a suitably gentlemanly level were hard to come by. The whole situation is an eloquent comment on the scarcity of middle-class salaried employment in early and mid-Victorian England.[16]

To the reformers, then, the Navy seems to have been something of a side-issue. On the one hand it was of limited interest as a source of employment: on the other, it was an arcane mystery best left untampered with if the safety of the State was to be preserved. After the battleship *Captain* foundered in 1870, was it not recorded on a brass plate in St Paul's Cathedral that she had been built to a faulty design in response to public clamour, against the better judgement of the Admiralty? If that could happen to a battleship, what might not public clamour do to the training of Naval officers? Best keep quiet, and let Their Lordships get on with it.

None of these considerations applied to the Civil Service. If criticism of the Navy was near to blasphemy, then the civil Service was the Aunt Sally of the Constitution: the traditional home of the patronage, jobbery and inefficiency which brisk reformers had long loved to castigate. Certainly there was no lack of justification for their abuse. Virtually every post was in some politician's gift and, as the two leading reformers, Northcote and Trevelyan, put it in 1854: 'admission into the Civil Service is . . . eagerly sought after . . . for the unambitious, and the indolent or incapable . . . those whom indolence of temperament or physical infirmities unfit for active exertions, are placed in the Civil Service, where they may obtain an honourable livelihood with little labour, and with no risk.'[17] Clerks in government offices must be literate and their arithmetic must be passable but young men of these very moderate attainments were not difficult to find among the 'friends' of public men, or among their needy relations. And occasionally there might be some deserving author or intellectual who needed an income, without any very pressing call on his time or talents, and who did not see fit to go into the Church.

The work in government offices – a great deal of copying and long addition sums – was dreary. On the other hand the hours were short – six a day, or so – and the pay, though no one could call it exciting, was not bad by the standards of the day. You might start as high as £100 a year and work up, over twenty years or so, to twice as much, or even more. And the job was absolutely safe. The attractions are obvious but, as Sir James Stephen said, 'the prizes to be won are not worthy of the pursuit of such young men as I am constantly observing among the forefront of the competitors for academical honours.'[18]

That was because nobody supposed that the young man who came in as a clerk had any serious chance of rising to the top of the Service. In any case while government was at a minimum, as it was in the eighteenth and early nineteenth centuries, there was nothing very much to be done there, either. But as the Victorian State began to grow, that began to alter. Against all the instincts of the English governing class, it became inescapably necessary to administer such things as the Poor Law and the health of towns. That meant making up one's mind, and making up ministers' minds, about drains, cholera, the design of workhouses, corrupt vestries, and the expense of it all. Especially the expense. Treasury officials, always important, became more important still. The best brains the universities could provide were not too good for that kind of appointment.

Men of this calibre were not often bred up within the Civil Service. They hardly could be, given its accepted standing and methods of recruitment. They were brought in at the top after they had made their mark elsewhere – at the university; at the Bar; perhaps in India, where public administration was already a profession.[19] And nobody despised them. 'All who are acquainted', said Edwin Chadwick, 'with the narrow circle of the highest class of permanent officers in the Civil Service will speak of them with respect.'[20]

Many influential people, among them Sir James Stephen, one of the most respected of Chadwick's 'narrow circle', did not want this system changed. They thought it was essential that the highest Civil Servants should, as a general rule, come to their posts from the world at large, and that it would be a disaster if the Civil Service were to become a closed corporation of good examinees. Moreover if the ordinary run of clerks were to be promoted on any other grounds than seniority they would immediately suspect favouritism (the same argument as was advanced in defence of promotion by seniority in the Army) and the most unholy jealousies would result. No office, they said, could be run on the basis of promotion by merit: feuds would tear it apart.[21] So far were they, in the mid-eighteen-fifties, from one of the central principles of modern competitive society.

But by the middle years of the century the pressure towards change – towards a competitive system – was growing too strong to resist. Sir Charles Trevelyan, speaking in 1875, said 'the revolutionary period of 1848 gave us a shake, and created a disposition to put our house in order.' One of the consequences was a series of investigations, lasting for five years, into the work of public offices. A Treasury Committee, with Trevelyan as a member, went from department to department, visiting some of them more than once. As they went on, Trevelyan recalled, they found 'the same evils, and circumstances pointing to the same remedies, with reference to every department.' The evils, broadly speaking, were the evils of patronage: the remedies, competitive examinations and promotion by merit.[22] The upshot was the *Report on the Organization of the Permanent Civil Service*, 1854, which we shall discuss in the next chapter.

Soon after the *Report* was issued, the first winter of the Crimean War began to reveal appalling depths of official incompetence, both military and civilian. The revelations set off a clamorous demand for wholesale reform, led, as demands for reform usually were, by men of the middle classes. The Administrative

Reform Association was founded. Samuel Morley (1809–86), a Non-conformist stocking-maker from Nottingham, took the chair. A 'monster meeting' was held to support the Association in Drury Lane Theatre, on 13 June 1855. Samuel Morley said 'he desired to see the offices of the State thrown open to public competition, believing that every man possessed of talent was responsible for its employment for the benefit of his fellow-men, and any barrier placed in the way of his so doing, either by the Legislature or by custom, was unnatural and suspicious.'[23] At a meeting in Birmingham, said to have been attended by six to seven thousand people, George Dawson, a surgeon, said: 'Now we demand that the whole system of England should be altered (Cheers). Not the Army only, not the Navy only, but all the Government affairs, all the Government offices; that all appointments shall be open to approved ability, tried by examination. (Renewed cheering).'[24]

The message was clear, and it could no longer be ignored.

Chapter 6

THE TRIUMPH OF COMPETITION

THE men mainly responsible for applying the principle of competitive entry to the public service, as distinct from the large number who simply agitated for it, were a small and close-knit group of officials, politicians, and academics. They were very clear-minded, very articulate, and they took care to explain themselves lucidly on paper at every step of their proceedings. Few major changes of public policy have been backed by more carefully reasoned theoretical considerations – which was one of the things their opponents held against them. Doctrinaires are not usually popular in England.

The *Report on the Organization of the Permanent Civil Service* was written by a rising politician, Sir Stafford Northcote (1818–87), and by Sir Charles Trevelyan (1807–86), the Assistant Secretary (permanent head) of the Treasury, who had long experience in India and at home. In 1853, the year before the *Report* was published, the reformers had scored their first big success when the principle of competitive entry to the India Civil Service passed into law in the Government of India Act. A Committee was set up to work out regulations for the competition, and the Chairman was T. B. Macaulay, Trevelyan's brother-in-law, who like Trevelyan had served with great distinction in India. Another member was Benjamin Jowett (1817–93), Fellow and Tutor, later Master of Balliol College Oxford, whose comments were sought by Northcote and Trevelyan when they had drafted their report. The Committee also included J. G. Shaw-Lefèvre (1797–1879).

In 1855, when the agitation for administrative reform was at its height, a Commission was set up, by Order-in-Council, to examine candidates for the Civil Service. One of the Commissioners was

Shaw-Lefèvre. Another was Sir Edward Ryan, a high official of the Exchequer who had been Chief Justice of Bengal. The third, Edward Romilly, was another Civil Servant – Chairman of the Board of Audit – but he soon resigned. Ryan and Shaw-Lefèvre had the shaping of the new system pretty much to themselves until 1862, when Shaw-Lefèvre's state of health caused him to resign.[1]

The men mentioned in the last two paragraphs had all been brought up to the strenuous academic competition, among a minority of brilliant undergraduates, which had been coming into fashion at Oxford and Cambridge since the beginning of the century. This was entirely confined to the old classical and mathematical course of liberal education. It represented the best aspect of that cast of mind which distrusted specialized training and what Gladstone (another product of it) called 'the low utilitarian argument in matter of education for giving it what is termed a practical direction.'[2]

For the few who were bright enough to become double-firsts, wranglers, university prizemen, and so forth, success offered Fellowships, Church preferment, a gateway to all the higher levels of the national life. The system was, in fact, a competitive selection device which by the fifties had already been operating, for the better part of half a century, over a wide unspecialized field. Why should not something like it be designed specifically for selecting the higher Civil Servants, Army officers, and anyone else who might be required for the middle and upper levels of the service of the State?

It will be observed that this was a different concept from the one which the reformers of the professions had been campaigning for. It was a competitive test in subjects of general education, not a qualifying examination in technical specialities. The two ideas, however, were sufficiently alike to appeal broadly to the same class of people, and in fact the effect of the new system, eventually, was to open fresh avenues of employment to the professional class and to those outside it who had sufficient academic ability and determination to thrust their way in. Sir Charles Trevelyan, speaking in 1875, recalled that among the early supporters of the competitive system, as soon as it was introduced, were 'a large and important class of clergymen and retired officers and persons of the middle class of all sorts, who are in the habit of giving a good education

86

to their sons, with a view to putting them out in life (in Ireland, especially, they at once took in the idea and saw the advantages of it).'³

What these people saw and welcomed was the shattering blow to aristocratic privilege and to closed systems of patronage like the East India directorate. Some of the ablest men of the day, nevertheless, were against the whole system of selection by competitive examination. The serious periodicals, especially the *Saturday Review*, were open to them, and during the fifties and sixties they repeatedly argued their case. They lost, and what they had to say against one of the most revered of present-day institutions – selection by examinable merit – has hardly had any serious attention since, which does not necessarily mean that it deserves none.

First and fundamentally, would competitive examinations produce men with the kind of ability the public service needed? Their opponents took leave to doubt it. Anthony Trollope and others were afraid that the junior posts in government offices would be filled with discontented bright young men who had been educated beyond their work, and whose only ascertained talent was the ability to pass examinations. 'The truth is,' said *The Economist* in 1862, 'it is simply *wasteful* and *cruel* to turn a young man of cultivated and aroused intellect into an ordinary Customs, War, or Admiralty clerk.' Sir Arthur Helps (1813–75), Clerk of the Privy Council and ghost writer to Queen Victoria, speaking to Lyon Playfair's Civil Service Inquiry Commission in 1875, was a good deal more picturesquely caustic: 'I believe that the present system of competitive examination is a dream of pedantry – dreamed by some Chinese philosopher – and that more witches and wizards were discovered by the notable system of pricking with pins, than judicious and capable men are likely to be discovered by the present system of competitive examination.'⁴

This criticism had particular force when it was levelled at the proposal to introduce competitive examinations for entry into the cavalry and infantry. Granted that it might be a good idea to get rid of purchase and the whole atmosphere of privilege and snobbery which centred round it, yet did it follow that a good examinee would necessarily be a good fighting man? Or even a gentleman? Wouldn't it, at least, be a good idea to make candidates for commissions take some sort of competitive test in physical exercises? This last suggestion had so much sense in it that in 1883 the Director-General of Military Education put forward detailed proposals, but nothing seems to have come of them.[5]

There were general misgivings, among supporters of examinations as well as among their opponents, about the effect of examination requirements on the educational system. 'If boys at school', said the *Report of the Schools Enquiry Commission* in 1868, 'are induced to view them as the be-all and end-all of school life, it is probable that the good which they do in stimulating study, will be very dearly purchased.' The Rector of Lincoln College, Oxford, quoted in the same report, sadly foresaw the time when schools would teach what they knew examiners required, rather than obliging examiners to test what the schools thought good for their pupils. The Civil Service Commissioners, fervently though they supported the examination principle, were well aware of the danger they were in of being deceived by cramming and superficial knowledge. Their usual remedy was to disallow marks in any subject they examined which did not reach a stipulated proportion of the total, varying between one-sixth and one-quarter from one examination to another.[6]

Even if examinations were an adequate test of intellectual qualities, what about character and morals? A patron, it was argued, usually took care to look into these matters and his nominees were often people he had known well for a long time, so that he would have much better opportunities for assessing their character than any stranger could have. Of course the authorities responsible for competitive entry would make enquiries, but were these really a substitute for the patron's detailed knowledge? And if a candidate were turned down after such enquiries, the replies to which were necessarily secret, admitting of no defence, would that not damage his reputation, perhaps unjustly?[7]

'For the moral character of the candidates', wrote Benjamin Jowett to Trevelyan, 'I should trust partly to the examination itself. University experience abundantly shows that in more than nineteen cases out of twenty, men of attainments are also men of character. The perseverance and self-discipline necessary for the acquirement of any considerable amount of knowledge are a great security that a young man has not led a dissolute life.'[8] Jowett's statistics are impressive in their precision, and no doubt the argument on behalf of patronage was to some extent a specious defence of nepotism. Before it is finally dismissed, however, it may be in order to question whether even yet any system of selection, however scientific, has provided an entirely satisfactory substitute for long personal acquaintance and shrewd judgement.

Finally, many people had grave doubts about the effect of the competitive system on the health of candidates. A generation which placed great emphasis on the muscular outdoor virtues, and on 'manliness', was very disturbed by the thought of lads of seventeen or so spending too long at their books and becoming over-anxious about the results of competitions they entered for. A committee reporting on the education of artillery officers in 1871 said: 'the severe competition for commissions during the latter part of the course at the Royal Military Academy has a severe though temporary effect upon the physical strength of the cadets'[9], and other commentators thought the results of this kind of exertion and anxiety might be permanent, not temporary. What a writer in the *Saturday Review* called 'undue forcing of the intellectual powers at a critical period of life' might permanently harm the individual.[10]

These fears were so often expressed, and were taken so seriously that at least twice the authorities comforted themselves by taking medical opinions. In 1875 Sir William Gull, MD, who had been examining ICS candidates for fourteen years, said: 'experience . . . abundantly proves that the course of life which conduces to some intellectual training is equally favourable to the physical health of the student.' In 1894 William Miller Ord, MD, FRCP, went much further, and his opinion so well expresses the later Victorian view of the proper relationship between physical and intellectual pursuits that it is worth quoting at length:

'I must confess that I had expected to find many of such candidates [for the ICS] more or less weakly, by reason of prolonged study and severe competitive examinations. I had also expected that by reason of close application to literary work, such as might have interfered with muscular exercise and also with the physical and moral development incidental to athletic exercises, the bookworm or the burner of midnight oil would more frequently present himself than the athlete. When, however, the candidates passed before me ... there was not one whom I would consider unequal to the requirements of a service calling for strength, endurance and activity. There was clear preceding evidence of their proficiency in a wide range of literary work, in mathematics, and in various departments of scientific education; yet to the eye of the medical examiner they presented no indication of physical depreciation or damage to be attributed to such influences. For the most part they presented the evidence of vigourous health, and bore the stamp of the University and the Public School ... it may be well to add that in the way of manliness their excellence is still more striking. They have commended themselves as excellent specimens of the English youth of today; for the most part well set-up, clean-skinned, clean-limbed, and in all ways wholesome.'[11]

Such whole-hearted exaltation of physical excellence would surely have surprised the original devisers of the ICS Competition, and might have disturbed them. It was a long way from what they intended. To their early struggles, with this glimpse of their later outcome, we must now return.

While many influential people remained dubious of the whole principle of competitive entry, or downright hostile to it, the early progress of the reformers was slow, even after the Civil Service Commission had been set up, rather tentatively, in 1855. The Commission was by no means empowered to bring in a competitive system straightaway, and apply it to the whole of the public service. The responsibility for appointing staff to the public offices still lay, separately, with the heads of each of the departments. The primary business of the Commission was to test candidates who were nominated and, if they passed, to certify that they were fit to be appointed. And they had to do this for candidates for thousands of positions of every sort, from village postmen, prison warders and wardresses, and minor customs officials upwards, though their main interest, as it is ours, was in the 'superior situations' – for which they devised tests very different from those imposed upon would-be Quarantine Mariners or Lady Scripture Readers in the Convict Service.

To some departments, however, right from the start, it was laid down that entry should be by limited competition. That is, the patrons who had the right to nominate candidates would still exercise the right, but they would nominate more than there were vacancies for. The Civil Service Commissioners would then run competitions – separately for each batch of vacancies to be filled – to determine who should be appointed. This meant a great number of small competitions (between 1858 and 1864, 774 for 1,836 'superior situations'), which led to some curious results. It was fairly easy, for instance, to rig one of these small competitions so that only one candidate could possibly get in. Again, it was easy enough for opponents of the system to show that it was unfair, since a candidate who failed to get into one department might have scored highly enough to get himself into another, in a competition run at the same time, but separately. And sometimes there simply were not enough candidates who were good enough. In 1863, eighty-six candidates competed for thirty situations, but the general standard was so low that only twenty-three could be filled.[12] So disastrously poor, in fact, was the general level of schooling revealed by these competitions – allegedly for the best educated young men of the kingdom – that the Commissioners very soon came to insist on a qualifying test before candidates were allowed to enter for the competitive examination.

This kind of competition, although an advance on undiluted patronage, was little more than half-way to what the Commissioners really wanted to see: open competition at a high level of intellectual effort. Apart from the fact that the competitions were open only to patrons' nominees, it is clear that the vast majority of the appointments to which they led were not of a kind to attract high talent, of the kind likely to gain high honours at Oxford or Cambridge. For that kind of young man, there were not more than ten or a dozen openings a year in the Home Civil Service, and so matters long remained, even after the Upper Division or Class I Clerkships were formally constituted in 1872. The immediate effect of that move, in fact, was actually to cut down the number of Class I vacancies offered, since heads of departments, to save money, offered as few as possible, preferring to get the work done by lower paid staff of a lower grade.[13]

The Commissioners' real showpiece was the ICS competition, which was from the first open, at a high intellectual level, and productive of sufficient vacancies to attract plenty of good candidates. In their annual reports during the sixties the Commissioners regularly discussed the competition in detail, building up, as they did so, a picture of the new kind of government service which was developing as the competitive system took hold. The features of the higher Civil Service which are familiar to us today, particularly the high standard and the wide range of subjects demanded by the examination, as well as the close connection with the universities, developed in the ICS long before they were much in evidence at home. In the Commissioners' reports on the early competitions, as well as in evidence from other sources, we see the modern Civil Servant of the administrative grade being born before our eyes: 'the virtual creation,' as George Brodrick observed in 1858, 'of a new profession.'[14]

The Commissioners were quite clear what they were about. Like management recruiters from large firms today – of whom, indeed, they were the ancestors – they were out to capture as much talent as they could from sources which had formerly supplied other needs. They offered good pay and prospects of 'steady advancement' – £300 or more a year to start with, and several times as much quite soon, at a time when £100 a year rising over twenty years or so to £200 was enough to attract plenty of well-educated applicants. They offered 'infinite opportunities of public usefulness': in other words, satisfying work. They offered 'dignity, honour and influence': in other words, status. On top of it all there was 'liberal and judicious provision for retirement at an early age.'

They required 'no particular course of special studies'. They felt that 'anyone well prepared to take high honours at any of the principal English or Irish universities has a good chance of success'. If he failed, he would not have wasted his time: his efforts 'would hardly at all interfere with his academical progress' (a point which was strenuously disputed by the university authorities). They felt convinced that 'when this system of competitive examination ... is generally made known and fully understood, the temptation thus held out will draw away many young university men from the severe and uncertain competition of the Bar, the moderate expectations of the Church, and still more from the laborious future which the various employments of a scholastic nature hold out.'[15]

The universities reacted variously. For all that the Commissioners might say, their examination requirements, which we discuss in the next chapter, went a lot wider than anything in the conventional university education of the day and their age limits conflicted with the universities' requirements for their degrees. Nevertheless the Commissioners were quite right about the attractions they held out to university men. They were so strong that the universities almost at once had to make provision for ICS candidates, especially at Oxford, under the influence of Jowett, and at Dublin where, as early as 1858, according to the *Saturday Review*, 'the Indian Civil Service appointments have become the true Fellowships.'[16] There was a native Indian professor at Dublin by 1862 and several at the University of London.

Cambridge, although bound like the rest to take the competition seriously, was inclined to be patronizing about the candidates – as, indeed, some people were at Oxford. 'When there are eighty vacancies', said the first edition of the Cambridge *Student's Guide* (edited by J. R. Seeley) in 1863, 'no very great ability or attainment is required . . . These appointments do not attract persons of first-rate ability from the Universities.' And in 1875 Lepel Griffin, ICS, in the *Fortnightly Review*, said: 'the probability is that always . . . men who have taken high honours at Oxford or Cambridge will find professional and political life in England both more attractive than an Indian career.'[17]

However that might be, the competition in its early years attracted university men in considerable numbers. Between 1855 and 1864, 101 men passed into the ICS from Oxford, 80 from Cambridge, 76 from Dublin, 37 from London, 27 from Edinburgh, 58 from other universities, and 79 from no university at all. By contrast, at the first open competition for positions in the Home Civil Service (nine writerships at the India Office) in 1858, only 9 of the 391 candidates had been to a university, and none of them got in.[18]

By 1875, though, the authorities were sufficiently disturbed by the relationship between the ICS and the universities to make it one of the particular subjects for investigation in a general enquiry into the selection and training of candidates for the Service. The root of the trouble was that, under pressure from John Lawrence and others, the upper age limit for taking the ICS examination had been lowered from twenty-three to twenty-two in 1859 and to twenty-one in 1865. This made it 'if not impossible, at any rate extremely difficult, to combine study at Oxford and Cambridge or any other university of great reputation, with the course of preparation required for the competition, or with the subsequent training ... to which the rules ... oblige the successful candidates to submit themselves.'[19]

This 'subsequent training', mainly in law and languages, lasted for two years. Since the men could not go to a university, they usually spent their time rather miserably in London lodgings, a way of life which contrasted very unfavourably with life at the East India Company's college at Haileybury before the days of the competition. Until this was put right, there could not be that close relationship between the universities and the public service which the founders of the competition had wished to see, and which did eventually grow up. At the same time, there was a risk that the universities would be as effectively separated from education for the government service as they already were from training for most of the professions.

Whether or not they went to a university, men reached the ICS from the whole range of English schools and from schools abroad as well. In a typical early competition there would be candidates from the ancient public schools and from the more ambitious recent foundations such as Cheltenham, Marlborough, King's College School and University College School. Then there would be a good many from grammar schools – not more than one or two from any single school, probably – including a largish Irish contingent. Another group would be from proprietary schools and there might be a few, with a very slender chance of success, from national, British or parish schools. There would always be some who had been educated at home or privately, probably as the pupils of country parsons.

The social background of the candidates interested the Commissioners very much. Year by year, they tabulated it in detail. Probably, although they do not say so, they wanted to show that the competition really was open and that patronage had gone. Probably, also, they wanted to make sure that they got at all possible sources of ability, even the most unlikely.

Successful competitors certainly came from widely varying social origins. In the *Report of the 1875 Enquiry into Selection and Training* there is a table which shows the profession or occupation of fathers of the 668 candidates who passed the final ICS examination between 1860 and 1874, and the coverage runs from members of noble families at one extreme to two gamekeepers at the other.

Mostly, as the Commissioners had predicted, and as Trevelyan recalled in 1875, the ICS drew on the class of men who otherwise would have gone into the commissioned ranks of the Army or Navy, or into one of the professions. Ten per cent of the fathers in the list appear to have been country gentlemen: another 63 per cent belonged to the armed services, some branch of the Civil Service at home or abroad, or to one of the learned professions. Much the largest group were the clergymen – 27·5 per cent of the total, whereas no other occupational grouping ran over 10 per cent. For this very large preponderance of clergymen there are presumably two main reasons: one, that clergymen, on the whole, were not rich and their sons had to earn their own living; two, that, as we have remarked earlier, in the early nineteenth century far more educated men, proportionately, went into the Church than subsequently, simply for lack of alternative occupation.

Some 30 per cent of the candidates were the sons of men who, by the standards of the day, came from the lower middle class or even further down the social scale. If we generously place with the professional class the 20 per cent whose fathers were merchants, architects and engineers (2 per cent), or teachers of one sort or another (4 per cent), and those who followed an assortment of occupations including accountancy, farming, land agency, and surveying, we are left with 10 per cent whose social pretensions, by any standard, were very modest indeed. It is perhaps a somewhat unfamiliar thought that the rulers of late Victorian India – the sahibs of the British Empire in its glory – included an appreciable number of men whose fathers had been bakers, butchers, tailors, shoemakers, upholsterers, cheese factors, and undertakers.[20]

John Lawrence, after the ICS competition was established, grumbled that 'the men came out too old'. Lepel Griffin said the new breed of civilians of whom he was one 'neither ride, nor shoot, nor dance, nor play cricket, and prefer the companionship of their books to the attractions of Indian society'. Lord Ellenborough warned: 'Recollect that the civil servant in England is a clerk; in India he may become a pro-consul.'[21] Yet in 1875, when the whole system was critically and exhaustively examined (district officers were encouraged to send in their opinions, and did so at great length), nobody was found to suggest seriously that the competitive principle was at fault. Its working could be improved, but no one wanted to do away with it.

The success of the new system was infectious, as its founders hoped, and during the sixties more and more departments in the home Civil Service accepted the principle of competitive entry. In 1870, by Order-in-Council, open competition was laid down as the method of entry to nearly all branches of the service. The Foreign Office, it is true, resisted successfully and preserved a system of limited competition for many years longer than anyone else. But then the Foreign Office, like the Navy, had a very special *mystique*, guaranteed by the principle that junior diplomats should be paid very little – preferably nothing at all – and should live very expensively, so that they would be bound to come from the very top. Everyone, even *The Economist*, admitted that diplomats had to be gentlemen, but *The Economist* did not see why they need be noblemen: 'the middle classes are perfectly able to furnish their contribution of highly polished and accomplished men' – but they ought to be properly paid.[22] This view was not taken seriously then, nor for many years. Diplomacy remained a profession of immense prestige and dignity, but not a way to earn your living.

The first competition for Class I Clerkships, in 1872, was an anti-climax. Twenty-two candidates competed for ten places. Soon there were more candidates, but sometimes even fewer vacancies. In 1876, thirty-eight candidates competed for four openings: in 1877, sixty-one for eleven. Between 1870 and 1881 (inclusive) 117 posts in the 'new higher division' were filled – and fifty-three were turned down. At about the same period the ICS was taking on thirty to forty men a year, out of perhaps two hundred competitors. The destruction of patronage did not open the way to large new fields of middle-class employment in the upper ranks of the Civil Service, which were very sparsely staffed. It did throw open a good many posts lower down – between 1876 and 1881, 1,270 men and 416 boy clerks were appointed after competition – but these jobs, though secure, were by no means well paid.[23]

The abolition of patronage and purchase in the Army opened a much wider gateway to talent, for the number of commissions granted every year ran into hundreds and increased as time went on, with the gradual build-up towards 1914. The first assault was on the Royal Military Academy Woolwich, where artillery and engineer officers were trained. Entry, under the old system, was by nomination and the Master-General of the Ordnance had the patronage. The course of study was a serious one and efforts were made to see that cadets took it seriously, though under the stress of war standards were from time to time relaxed.[24]

Warning was given in 1856, during the wave of reform about the time of the Crimean War, that patronage would be replaced by competition, and by 1857 an examination of considerable severity had been devised, placing great emphasis on mathematics. By 1863 the changeover was complete and every cadet then at Woolwich had come in by competition. The Woolwich competition very quickly attracted attention, in much the same way as the ICS competition did, though it was aimed at men with a scientific cast of mind rather than a literary one.

The artillery and engineers were not socially so distinguished as the rest of the Army. Their officers were not expected to live quite so expensively and that was a positive advantage to country clergymen or doctors with several sons to provide for. Moreover Woolwich was for many years one of the very few establishments in England giving anything like a serious scientific or technical education, which meant that RE officers, in particular, often got the chance of attractive appointments of a civilian or semi-civilian character. Many were in India, but at home the Ordnance Survey was in the hands of engineer officers; engineer officers became inspecting officers of railways, responsible for official enquiries into accidents, and a large variety of other appointments were held by officers trained at Woolwich. Professor W. L. Burn, in *The Age of Equipoise*, gives a considerable list, and in the latter part of the century Sir John Donnelly (1834–1902), an engineer officer, was head of the Science and Art Department and Sir Vivian Majendie (1836–98), an artillery colonel, was Inspector of Explosives at the Home Office, to name but two.[25]

In 1867 Sir Charles Trevelyan wrote '. . . when, by the abolition of purchase and the increase of pay, the army shall become an open, remunerative profession, it will be an object of desire for the best class of our young men who now enter the artillery and engineers, the Indian Civil Service, the law, civil engineers, or any other line of life.'[26] With others of like mind he campaigned actively for the end of purchase, and in 1871 he saw it brought about.

The thought that the award of commissions in the most fashionable regiments of horse and foot should be subject to competitive examination was intolerable to conservative upper-class minds. The defenders of the old system, who included the Commander-in-Chief (Queen Victoria's cousin the Duke of Cambridge), were well entrenched in the House of Lords, as well as having a strong force in the Commons. Gladstone's Government, therefore, abolished purchase not by Act of Parliament but by a Royal Warrant, which the Lords could not challenge. This was regarded as a very dirty trick indeed, and the resulting bitterness split society in a way in which it was seldom split by late Victorian politics, unless Ireland was the issue.

Between 1876 and 1882 over eighteen hundred cadetships were offered at Sandhurst: seven hundred at Woolwich. These numbers no doubt help to explain why so many people were so anxious to prise the Army open. The Navy, meanwhile, went quietly on to a system of limited competition after nomination: very much the same system as that at the Foreign Office.

The effect of competitive entry on the Army was less devastating than the opponents and defenders of purchase respectively hoped and feared. It remained an expensive occupation, except in India, and it was still difficult for an officer to live on his pay. The 'best' regiments were still guarded by considerations of wealth, social standing, and family connections. The cavalry's magnificence remained, on the whole, undimmed by brains. Nevertheless, under the influence of Wolseley and those who thought like him, the idea that an officer was a professional man was firmly insisted upon. From 1874 onwards all officers of cavalry and infantry had to take a course of professional education at Sandhurst before they took up their first appointments. Only one way remained of avoiding the open Sandhurst competition. That was to persuade a colonel of militia to nominate you to a militia commission, from which it was fairly easy to proceed to one in the regular forces. That was the last remnant of patronage in the appointment of officers to regular commissions in the British Army, and by it the nation gained the services of Marshal of the Royal Air Force Lord Trenchard (1873–1956).

Between 1855 and 1875 the old official world of patronage, purchase, nepotism, and interest was turned upside down. Only the Church escaped. Otherwise, these things lived on outside public life, in what is nowadays often called 'the private sector', where no one complained overmuch about them – no one, at any rate, who was in a position to do much about it. Examinations, both qualifying and competitive, came into the centre of the stage for the classes which looked for a living either to the public services or to the open professions. Success in the ICS competition opened up a prospect of great rewards, and at the least it guaranteed a competence for life. Success in the competition for Woolwich was less exciting, but it meant that a boy was decently and honourably provided for. More and more these two competitions and, after 1871, the competition for Sandhurst as well, began to enter into the calculations of clergymen, doctors, lawyers, army officers, and others of similar social standing who were seeking a career for their sons. There was no longer so high a barrier of 'influence' and 'connections' to keep them out of the world of official employment. With this much wider prospect before them, what educational system existed, or could be built, to serve their needs?

Chapter 7

PROFESSIONAL MEN AT SCHOOL

PARENTS of boys intended for the reformed professions and for the new public service soon found that the examiners were making demands which mid-Victorian schools, especially the most respected, were ill-fitted to supply. The schools themselves had been reformed, and the best headmasters were full of the same kind of self-confident energy which the reformers of the professional world possessed. But they were far from believing that preparation for qualifying or competitive examinations was a proper function for the English public school. At the heart of upper-middle-class education, therefore, as Victorian England faced the growing challenge of the later nineteenth century, there was a conflict of purpose.

In their *Report on the Indian Civil Service* of November 1854 Macaulay and his Committee explained the reasoning behind the regulations for the newly devised competition. They amounted to a thorough-going assault on the foundations of the established system of English liberal education. The members of the Committee were themselves distinguished products of that system and the last thing they intended, according to their own account, was its overthrow. Yet what they asked of it it could not possibly deliver without, to say the least, very drastic changes in what was taught and in the methods of teaching.

The Committee said they set out to find young men who had had 'the best, the most liberal, the most finished education that their native country affords.'[1] They thought it desirable that a considerable number of them should have taken first degrees in Arts at Oxford or Cambridge. They therefore fixed their upper age limit at twenty-three. When the age limit was brought down successively to twenty-two (1859) and twenty-one (1865) the Committee's desire, as we have seen (above p. 93) was seriously interfered with.

They emphatically did not intend to create anything in the nature of a specialized professional qualifying examination. The examination they proposed, they said, ought to test general education – 'those branches of knowledge to which it is desirable that English gentlemen who mean to remain at home should pay some attention.' They set a high standard and realized that most of those who entered would fail – 'among them many young men of excellent abilities and laudable industry' – and it would be undesirable to call on them to waste time on subjects which could be of no use unless they succeeded. Professional training as Indian administrators was to begin after selection.

Working on these principles, the Committee devised an examination which centred on the mastery of English rather than the classics. This was revolutionary, as they must have known. It flew in the face of the public schools and the ancient universities. Nevertheless the committee quite firmly declared their belief that English subjects, in which they included history as well as literature, were the essential basis of the kind of general education they sought.

After that, their object was to give an equal chance to candidates from all parts of the United Kingdom, so they were careful to give due weight to all the subjects in which the English, Scottish, and Irish universities were known to specialize. They went out of their way, also, to cater for native-born Indians, who were allowed to take the classical languages of India instead of Greek or Latin. 'The whole examination,' they said, 'ought . . . to be carried on by means of written papers. The candidates ought not to be allowed the help of any book; nor ought they, after a subject for composition has been proposed to them, or a paper of questions placed before them, to leave the place of examination till they have finished their work.'

From these considerations there emerged a list of subjects for candidates to choose from. None was compulsory, and the marking system was carefully weighted to give an equal chance to English, Scots and Irish, provided that each of them had taken sufficient trouble over English language, literature and history.

In the early competitions the choice of subject and the maximum marks attainable were:

English and English History	1,500 marks
Classics	1,500
French, German, Italian, each	375
Mathematics	1,250
Natural Sciences	500
Logic, Mental, and Moral Philosophy	500
Sanskrit, Arabic, each	375

The results were determined simply by adding up the marks gained by each candidate, but 125 marks were knocked off the total gained in each paper in order to discourage candidates from attempting subjects which they did not really know. Thus it was hoped to defeat the evils of 'cram' and 'smattering', two of the examiners' favourite bogeys.[2]

The Woolwich examination, likewise, demanded evidence of a respectable general education, but beyond that it required a marked leaning towards science and mathematics, which placed it much farther beyond the range of a conventional liberal education than the ICS competition. In 1857 the subjects that might be taken, and the marks that could be gained, were:

Pure and mixed mathematics, i.e. statics, dynamics, hydrostatics	3,500 marks
English language, literature, composition, history, geography	1,250
Language, literature, history, geography of:	
Ancient Greece and Rome	1,750
France	1,000
Germany	750
Experimental sciences (chemistry, heat, electricity including magnetism)	1,000
Natural sciences, mineralogy, geology	750
Drawing (mainly technical)	1,000
Moral and political sciences	1,000

Mathematics was compulsory and candidates were permitted to take up to four more subjects. No one was to be admitted with less than seven hundred in mathematics, or three thousand in all. Marks which came to less than one-sixth of the total for any subject were to be disallowed – another anti-smattering device.[3]

These two competitions came in on top of the rising demand of the professions, particularly medicine and law, for qualification by written examination. Nobody expected the schools to prepare boys directly for the technical parts of these examinations, but the professions did feel, not unreasonably, that by the time boys became articled clerks or medical students they should have had a decent general education. How far the general run of schools, including the public schools, were from supplying that elementary requirement was demonstrated by the Civil Service Commissioners. They swiftly revealed how badly middle-class boys wrote, spelled, and above all figured, since arithmetic was widely neglected, except in 'commercial academies' which single-mindedly set out to produce clerks. 'There is scarcely any branch of human learning more generally useful than numbers', wrote Thomson in 1857, '. . . yet there are few more inefficiently taught', and university witnesses, about five years later, told the Clarendon Commission that at the first examination at Oxford, where arithmetic ran to vulgar fractions and decimals, algebra to simple equations, about a quarter of the candidates usually failed or withdrew.[4]

Moreover, even if school were not the place to begin professional studies, it was surely reasonable to expect the schools to lay a foundation on which professional studies could be built. Thus Sir John Rennie, writing in 1867, suggested that a boy intending to be a civil engineer ought to have a sound elementary education in 'arithmetic, algebra, geometry, natural philosophy, geography, geology, astronomy, chemistry, land and hydrographical surveying, as well as grammar, English composition, history, French, German, and Latin', and concluded, optimistically, 'every youth of ordinary talents has a tolerably fair knowledge of these at seventeen or eighteen.'[5] Rennie's list, it will be observed, covers much the same ground as the requirements for Woolwich, and careers advisers generally, writing in the third quarter of the century, emphasized the desirability of good general education for the professional man, with a grounding in technical subjects before he came to his specialized training.

Parents naturally took up the demand, and it was noticed by the Schools Enquiry Commissioners of the later sixties, who spoke sympathetically of those who intended their sons for 'employ-ments, the special preparation for which ought to begin at sixteen; as, for instance, the army, all but the highest branches of the medical and legal professions, civil engineering, and others.' Parents in this position were impatient of the traditional classical training. Latin they would accept, so long as it did not interfere with 'modern subjects': hardly Greek at any price. The kind of education they sought was increasingly tested, from 1860 on-wards, by the Oxford and Cambridge Local Examinations and by the examination for matriculation at the University of London. Professional bodies began to accept the results of these examina-tions as evidence of sound preliminary schooling, often as adequate substitutes for their own preliminary examinations, and schools began to be judged, partly at least, by the number of boys who got through.

But the education of the professional classes was dominated by the public schools, and to the orthodox public-school master of the fifties and sixties the demand for 'modern' education was most unwelcome. He would be a classically-educated clergyman with a good academic record, perhaps on his way to a bishopric. His idea of the purpose of public-school education would be to pro-duce Christian gentlemen. Whether the Christianity or the gentle-manliness should come first would depend on whom you were speaking to, and Thomas Arnold was aware that there might be a contradiction between the two. It was generally agreed, however, that the overriding purpose of education ought to be religious and moral; certainly not, except incidentally, to produce Indian administrators, engineer officers, doctors, or lawyers.[6]

Those who held this view laid great stress on 'character-build-ing'. By the fifties it had come to be looked on as much the most important activity of the English public school. Character was built mainly by the monitorial system, commonly reinforced by fagging, which gave almost the entire responsibility for the discipline and daily running of the school into the hands of the senior boys, backed by the remote authority of the headmaster. The monitors' power astonished foreign observers like Hippo-lyte Taine, who approved of it,[7] and the monitors set the tone of the school far more than the masters. 'Character-building' was almost entirely a non-intellectual process and it could easily become anti-intellectual. '[It] is of much more importance than the acquisition of mere knowledge', said Lord John Russell.[8]

As time went on this attitude led, by devious and fascinating paths which here we are not called on to explore, to the extreme games-worship of the latter part of the nineteenth century and the early part of the twentieth. 'We do not suppose', said the *Saturday Review* as early as 1857, 'that anyone hesitates to admit the great importance of keeping the proficiency of schoolboys in manly exercises up to the highest possible pitch. It is in these sports that the character of the boy is formed. It is from them that the readiness, pluck and self-dependence of the English gentleman are principally caught.'[9] And by 1864 it was estimated that Harrow boys, on an average, spent fifteen hours a week at cricket. A boy 'who took every opportunity' might spend twenty.[10]

The mental training which accompanied the building of character was overwhelmingly classical. Boys at Rugby in the early sixties, taking an average through the school, spent seventeen hours out of twenty-two on the classics, leaving three for mathematics and two for modern languages or 'natural philosophy', which meant chemistry and electricity – and Rugby was exceptionally advanced in the teaching of science. The Clarendon Commissioners asked headmasters why subjects other than the classics were not taught, and they replied, apparently with an air of putting an end to the matter, that there was no one to teach them and no books for them to be taught from.

When masters for modern subjects were found, they were often treated with an ostentatious condescension which must have ruined their chances of exercising any authority. Mathematics masters at Eton in the fifties were known as 'Assistants in the Mathematical school', not as 'Assistant Masters'. They were permitted no authority over the boys out of school, so that the boys, quite naturally, did not regard them as 'real' masters nor their subject, presumably, as a 'real' subject. As for modern languages, the unfortunate French master was long a stock figure of fun in public-school mythology, which may be one reason why Englishmen have traditionally been so good at spending so long at French without learning any.[11]

Nor does it seem that the classics were taught well. The basis of the teaching method was 'construing': that is, the literal word-by-word rendering of passages into English. Minute accuracy was aimed at and a detailed knowledge of the structure of the language. Appreciation of the subject matter was secondary. There was a great deal of learning by heart: a great deal, higher in the school, of composition, both in prose and verse. Some tough intellects survived it all and emerged magnificently trained.

With the majority the results were abysmally bad. So, at any rate, the Clarendon Commissioners reported, and it is significant that none of the schools would allow them, as they wished, to test a proportion of the boys by direct examination. Gladstone remarked 'the amount of work which we get out of the mass of the boys at our public schools is scandalously small.' Anthony Trollope, in 1865, maintained that there was no true teaching. He said there were too few masters to do the job properly (in the ancient public schools, a ratio of about one to twenty-two), and there were too few masters because those who were in office, dependent for their very comfortable incomes on the schools' endowments, were unwilling to share them with newcomers. 'Who', he asked, 'is going to give up his wife's carriage or his own bottle of claret, because somebody else thinks that the world might be improved by such sacrifices?'[12]

There was no reason why public-school masters should be good teachers. Teaching as an occupation had a very low standing indeed and was no profession for a gentleman. Hence there was even less provision for training teachers than for training doctors and lawyers. When teacher-training did come in, during the seventies, it was a process to be undergone by the despised teachers in elementary schools – many of them women – and it would never have occurred to a university man to submit himself to anything so degrading.

Teaching was, however, one of the traditional functions of the clergy, and masters in Victorian public schools were usually clergymen or, towards the end of the century, university men of the same social standing. By taking up the profession they conferred lustre upon it rather than the other way round. So far as the young clergyman was concerned, and sometimes the young layman too, teaching might be, in the words of the *Contemporary Review* in 1866, 'a pleasing and useful mode of filling up the vacant time between the taking the degree and the entry upon the life-profession.'[13]

An advertisement for an under-master at Merchant Taylors' in 1857 asked for a clergyman who had taken a first or second in classics at Oxford, 'fully competent to take a part in the Classical and lower branches of the Mathematical department of the School.' The salary offered was £250. This was quite good for a start, but scarcely a competence for a married man, and a clergyman of the academic standing required would certainly be looking well beyond it. He might stay in teaching for life, going on in due course to a headmastership, but it was equally possible that he would look on a spell of teaching as a step towards preferment rather than as a career in itself. In either case he would almost certainly have been scornful of anyone who suggested that he needed specialized training. Indeed the public-school master's view of his job displayed to an extreme degree that contempt for specialized training which was characteristic of the Victorian upper classes.[14]

To promote the study of the classics – the product of a pagan culture – as the essential education of the ruling classes of a self-consciously Christian nation might be thought a difficult intellectual exercise, especially considering the subject-matter of some of the most admired Roman authors. It was a difficulty resolutely disposed of. We have seen what Whewell thought (above p. 10). Mr Gladstone wrote: 'The materials of what we call classical training were prepared, and we have a right to say were advisedly and providentially prepared, in order that it might become ... the complement of Christianity.' Frederick Temple, Headmaster of Rugby and later Archbishop of Canterbury, was the more telling through not attempting to fly so high: 'The real defect of mathematics and physical science is that they have not any tendency to humanize. Such studies do not make a man more human, but simply more intelligent ... The fact is that all education really comes from intercourse with other minds.' He told the Clarendon Commission that he once asked a tradesman who had been at Rugby whether he learned anything useful there. ' "I was at school several years," the man answered, "and I have never regretted it; I learnt there what I don't think I could have learnt as well anywhere else, how to learn anything I wanted." '[15]

This tradesman was no doubt able and intelligent, with an exceptional aptitude for the classics. For such minds as his the old classical education, once you got beyond the stage of elementary drudgery, provided a very fine general training in the use of language and the handling of ideas. But very few boys ever did get through the stage of elementary drudgery, even at the university, and it is difficult to believe that they were all dunces, competently taught but incapable of learning. This, nevertheless, seems to have been what many of the great Victorian headmasters really believed. They steadily refused to admit to the Clarendon Commission either that anything could replace the classics as the best training for a first-class mind, or that anyone with a first-class mind could fail to be good at classical studies.[16]

It followed that 'modern studies' and anything in the nature of professional training were for the boobies, or at least for the second-rate. They could never be admitted to have any high educational value. If enough parents demanded them, however, they would have to be provided, albeit grudgingly. Thring, energetically developing Uppingham from a small country grammar school, described his response to the demand as follows:

'The question of professional training still remains. It has been shown above [in discussing the classics] to be absolutely impossible to direct the studies of a great school to this end beyond a certain degree, without destroying the object of a great school, which is, mental and bodily training in the best way, apart from immediate gain. Still there are very many who wish to have a good education, and at the same time to graft some professional knowledge upon it. This can be done ... If the extra subjects form so valuable a component part of the school, and are generally studied as filling-up work, there will be funds to support first-rate teachers, not inferior in any respect to the regular masters; and this will make the giving professional training, as far as it is desirable to do so, easy. It secures competent teachers.'[17]

The 'extra subjects' which Thring contemplated seem to have been 'Music, French, German, Drawing, and various branches of Natural Science, such as Botany, Natural History, &c.; or of Physical Science, as Chemistry, Electricity, Statics, Dynamics, &c.' – in other words, very much the kind of subjects asked for by the ICS and Woolwich competitions. Thring's opinion of them was revealed when he said that in them 'the most backward in Classical knowledge can take refuge. There they can find something to interest them; something too which others do not know, something in which they can attain distinction, and by so doing restore the balance of self-respect, or at least make some progress where many are quite ignorant.'[18] In other words, if parents insisted, he was willing to pay teachers of modern subjects quite well to keep the dunces happy while classical masters got on with the serious work of educating clever boys. With this attitude prevalent it is hardly surprising to find Jowett saying in 1875, of the ICS, 'The masters of public schools are set against the service, and are naturally indisposed to send up their best pupils as candidates because ... they gain no credit from them.'[19]

Parents could hardly be expected to accept so whole-heartedly as Thring and his brethren the idea that education at a 'great school' was to be 'mental and bodily training in the best way, apart from immediate gain.' They were very conscious of the need for immediate gain, and if the schoolmasters could not or would not put their sons in the way of acquiring it by teaching the subjects which examining bodies required, then they would find someone who would. Thus arose cramming: a characteristically Victorian branch of the educational industry.

It had a fairly respectable ancestry in the universities. In the fierce academic competition of the early nineteenth century it was generally recognized that private coaching, very much on the lines of the present-day tutorial system, was essential if you meant to take high honours, especially in mathematics. Alongside the official and somewhat decrepit teaching system of the universities and colleges there grew up an unofficial and highly lucrative system which was anything but decrepit. The coaches were men of high academic standing and often examiners – a point which did not go unremarked – and of one of them, second wrangler in 1877, a diarist observed 'this youth has already got a Fellowship and earns £800 besides by taking pupils.'[20]

As the competitive examination spread from the universities outwards into the professional world, it was natural that cramming should follow it. The headmasters of the great schools looked rather loftily upon it, but they did not hesitate to advise parents to take their boys away and send them to crammers if they wanted them to do well in the competition for the ICS or for Woolwich. Six months at a crammer's, therefore, became an accepted if not very dignified episode in the education of a Victorian gentleman, and there are many jocular references to it in the reminiscences of the great. Sir Winston Churchill called it 'this renowned system of intensive poultry-farming.'[21]

It was contended, particularly by those who distrusted the whole competitive system, that crammers were the ruin of good education and that all they did was to force enough knowledge into stupid boys' skulls to get them through whatever examination happened to be in prospect. Certainly the science of examination-passing, as distinct from the science of education, was more and more closely studied, more and more highly developed, as more and more careers came to depend on it. But there was more to be said for the crammers, some people thought, than merely this. Jowett himself admitted that crammers were 'excellent teachers' and Lepel Griffin (1838–1908) went further.[22]

Griffin, who had a distinguished Indian career, had been educated privately and then at Harrow. He left Harrow because of his health and went to a crammer, Mr Whitehead, of Chatham House, Ramsgate, from whose hands he passed into the ICS in 1859. He said that crammers were usually men of high academic attainments; that they were assisted by 'the most competent masters procurable'; that they got eight or ten hours' work a day out of their pupils. But his main point was that 'the results so much criticized are attained not so much by the excellence of the instruction as by the care taken to ascertain the peculiar bent of each mind, and to cultivate those particular subjects which are most congenial to it. This, which is neglected in the system of our public schools and colleges, is at the root of all intelligent education. The instruction given . . . is scientific in *method*, as opposed to ordinary English education, under which boys are taught Greek and Latin by a system which any man of sense, learning a modern language, would reject as ridiculous.'[23]

Many others besides Lepel Griffin were uneasy about the state of public-school education, and of English secondary and higher education generally. They found it deeply disturbing that the established educational authorities should be so scornful of almost all knowledge that was of direct practical use in the modern world. The Royal Commissions which investigated Oxford and Cambridge in the early fifties urged them to apply their resources to professional education. The Clarendon Commission expressed uneasiness about the overwhelming classical bias of the great public schools, though in mild and respectful terms. The Schools Enquiry Commission, a few years later, called for drastic reforms, but their report we shall return to (p. 114)

Dean Farrar, himself a public-school headmaster, was quite prepared to accept the view that there were subjects, particularly in science, which could provide an intellectual training as good as that provided by the classics which, anyhow, he thought badly and unimaginatively taught. Moreover a scientific education would be useful – 'and no sooner', he wrote, 'have I uttered the word "useful" than I imagine the hideous noise which will environ me, and amid the hubbub I faintly distinguish the words, vulgar, utilitarian, mechanical ... Well, before this storm of customary and traditional clamour I bow my head, and when it is over, I meekly repeat that it would be *more useful* – more rich in practical advantages, more directly available for health, for happiness, for success in the great battle of life. I for one am tired of this "worship of inutility". One would really think that it was a crime to aim at the material happiness of the human race.' He went on to say 'two or three truths ought now ... to be regarded as axiomatic: First, that science is as important a means of training as literature; secondly, that every education is one-sided and most imperfect which does not add science to literature; thirdly, that our present system is neither literary nor scientific; and fourthly, that it is perfectly possible for it to be both.'24

Some of the newer public schools, particularly Marlborough, Wellington and Cheltenham, were willing to experiment, as Thring was at Uppingham, with 'modern studies'. They depended more heavily than the ancient foundations on the professional classes, and they could not afford to treat parents' wishes so cavalierly. On the whole, though, their headmasters' enthusiasm was rather pale.

Barry, of Cheltenham, with some misgivings, was prepared to tell the Clarendon Commissioners that he felt sure (which may have meant that he felt nothing of the sort) that education in the Modern Department gave 'a true education, and not mere instruction in various subjects.' On the other hand the future Archbishop Benson, at Wellington, thought 'no boy has yet been placed in [the mathematical forms] by his friends from a conviction of the superiority of this mode of education', but simply in order to pass examinations, and it was evident what Benson thought of that. Only J. F. Bright, head of the Modern School at

Marlborough College (Sixty-two boys, against 315 on the classical side), was whole-hearted in his support. If, he said, there were equally good appliances for the modern as for the classical teaching, if there were equally good textbooks, grammars, and so on, then 'an education might be given in modern as accurate as in ancient subjects, while in comprehensiveness, in so far as it would be concerned with the wider field of modern thought, it might even have the advantage.'[25]

What particularly worried the critics of traditional education was that England was falling behind continental countries in the provision of secondary education in general and technical education in particular. As early as 1852, the year after the Great Exhibition – that grand demonstration of England's industrial supremacy – William Fairbairn (1789–1874) the engineer was complaining that in England there was nothing to compare with the Conservatoire des Arts et Métiers and the Ecole Centrale des Arts et Manufactures in France, nor with the educational institutions of Prussia. There, he said, the Government 'in its solicitude for the well-being of society, renders it imperative that every person in the Prussian dominions should be educated.'[26]

This unaccustomed feeling of insecurity was behind much of the investigation of the English educational system which went on in the sixties. It is expressed in particular in the monumental labours of the Schools Enquiry Commission, which in 1868 reported in great detail on the grammar schools, proprietary schools (many being what are now called public schools) and private schools of England. They found most of the grammar schools far in decay, most of the private schools deplorable, and most of the vigour among the proprietary schools and those grammar schools which, like Uppingham, were being rescued and turned into public schools by energetic headmasters. Of anything approaching a national system of education, except among the public schools, they found not a trace, and most of the public schools, new or old, were heavily influenced by the 'nine great schools' whose educational ideas we have already examined.[27]

One of their Assistant Commissioners was Matthew Arnold. They sent him to examine the education of the middle and upper classes in France, Italy, Germany, and Switzerland, a task which he accomplished in 1866. As well as being Thomas Arnold's son he was a school inspector, and in his report he compared the English system which he knew with the foreign systems he had just seen, and he was especially at pains to bring out the differences in the approach to professional education.

On the Continent he found the upper and middle classes brought up, as he put it, 'on the same plane'. In England the middle class as a rule was brought up 'on the second plane'. This, he said, was because 'half a dozen famous schools, Oxford or Cambridge' gave 'a training, a stamp, a cast of ideas, which make a sort of association of all who share them, and this association is the upper class. Except by one of these modes of access', he went on, 'an Englishman does not ... become a vital part of this association, for he does not bring with him the cast of ideas in which its bond of union lies.' That cast of ideas, he maintained, was aristocratic, not professional.

In consequence there was no country in Europe where the professions so thoroughly shared the outlook of the upper class as in England. Matthew Arnold did not deny that this outlook had its good points – 'a high spirit ... dignity ... a just sense of the greatness of great affairs – all of them governing qualities.' But he did point out that 'judged from its bad side, this cast of ideas is characterized by its indisposition and incapacity for science, for systematic knowledge.'

For this reason, he thought, the English professions were not, like the professions on the Continent, 'the stronghold of science and systematic knowledge. Moreover they were

'separate, to a degree unknown on the Continent, from the commercial and industrial class with which in social standing they are naturally on a level. So we have amongst us the spectacle of a middle class cut in two in a way unexampled anywhere else; of a professional class brought up on the first plane, with fine and governing qualities, but without the idea of science; while that immense business class, which is becoming so important a power in all countries, on which the future so much depends, and which in the leading schools of other countries fills so large a place, is in England brought up on the second plane, cut off from the aristocracy, and the professions, and without governing qualities.'[28]

These were serious charges. Arnold accused English education of snobbery, of neglect of science, of perpetuating and reinforcing the damaging division between 'professions' and 'trade'. In general the Commissioners agreed. Certainly they recognized and deplored the class basis of English schools, but they feared there was little to be done about it. 'Much of our evidence', they said, 'tends to show that social distinctions in education cannot be ignored.'[29] They sympathized with the desire of parents of good social standing to see modern subjects taught alongside the classics, but they pointed out that these parents 'would not wish to have what might be more readily converted into money if in any degree it tended to let their children sink in the social scale.'[30] They were very clear about the threat of foreign industrial competition.[31]

The Commissioners were disturbed by their findings. They made thorough-going recommendations for setting up a national system of secondary education. It took thirty years and another Royal Commission before a national system of secondary education, state-supported, was in fact set up.

For this there seem to have been two important sets of reasons. The first was the Victorians' intense dislike of state control, especially when it meant spending the taxpayers' money, as it usually did. They were most unwilling to see education run by the State and they were only prepared to spend on it sums of money which were ludicrously small by comparison with sums spent elsewhere, especially in Germany. And the whole conception was made even less attractive to politicians by the certainty that it could be relied on to stir up strife between Church and Dissent, to say nothing of the Catholics.

Even in spite of this group of obstacles, something might have been done if it had not been for the immense and growing prestige of public-school education, which was particularly attractive to the socially ambitious middle-class people – many of them rooted in trade – from whom the professions were so largely recruited. There was no national system for these people, as there was for people like them in Scotland or in Germany. There were, however, the ancient public schools and the growing throng of imitators by which alone, as Matthew Arnold so acutely pointed out, it was possible to pass, or to persuade others that one had passed, from the middle to the upper class.

The professional classes in England, therefore, and those who aspired to join them, could see no reason to take any interest in setting up a state system of education, and all their instincts were against state systems of any kind. On the other hand they found a very strong interest in maintaining, enlarging and multiplying the public schools. In 1866 a contributor to the *Contemporary Review* said: 'there is no doubt that the middle and professional class in England has either anticipated or is now endorsing his theory [the article was a review of Thring's book on public-school education]. To prove this we have merely to point to the unprecedented – almost mushroom – growth of the great modern public schools of Rossall, Marlborough, Wellington College and Haileybury.'[32] He might have added a couple of dozen names to that list without any difficulty at all, including the name of Thring's own school.

Public-school education, far more than university education, became the hall-mark of the later Victorian professional man, if by any means his parents could contrive it for him. The public schools had therefore to adapt themselves in some degree to the demands of professional life as expressed by examining bodies. We have seen the spirit in which most of them did it. The professional classes, for their part, had to adapt themselves in some degree to the demands of aristocratic education, in its late Victorian form, which they did with great eagerness. The compromise thus reached was not altogether favourable to the development of professional and technological skill, however admirably it may have developed other characteristics of mind and body.

Chapter 8

PROFESSIONAL MEN APPRENTICED

THE triumph of the examination system is a major historical landmark. It marks the end of a whole set of social assumptions; England had left the eighteenth century behind. But to go forward in the same spirit into the nineteenth and twentieth (not very far below the economic horizon by 1870), the country needed drastic reform of her educational institutions and the ideas behind them, especially at the higher end of the scale. For perhaps ten or fifteen years in the sixties and early seventies, it looked as if she might get it. Why else all those commissions of enquiry, investigating everything from village schools to universities? Why else so much discussion in print?

The movement petered out. Why, it is difficult to say, though some reasons have been suggested in the last chapter. The fact is certain. We must trace its consequences for the education and training of the professional classes after their schooldays ended.

The new competitive examinations set the schoolmaster a problem. On the whole, he evaded it and passed it to the crammer. Educationally that was not a very satisfactory answer, but it worked, in the sense that it got the boys off the schoolmaster's hands and launched on their careers. So far as the boys themselves and their parents were concerned, too, it worked in so far as the problem of 'getting a start' was solved. The young man might need support for a few years, but his professional training was assured and his prospects were reasonably clear. The cadet went off to Sandhurst and later to his regiment; the ICS probationer to a couple of years' study and then to Dustipore. After that it lay with their superiors to teach them their job and with themselves to learn it.

By the time the successful competitor was safely commissioned, or covenanted, or established, most of the sting of the competitive principle had been drawn. The officer or Civil Servant might be overtaken by the able, the ambitious, or the lucky. His progress, in the Army, would govern the age at which he would be retired. But the threat of the sack could hardly in any conceivable circumstances arise unless, like Valentine Baker Pasha, he tried to kiss a reluctant young lady in a train. And after retirement a pension was guaranteed: in the ICS, £1,000 a year. The public service, in fact, offered security as great as the parson's, and much better pay.

In the open professions, how different. Nothing was certain, nothing guaranteed; least of all, the proper course of training and a prospect of security after qualifying. When examinations were devised, with their accompanying requirement of a prescribed course of study, and when professional bodies proclaimed their intention of cultivating the scientific study of their functions, it might be thought that the next step, in logic, would be to establish institutions where study and research could single-mindedly be pursued under proper teachers. The Germans were showing the way, in their technical high schools and universities, and what they were doing was repeatedly recommended in England. What actually was done in English professional education, this chapter and the next will discuss.

The leading principle of professional education was apprenticeship: learning by doing. In so far as the professions were skilled trades, earning their living by the right use of applied knowledge in the workaday world, that was very reasonable. The doctor must cope with his patient as well as cure his disease; the lawyer must understand his client as well as his case; the engineer must handle tools. All must understand practice as well as theory, but as much could be said of a plumber. It is in depth of theoretical knowledge, as much as in anything else, that a professional man differs, or ought to differ, from a tradesman. And theoretical knowledge is not easily acquired by apprenticeship, as the doctors were well aware by 1834.[1]

Nevertheless in nearly all professions, when examinations were introduced, a period of apprenticeship or pupilage was required as well, and it was assumed that the study required for the examinations would be fitted into the interstices of work in the office or workshop. In medicine only was apprenticeship allowed to wither away, being replaced entirely by the mid-seventies by full-time studentship.[2] In engineering, on the other hand, there were no qualifying examinations until 1898; apprenticeship was all. In between were professions like the Bar and architecture, which for about twenty years in the mid-century got on with a system of pupilage combined with voluntary examinations. Compulsory examinations for membership of the Royal Institute of British Architects were started in 1882, but the RIBA's authority was by no means undisputed, and apprenticeship, more or less unregulated, continued to be a sufficient ground for qualification throughout the century.

When governing bodies came to fix the length of time required for articles, or whatever term they employed, they were not inclined to underestimate the abstruseness of their craft, nor to over-estimate their pupils' ability to unravel it. Five years was a favourite period, as with the solicitors, the architects, and eventually, the accountants. Whether the full period could be enforced or not depended on whether it had any legal backing. The solicitors' five years and the barristers' three were absolute, but there was nothing to prevent anyone setting up as an engineer or an architect or an accountant after any term of pupilage he liked, or none at all. Thomson, in 1857, recommended not less than four years' training for an architect, but the length of father's purse would in the end decide.[3]

The first problem, then, for anyone hoping to enter a profession, was to find someone to teach it to him: normally an established practitioner. Outside medicine and the law, until very late in the century, most professional and near-professional activities were not defended by recognized qualifying examinations – though they were increasing in number all the time – and then the principal's name and reputation, as Thomson says, 'supply the place of the college', and were of the greatest importance when the pupil came to look for employment or to set up in practice afterwards. So far, indeed, was this principle carried that while surgeons' examinations were still oral, and the examiners signed each diploma, some signatures carried far more weight than others.

In all professions, eminent practitioners were much sought after to take pupils, and by training young men who themselves became eminent they could found schools of thought and originate controversy as surely as any professor in the universities. Among the engineers of the early nineteenth century Henry Maudslay (1771–1831), the great machine-tool maker, was trained by Joseph Bramah (1748–1814) and himself trained, among others, Nasmyth (1808–90) the inventor of the steam hammer and Joseph Whitworth (1803–87) who standardized screw threads and built cannon in the second half of the century. The railway works, where locomotives were built, naturally became centres of teaching, especially under such men as F. W. Webb (1836–1906) at Crewe, his pupil H. A. Ivatt at Doncaster, and other great builders of railway engines. Nor was the influence of the railway engineers confined to the railways. Both W. O. Bentley (*b.* 1888) and Sir Henry Royce (1863–1933) had their early training on the Great Northern Railway, the one at Doncaster and the other at Peterborough.[4]

Architects similarly attracted pupils and disseminated ideas through them. G. E. Street (1824–81), the designer of the Law Courts in the Strand, London, had a hand in the training of William Morris (1834–96), Philip Webb (1831–1915), and Richard Norman Shaw (1831–1912), all men of very great influence themselves, and in their turn teachers.[5] Successful training under some recognized master, with his backing at the end of it, might be to an architect, as Thomson suggests, what academic success at Oxford or Cambridge might be to a rising clergyman: the starting point for an impressive professional career.

It was quite easy to make terrible mistakes. A boy might fall into the hands of some man whose main interest in pupils was the premium to be extracted from their parents. Having pocketed that, he would use a pupil as cheap labour in his drawing office (if he were an architect or an engineer), pirate any ideas he might have, and turn him loose at the end of his time with nothing more than a lukewarm testimonial. Both Thomson and Davenant, the one in 1857 and the other in 1870, warn their readers against such principals, especially in architecture and engineering. Against them, qualifying examinations were some protection, for at least their results gave a standard for measuring a principal's performance as a teacher. Also they protected the pupil against himself, for he was less likely to idle his time away if he had before him the prospect of a day of reckoning in the examination hall.[6]

To get a good start family connections in the professions were highly desirable. A boy in a professional family, whose father knew his way about the world of law, say, or of the Church, medicine, or engineering, was far better placed than an outsider. There might be an uncle or a cousin with whom he could serve his articles; if not, his father could probably find a good principal for him. Robert Stephenson (1803–59), I. K. Brunel (1806–59), and Sir John Rennie (1794–1874) weree all imnent engineers whose fathers had been eminent engineers, and though all of them no doubt had enough ability to have carried them through unaided, they were none the worse for parental backing. Moreover the professions tended to cross-fertilize each other. Sir Gilbert Scott (1811–78), the architect, was the son of a country parson. Lord Chancellor Westbury (1800–73) was the son of a physician, though not a prosperous one. Once a family had arrived in the professional class it was reluctant to leave, and well placed to stay. 'Clergymen beget clergymen and barristers', said a writer in the *Saturday Review* of 1857, 'barristers beget barristers and clergymen and the scions of the professional classes have generally to get a draught of the Lethe of penury before they desert their conventional status, and take to selling anything but their wits ... The professions absorb aspirants from all classes, but return few or none to their source.'[7]

If much could be done with family connections, even more could be done with money, and precious little without it, except by altogether unusual exertions, ability, or good luck. The father of a prospective professional man had usually to reckon with a heavy premium for articles, something for equipment, and maintenance while the articles ran their course, to say nothing of optional extras like travel. As with all commercial transactions, you got what you paid for, and in most professions it was possible to get some form of training on the cheap, but for good-class training, with all that that implied in the way of introductions and opportunities, as well as straightforward technical competence, it seems to have been unwise to budget for an outlay of less than £1,000.

That was the figure mentioned by W. S. Cookson, an attorney who gave evidence before the Inns of Court Commission in 1854, as the sum required for training in his branch of the legal profession. It was, in fact, a minimum. He thought the total would be higher by the time you had taken account of three hundred guineas for a premium and of the heavy stamp duty payable on taking up articles and on admission to the rolls. It was suggested, and the suggestion has been repeated as recently as 1933, that the intention behind the heavy duties was 'to increase the respectability of the Profession' by keeping poor men out of it, and it was insinuated that established attorneys were quite pleased to see the rates so high. Their level had been set by the younger Pitt and before 1853 they came to £145; after, to £109. Cookson's comment was simply that it would be better to let the money go into the articled clerk's education. The premium and stamp duties were only the start of the expense. To them must be added the cost of maintenance for five years while the young man served out his time and, as Cookson said, 'he mixes among gentlemen, and must support the position of a gentleman, which is a considerable expense.' He might reduce the term of his articles from five years to three if he went to a university, but that certainly would not reduce the expense. And to complete the attorney's professional education there might be six months or a year in chambers with a barrister or special pleader.[8]

This would bring a young man into the highest class of London attorney. You could do things more cheaply in the country, and finish on a very different social and professional level. The sort of money Cookson spoke of implied an attorney who was the social equal of most barristers and considerably better educated, professionally. Certainly more would have been spent on his training than most barristers spent on theirs, such as it was.

Thomson, writing three years after Cookson's evidence, gives figures for the training of architects and engineers. For architecture, he suggested, the premium would range from £100 to £500. 'When the higher premium is given, it is because the pupil at the expiration of his articles, is usually installed in some situation where he is in receipt of an income.' A writer in 1870 gave an estimate between one hundred and three hundred guineas, according to the standing of the principal. He would no doubt have agreed with Thomson that any attempt to save on the premium was 'a very false economy'. To the premium Thomson added £100 for books, instruments and apparatus and £150 for living away from home – 'and on that he must be economical'. With four years' articles, all these items made a total of £1,100.

When the young man finished his articles, he would do well to travel a couple of years, to Greece and Rome. 'As living is very cheap in those countries, £100 a year, with the expenses of transit, ought, with care, to be sufficient.'[9]

An engineering apprenticeship might require a premium between £200 and £500. Otherwise the expenses would be much the same as those of training an architect, 'to whom, indeed, he is allied in many points. Both build, but with different objects.'[10] Thomson meant civil engineers. Mechanical engineering was hardly a profession. What he said was uncomfortably true for architects who, as the more specialized of the two, and also priding themselves on their artistic aptitude, resented engineers doing work they claimed as theirs.

It may be supposed, then, that Thomson expected an engineering or architectural education, of the top class, to cost over £1,000, and that is certainly unlikely to have been an over-estimate, if we look at Sir John Rennie's recommendations, published in 1875. His ideas on schooling (above p. 103) were ambitious; on what ought to follow, no less so. After leaving school at seventeen or eighteen (Thomson says most engineers left 'much earlier'), the boy should do two or three years' apprenticeship with 'some good steam engine and machinery manufacturer' so as to become 'a practical as well as a theoretical mechanician which is the soundest basis for good engineering.' Then he should go for three or four years to 'some well known civil engineer' for experience of railways and public works.

That was not all. The engineer should be architect enough to design buildings 'with a certain degree of symmetry and dignity, so as to impress upon the spectator the idea that they are thoroughly adapted for their purpose.' His professional knowledge should also cover surveying, geology (so that he could judge the nature of ground on which he might be required to build) astronomy (so that he could calculate tides in building harbour works), and mineralogy.[11]

Education for medicine was on a rather different basis from education for other professions, in so far as apprenticeship had been commuted into studentship (though the principle remained in the clinical teaching of the hospitals), and there was a regular academic course of study to be followed. This meant that there was no premium to be paid, but there were fees for lectures, demonstrations, dissection, and all the other necessary activities of a medical course – including, if the student were ambitious, foreign travel to study at Paris or in Germany. And to this, as with all the other professions, maintenance would have to be added since the medical student was no more in a position to earn his keep than the engineering apprentice.

Professional education, then, was not cheap. Indeed it must have been the cost of it, as much as anything else, which kept the professional classes relatively small. Not many families in Victorian England could afford £1,000 or more for the education of one son, let alone two or three, and the likelihood of a boy getting help from anyone but his family was small in the extreme. It was possible, as we have seen, for boys of very humble origins to work their way into the public service, after it was opened to competition, but no question of a premium arose there, nor maintenance for four or five years in the late 'teens and early twenties of a man's age.

The figures we have been discussing, however, are for the highest class of professional qualification. As long as the professions were ill-defined, and the qualifications for entry equally so, a determined, able, ambitious man could establish himself without the heavy capital expenditure discussed above. Moreover, training for one occupation might be made to serve the purposes of another. There was nothing to stop a surveyor practising as an architect or an engineer, or both, and the census authorities found it impossible to distinguish these professions clearly until well into the twentieth century.[12] In the church at Avebury, Wiltshire, there is even a monument to a mid-century doctor (*d.* 1877) who is called 'an able . . . architect,' though there is nothing to suggest that he practised architecture for gain. A far more common extension (or confusion) of professional identity was – and is – the link between surveying and auctioneering, an undoubted trade.

Of all major occupations which had any claim to be considered professions there was none, in Victorian England, in which a capable man without much money could more readily establish himself than engineering, if only because no one could draw a hard and fast line between any of the rungs of the ladder which ran upwards from dirty-handed fitters like the young George Stephenson to the proudest consulting engineer who ever graced the Institution. Although theoretical training and formal qualifications, as prescribed by Rennie, were desirable, they were not absolutely required, as medical and legal qualifications were, and it was possible to be trained as an engineer for very much less than the sums quoted by Thomson.

In 1860, in Glasgow, a pupil might be articled to Randolph and Elder, consulting engineers, for 5s. a week, the term of the articles being three years. The evening classes of the Glasgow Mechanics Institute were open to an ambitious pupil cheaply, and he might go on from his apprenticeship to gain practical experience at sea. James Weir (1843–1920) passed through all these phases and eventually, with his brother, became immensely successful as an inventor and manufacturer of ships' machinery. Few rose so high as Weir, but the self-made Scottish engineer was familiar wherever British ships steamed, wherever British machinery was erected, wherever bridges, canals, railways, and harbours were built by British firms, and wherever mines were dug; that is to say, throughout the world.[13]

In England, too, an engineer's career could be built from inexpensive materials. Henry Royce ran out of money before he could finish his term as an apprentice at the Great Northern Railway works at Peterborough, so he became a tester with the London Electric Light and Power Company, going to night classes (run by the City and Guilds of London Institute) in his spare time. O. V. S. Bulleid (b. 1882), one of the last great builders of steam locomotives, became a 'premium apprentice' in the Great Northern's Doncaster works, in 1899, for £50. He got the chance, after the fashion of the day, because a Doncaster clergyman was a friend both of Bulleids family and of H. A. Ivatt the Locomotive Superintendent. The Bulleid's rather disapproved of the whole transaction. They considered engineering 'rough and common', but being in reduced circumstances they had not much choice in the matter.[14]

The dark side to these shining stories of triumph over adversity was that many British engineers, in the view of contemporary critics, were ill-qualified. Matthew Arnold, in 1868, quoted 'one of the first mathematicians in England . . . and a practical mechanician besides' as saying:

'Our engineers have no real scientific instruction, and we let them learn their business at our expense, by rule of thumb; but it is a ruinous system of blunder and plunder. A man without the requisite scientific knowledge undertakes to build a difficult bridge; he builds three which tumble down, and so learns to build a fourth which stands; but somebody pays for the three failures. In France or Switzerland he would not have been suffered to build his first until he had satisfied competent persons that he knew how to build it, because abroad they cannot afford our extravagance.'[15]

The same view was held by eminent figures within the profession. Both Henry Bessemer (1813–98) and Joseph Whitworth among others were disturbed by the lack of facilities for professional education for engineers, and in 1868 Whitworth offered £3,000 a year to endow thirty scholarships for the study of 'the theory and practice of mechanics and its cognate sciences'. In his will he left £100,000 more for education.[16] Sir John Rennie, writing mainly from the standpoint of the civil engineer, though with an eye to other branches, urged that no one should be allowed to practise as an engineer without a certificate of competence granted after proper examination.

'This is the rule', he wrote, 'in every other learned profession, and there can be no reason why it should not be adopted by the engineers ... at present ... any man without business, competent or not, dubs himself engineer, starts a project, well or ill founded ... *generally the latter*, and issues a prospectus to the public ...'[17]

During a gale in 1879 the new Tay Bridge, in Scotland, collapsed with a train on it, which seemed to confirm the worst that had been said or suspected about the competence of British engineers.[18]

It was becoming apparent that professional education, at least for those professions based on science and technology, could not be raised to a proper level by apprenticeship alone. The system did not provide well enough for the study of theoretical principles and scientific method, which were increasingly important as they were increasingly applied to the practical problems of manufacturing industry. And in engineering all the sciences met, for it fell to the engineer, as the designer of plant, to transform laboratory successes into commercial propositions.

The shipbuilder was faced with the change-over from wood to iron; from sail to steam. The builder of heavy ordnance had to keep pace with the development of modern explosives. The electrical engineer had to be a physicist as well as a mechanic. In the chemical industry the engineer who built the plant had to understand the processes which it would have to deal with. It may be significant of the general state of British engineering in the early seventies that the firm of Brunner Mond, starting operations in Cheshire – long a centre of chemical industry – for the production of soda ash by a new process, had far more trouble with their machinery than with any of their chemical problems.

Chapter 9

APPRENTICE INTO STUDENT

It was already beginning to be thought by 1850 that Oxford and Cambridge might reasonably be expected to do more for professional and scientific education. Views of this kind were held among the group who promoted the idea of the Great Exhibition of 1851 – the Prince Consort, Sir Henry Cole, Lyon Playfair, and others – and on the liberal side of politics. Demands of this sort, it was argued, far from asking for something new and revolutionary, simply represented a desire to revive the true and ancient purpose of the universities. Some people in the universities agreed, but not the majority, and in general the academic authorities took a high but narrow view of their proper function.

When, therefore, in 1850, under the influence of the reformers, Royal Commissions were appointed – not in the most tactful manner – to investigate the state of affairs at Oxford and Cambridge, they were bitterly resented, especially at Oxford. The University disputed the legality of the Commission and refused to co-operate officially. So did most of the colleges. Witnesses, therefore, appeared in their private capacity and not as representatives of corporate bodies, and it must be supposed that reformers generally got a fuller hearing than conservatives. At Cambridge, hostility was not quite so violently and flamboyantly pursued.

As a result, perhaps, the Commissioners who reported on Cambridge, in 1852, were comparatively mild in their comments. They were anxious to see undergraduates encouraged who were not ambitious for high academic honours, as the term was then understood – that is, honours in classics and mathematics – but who simply wanted a good general education, perhaps scientific. They noticed the fact that new triposes (honours courses) had been started in 1848, and that they catered for Moral Sciences (mainly philosophy, economics, history, and law) and Natural Sciences, which were obviously moves in the general direction which the reformers desired. They deplored the neglect of civil engineering, and likewise of medicine (over ten years there had been an average of four MB degrees granted annually).[1]

The Commissioners who reported on Oxford, also in 1852, were far more cutting. Their report, in fact, amounted to an accusation of malversation and breach of trust, for the essence of it was that the wealth of the university and colleges – particularly the colleges – was being used for the advantage of a narrow clerical clique rather than for the nation as a whole.

> 'The education imparted', they said, '. . . is not such as to conduce to the advancement in life of many persons, except those intended for the ministry of the Established Church. Many are now called to the Bar, and raised to the highest judicial functions, who have not been members of any University . . . Few Physicians are now educated at Oxford. Nor do many persons take a Degree with a view to enter into the legal profession as Solicitors, though the Legislature has given to Graduates an advantage as regards the duration of their articles.'

'The great bulk' of Oxford men, according to the Commissioners, became parsons, but 'no efficient means at present exist in the University for training Candidates for Holy Orders in those studies which belong peculiarly to their profession.' 'But', they went on, 'the number of Students intended for Holy Orders would, we believe, become much greater if the expenses were considerably reduced. Indeed, the foundation of such institutions as Durham, Lampeter, and St Bees' – one university and two theological colleges, all founded in the nineteenth century – 'is probably owing in part at least to the great cost of an Oxford or Cambridge education.' Both lawyers and doctors, the Commissioners thought, would do well to spend three or four years at Oxford before passing to the Inns of Court or the teaching hospitals. 'The changes', they said, 'which are taking place in the administration of justice seem to render it necessary that persons in all grades of the Legal profession should receive an Academical education', but 'the connection of Oxford with the Profession of the Law is unsatisfactory', and as for doctors, 'Oxford has ceased altogether to be a school of Medicine. Those few persons who take Medical Degrees there with a view to the social consideration which those Degrees give, or the preferments in the University for which they are necessary, study their profession elsewhere.' Altogether, they concluded, 'the Education given has hitherto been the same for all, whether clergymen or barristers, medical men or private gentlemen . . . and no one has left Oxford . . . much more fitted for one profession than for another . . . the University is for the majority . . . a mere Grammar School from first to last.'

And even this unsatisfactory education was far too expensive. The Commissioners made lengthy observations on the extravagance and immorality of the undergraduates which provide an interesting side-glance at the education of Victorian clergymen. This kind of conduct led to expense which, naturally, they considered quite unjustifiable, but even when they looked at those who were 'studious . . . moral, and frugal' they were not much comforted. 'The whole expenses', they said, 'even of prudent and well-conducted Students greatly exceed £300.' This figure (which is for the whole course at the University) they considered much too high; so high as to shut out many who ought to be allowed in. The reason why Oxford was so expensive, in the Commissioners' view, was that most scholarships (as well as Fellowships) were restricted by statute to certain classes of people, usually from particular schools or localities, or of the 'Founder's kin', so that they could not be freely granted to able but needy applicants. At Cambridge there were more open awards, and it was possible to go through the University for less than £300. The Cambridge Commissioners, however, like the Commissioners at Oxford, considered that the cost to the average undergraduate would be somewhere between £300 and £400. In looking at all these figures it has to be remembered, as the Commissioners at both Universities were well aware, that the way in which bills were run up, both at Oxford and Cambridge, made it almost impossible to say what the minimum cost of education there would be, and the maximum could run to almost any figure.[2]

Two important general points emerge from these reports. One is that up to 1850 professional education was not being taken seriously either at Oxford or Cambridge. The other is that education at Oxford and Cambridge was extremely expensive. It may be observed, in passing, that it was not more expensive than the costs of top-class professional education by apprenticeship, considered in the last chapter, but this does not alter the fact that it was a great deal dearer to go to the great English universities than to universities of comparable standing in other countries, notably Germany and Scotland. The expense, and the general air of social privilege which went with it, astonished foreign observers, and in spite of the criticisms of the Commissioners and others, it did not diminish, so that as late as 1885 Paul Vinogradoff was remarking: 'academical education in England is more a kind of luxury for the select few, than the necessary starting point for the many.'[3] This was a serious matter, as some contemporaries realized, if the nation was to have to live by its brains, for it was by no means certain than only well-to-do parents' sons had them. In 1868 Matthew Arnold pointed out that England, with a population of just over 20 million, had 3,500 matriculated university students against 6,362 in Prussia (18½ million.)[3]

The Commissioners' reports gave great offence, particularly at Oxford. It has been argued that the Commission on Oxford ought never to have been appointed.[4] Reforms were going ahead under internal pressure, and the intrusion of outsiders, politically opposed to the great body of Oxford opinion, may merely have exacerbated opposition instead of smoothing the way for reform. In particular, Dr Newman suggests that the Commissioners were unfair in their remarks about medicine at Oxford, in spirit if not in hard fact, because Henry Acland was already at work reviving medical studies in the University, and other movements were afoot to improve the standing of natural science.

However that may be, the progress of the universities towards a wider view of their functions was not dramatically rapid. At Cambridge they founded the Moral Sciences and Natural Sciences Triposes in 1848, but it was half-way through the sixties before they modified the course for the Ordinary Degree with the deliberate intention of helping the undergraduate who was aiming at a professional career. They framed new regulations, says the *Student's Guide* of 1866, which compressed into two years 'the reading which was formerly spread over the whole time of residence . . . thus leaving the last year of the University Course open for the pursuit of professional studies.'

What this meant was that in three examinations during his first two years the undergraduate reading for the ordinary degree – that is, not for honours – dealt with Paley's *Evidences of Christianity*; with a good deal of Latin and Greek, including two Greek classics, a Gospel and the Acts; with Arithmetic ('public schools have as yet given little attention to this subject'); and he could, if he wished, submit an English Essay. The third year was, in effect, two terms, since the 'special examination' (as opposed to the 'general examination') was held in the Easter Term – that is, the summer term. In these two terms the undergraduate destined for a profession had a choice between theology, moral sciences, law, natural sciences, and mechanics combined with applied sciences. 'And though one entire year is given up to professional pursuits', the *Student's Guide* concludes, 'nearly the same amount of work is accomplished in two years which formerly occupied three, and the University has at the same time retained her academic training and yet adapted her teaching in a very great degree to the spirit of the times.'[5]

One cannot help suspecting that one hears, in the tone of this last remark, the voice of the schoolmaster, harried by parents, who unwillingly sets up a 'Modern Side' and condemns his dunces to it. Nevertheless it was a step forward. It was followed during the seventies by a crop of new triposes. In 1875 a Chair of Civil Engineering was at last established, with small encouragement from engineering employers, most of whom for many years continued to regard university men with grave suspicion. There was no engineering laboratory until 1894.

The provision of laboratories and specialized libraries was slow and sparing. Under the influence of the seventh Duke of Devonshire, James Clerk Maxwell (1831–79) was appointed first professor of experimental physics in 1871 and proceeded to supervise the building of the Cavendish Laboratory, opened in 1874, which was financed by the same nobleman. In the Cavendish, Cambridge physics flowered, but the wonder is less that so much was achieved than that so much was achieved with so little in the way of equipment and encouragement. There was no chemical laboratory until 1887.

At both Oxford and Cambridge medicine gradually came back into university life over a long period of years, but neither University could rival Edinburgh or London in medical education, if only because the towns were too small to provide enough cases for clinical teaching. It remained the rule for medical students of Oxford and Cambridge to do their hospital work elsewhere.

Oxford was less receptive to science generally than Cambridge. The Final Honours School of Natural Science was started before the Commission of 1850, a Museum was set up in 1858 and the Clarendon Laboratory in 1872 but in general science did not loom very large at Oxford until well on in the twentieth century. Nevertheless by the eighties Oxford was far more aware of the outside world than in the fifties. W. J. Ashley, Fellow and Tutor of Lincoln College, Oxford, writing in 1887, went so far as to suggest that history might be a good subject to read if you were thinking of going into business, and for a don to conceive of an Oxford man going into business was a notable advance.[6] Moreover, as we have seen, Oxford gradually developed a close connection with the public service, both at home and overseas.

In the later sixties both universities were still being criticized for the neglect of professional education which had attracted the attention of the Commissioners of 1850. Matthew Arnold, in spite of his affection for Oxford, seems to have considered both the ancient universities played out. He suggested breaking them up. 'Oxford and Cambridge', he wrote in 1868 in his capacity as an Assistant Commissioner to the Schools Enquiry Commission, 'can from the nature of things be now-a-days important schools only in theology, arts, and the mathematical and natural sciences . . . They are actually bad places for schools in law and medicine, and all their professors in those faculties they might with advantage employ where there would be a better field for their services.' Faculties, or groups of faculties, might be established in the great towns, staffed by redundant (and no doubt recalcitrant) dons from Oxford and Cambridge. Even in the faculties that would be left to them, Arnold thought they would not 'really need half their professors . . . and could spare half of them for use elsewhere.'[7]

Dean Farrar, like many other critics of Oxford and Cambridge, looked with mingled apprehension and enthusiasm on the revived German universities. In 1868 he wrote of the mood of 'astonishment and admiration' which their professors and lecturers created among the students, and contrasted it against what he said was the state of affairs at Oxford. There, he asserted, the dons admitted that most of the undergraduates had no interest in intellectual pursuits at all, largely because almost nothing but classical studies was admitted.[8] A. H. Sayce, writing seven years later, asserted that 'it is not from Oxford and Cambridge that the great writers and thinkers of the present generation have come.' He named Mill, Herbert Spencer, Buckle and Tyler, and finished by accusing the ancient universities of intellectual stagnation.[9]

Even in 1889, after Oxford and Cambridge had made, or had been jolted into making, considerable changes in their methods, Lyon Playfair was not satisfied. A Scot, speaking to a Scottish audience, he said 'The old English universities have not the same function as the Scottish and Irish universities. The former teach men how to spend a thousand a year with dignity and intelligence, while the latter aim at showing men how to make a thousand a year under the same conditions.' He went further. He said that universities had been founded by 'the professional classes . . . to glorify their professions by raising them above mere empiricism', but that nowadays 'new professions are arising and for these our old universities make no provisions; old professions have completely changed their aspects, yet the schools and colleges remain as of old. Perhaps the most robust men of our time have been our engineers and mechanicians [but] I look in vain for a single representative man among our Telfords, Watts, Stephensons, Arkwrights, Wedgwoods, whose intellect was nurtured on classical learning,' and he said the same about scientists and 'medical discoverers'. The classics, he was prepared to admit, might be a good training for statesmen: perhaps also for priests and lawyers, though he was very doubtful about the latter. 'The fact is', he concluded, 'that all professions have reached a stage when a single curriculum for an arts degree is neither possible nor tolerable for them, if universities intend to maintain their chief function of liberalizing the professions.'[10]

This was a partisan speech delivered during a controversy over medical education. It displays a good deal of oratorical licence and a distinct tendency to choose facts which fitted the speaker's case. Nevertheless it is a strong indictment with an uncomfortable degree of truth in it. It was delivered nearly forty years after the Royal Commissioners had complained of the neglect of professional education at Oxford and Cambridge and at a time when foreign competition, then a distant threat, had become a triumphant reality, above all in industries, such as the chemical industry and electrical engineering, which depended on the application of science to manufacture.

Of course the ancient universities were delightful places where life could be lived graciously and all sorts of manly sports pursued. At the same time the intellect might be trained, sharpened, and practised – or not, as the case might be. Above all the young gentlemen of England could gain social poise and meet one another, to the infinite advantage of their future careers, and, perhaps, of the conduct of public affairs. All this was pointed out, time and again, and many people thought it an entirely adequate defence. But was it? Was this all that a university was for? Matthew Arnold had not thought so in the sixties and in the mid-eighties Vinogradoff, looking at the universities as a foreigner, echoed Arnold's complaint when he remarked 'liberal and professional education are indissolubly connected on the Continent, they are separated in England.'[11]

Outside the charmed circle of the ancient English universities, as Lyon Playfair pointed out, stood the universities of Scotland and Trinity College Dublin: ancient also, but with a very different tradition. The Scottish universities, like the Scottish educational system as a whole, had none of the social overtones so conspicuous and valued in England. They were cheap to attend, so that the poor, or at any rate the fairly poor, could attend them in far larger numbers than could get into Oxford or Cambridge on scholarships and exhibitions. As a consequence, no doubt, they had far fewer inhibitions about teaching their students directly to earn a living. The Scottish medical schools, whether part of the universities or run by the medical corporations, had long been famous, though towards the middle of the nineteenth century some people – English people, mostly – were inclined to say that they were not what they used to be.[12] They were ahead of Oxford and Cambridge in paying serious attention to the engineers. Glasgow had a Chair of Civil Engineering in 1840: Edinburgh in 1868. Trinity College Dublin also catered for students far less affluent than undergraduates of Oxford and Cambridge. It was a Protestant institution, founded in the sixteenth century, and its students therefore came from the families of the Anglo-Irish 'ascendancy' who, although vastly better off than the Catholic Irish, were not on the whole so wealthy as their social equals in England.

Certainly the young men who went to Dublin virtually all expected to earn their own living, whereas a fair proportion at Oxford and Cambridge did not. For that reason, if for no other, Trinity College was even more professionally-minded, if that were possible, than the universities of Scotland.

[handwritten margin note: confusing "prof" w. technical]

The university was investigated by a Royal Commission at about the same time as Oxford and Cambridge, with very different results. The Commissioners found that since 1848 the Law School, with two professors, had established a close connection with the King's Inns (the equivalent of the Inns of Court in England). There were six professors in an active medical school. In 1844 a School of Civil Engineering had been founded with seven professors and lecturers. Two held Chairs in Civil Engineering and the others taught applied chemistry, mineralogy and geology. The course lasted for three years. In general, undergraduates did a four-year course, but in the fourth year there were special concessions to students aiming at the professions, who might concentrate on the subjects of direct interest to them. There were about fifteen hundred students in 1850 (Oxford, at the same date, had about thirteen hundred, Cambridge about nineteen hundred) and the cost of the complete course, to an ordinary paying student, was given as £83 17s. 6d., though a sizar could do it for less than £5. The Commissioners commented: 'There is great activity and efficiency in the different departments, and the spirit of improvement has been especially shown in the changes which have been introduced in the course of education, to adapt it to the requirements of the age.'[13] Evidently the economic urge was a powerful one, and we have seen that Irishmen were quick to seize on the potentialities of the ICS competition. Trinity College was equally quick to meet their needs: so much so that as early as 1858 a writer in the *Saturday Review* remarked that in substituting competition for patronage 'we are substituting Irishmen for Scotchmen in the Civil Government of India.'[14]

In England during most of the nineteenth century higher education was so dominated – 'overshadowed' would perhaps be an apter word – by Oxford and Cambridge – that to contemporaries other universities and university colleges did not seem of much account. In any case, until 1880 there were only two other universities (London, 1828, and Durham, 1837), and only one university college (Owens College Manchester, 1851) was

founded before the seventies. In these institutions, few and un-
prestigious as they were, professional and scientific education
were taken seriously from the start. Together with the Royal
College of Chemistry (1845), the Royal School of Mines (1851),
and the Royal Military Academy at Woolwich they represented,
until the last quarter of the century, virtually the whole of
England's regular organizatio forn scientific and technological
studies at anything like a university level.

The Victorian University of London only conducted examinations and conferred degrees until after the passing of the University of London Act in 1900. It did not teach. Teaching was the
business of its constituent colleges, principally University College
and King's College. University College had been founded in 1828
in protest against the Anglican exclusiveness of Oxford and
Cambridge, and it had an inherent bias against their system of
education. King's College (1834), in its turn a counter-protest
against the 'godlessness' of University College, was also less
devoted to academic purism than the ancient universities. Neither
college, in fact, could afford to neglect 'practical' studies, for both,
like the Scottish and Irish universities, catered overwhelmingly
for students who would have to earn their own living. King's
College had a department of engineering as early as 1838, and it
also specialized in the professional education of Anglican clergymen, rather than simply educating them generally in the manner
of Oxford and Cambridge.

The great speciality of London University as a whole, as of the
Scottish universities, and in rivalry with them, was medical
education. The older teaching hospitals and the medical corporations were established long before the University. To them were
added the medical schools and teaching hospitals of University
College and King's College. By long-drawn-out stages all were
eventually brought to co-operate in a scheme of medical training which comprehended both the degrees of the University and
the diplomas of the corporations, though the matter was not
brought to finality until the setting-up of the Conjoint Board
in 1886.[15]

Medical students had a tradition of bawdy boisterousness, so
much so, it was said, that in respectable company some were
unwilling to admit to being medical students. Teachers of anatomy,
in which a great many very dull facts had somehow to be com-

mitted to memory, relied heavily on indecent mnemonics, and when the admission of women was being debated they argued quite seriously that the presence of girls would prevent anatomy from being properly taught. And medical students seem to have been even more given to uproarious behaviour in public than other students, for an article in the *Fortnightly Review* in 1879 deplored their reputation and said that after a riot in that year, at the City Tabernacle against the preaching of C. H. Spurgeon, some four hundred out of two thousand medical students in London had come to the notice of the police.[16]

The results of medical examinations were bad. In 1875, at the pass examinations conducted by the College of Surgeons, 10 per cent of University College Hospitals' students failed, 17 per cent of St Bartholomew's, 30 per cent of St George's, 44 per cent of Charing Cross's, and 56 per cent of St Thomas's. These figures were enormously higher than the failure rates of the early part of the century (above p. 53) and no doubt they represent a much higher standard of qualification. But the *Fortnightly Review* also thought they reflected the students' behaviour, particularly their addiction to 'the music-halls and places of amusement of the same description.'[17]

Apart from London, only one other university was set up in England before 1880. This was the University of Durham, opened in 1833. It was an Anglican foundation under the control of the Dean and Chapter of Durham Cathedral and it was intended to provide 'a general academical education, similar to that which is given at Oxford and Cambridge.'[18] It was a dismal failure. In the academic year 1862–3 it had 44 students, against 120 ten years earlier. A Royal Commission was set up to investigate it.

The Commission's Report (1863) throws a clear light on the demand for higher education, not of the kind given at Oxford and Cambridge, which existed in England at the time. There were internal reasons for Durham's decline which do not concern us here, but on top of these the Commission concluded broadly that the University was ill-adapted to the needs of the people of the North of England, whom it had explicitly been founded to serve.

It was too expensive. There were a college and two halls: in college, fees might run between £100 and £140; in the halls, between £60 and £75. Moreover a three-year course was beyond the resources of most of the students whom it was hoped to attract, and the age of admission had been 'such as to preclude the hope of the University being frequented by the sons of persons engaged in industrial pursuits.' There was not enough provision either for theological students (and Dissenters were virtually excluded by the requirement to attend Anglican services) or for students of physical science or engineering. In general, an imitation of Oxford and Cambridge was not suited to the needs of the North of England and the imitation – Durham – could not survive the competition of the originals for those students who wanted what they provided. Durham at first had a School of Civil Engineering, which in 1840 had twenty-six students, against thirty-four in Arts and twenty-nine in Theology. But it never had enough money to pay really good staff: nor were there scholarships to help poor students with the fees for the three-year course – thirty guineas a year for two years: then twenty. Worse still, those who took the course found it of no professional advantage afterwards. Employers usually required them to pay a premium, and then put them into the shops or mines on the same footing as boys fresh from school. By 1863 the School had ceased to exist. 'The partial and immediate success which attended its institution', observed the Commissioners, 'appears to us to point conclusively to the existence in the North of the want of some similar education.' Nevertheless a School of Physical Science started in 1865, with a lecturer on civil engineering, including mechanics, hydrostatics, hydraulics, and mining, also failed, and when the lecturer's three-year contract (at £250 a year) was up, no one else was put in.[19]

Until the seventies the only other institution which went any distance to meet the 'want' of technological education in the North was Owens College, founded under the will of James Owens and opened in 1851. J. J. Thomson (1856–1940) was there before he migrated to Trinity College Cambridge. A Chair of Engineering was established in 1868. Henry Roscoe (1833–1915) began to supply the English chemical industry with chemists trained in England rather than at Göttingen or Giessen. The more enlightened chemical manufacturers, such as Ludwig Mond and Ivan Levinstein, supported the College and served on its governing body. But it was alone in the North for over twenty years.

In London two scientific and technological foundations came

into being about the same time as Owens College. The first was the Royal College of Chemistry, founded with the backing of Prince Albert and his circle, especially Sir James Clark, the Queen's physician. The professor appointed to run it was A. W. Hofmann, a German from the University of Bonn, a pupil of Liebig full of the spirit of the German universities, with their zeal for research and applied science.

In 1851, on foundations laid by Sir Henry De la Bèche in the Geological Survey, the Museum of Practical Geology, and the Mining Record Office, the Government School of Mines and of Science applied to the Arts (after 1862, the Royal School of Mines) was opened. Perhaps the most remarkable thing about it was that it was a *Government* school, but to that we shall return. Its purpose was explicitly stated to be 'to give a practical direction to the course of study, so as to enable the student to enter upon the actual practice of mining, or of the arts which he may be called upon to conduct.'[20]

Hofmann, at the Royal College of Chemistry, quickly attracted pupils. Among the men he taught during his years in England (1845–63) were William Perkin (1838–1907), Henry Bessemer, and many of the leading spirits in the British chemical industry. It is impossible, in fact, to read much about the chemical industry in the later nineteenth century without becoming aware of his influence, which was by no means confined to the United Kingdom but was also powerful on the Continent.

The Royal College of Chemistry, however, was a private institution without government backing or massive endowments. The building, in Oxford Street, and the laboratories cost £5,000, of which only £2,500 was subscribed. Hofmann himself gave up part of his salary, then his share of the students' fees, and finally the house assigned to him to live in, but the debt was fatal to the independence of the College. In 1853, on De la Bèche's suggestion, it was merged with the School of Mines as the Chemical Department of the Metropolitan School of Science applied to Mining and the Arts. Hofmann stayed on as Professor of Chemistry, but in 1863 the University of Bonn recalled him and in 1866 he accepted the Chair of Chemistry at the University of Berlin on terms very much more attractive than anything ever offered to him in England. From Berlin he continued to impress his ideas on the chemical industry until he died in 1892.

The story of the Royal College of Chemistry, the treatment of Hofmann, and his final return to Germany are symptomatic of the English attitude to higher technical and scientific education during the third quarter of the nineteenth century. Almost everything that was done had to be done by private initiative, and that was not always over-generous, as the tale of the College of Chemistry's debt shows. The Government refused as a matter of principle to apply its resources seriously to the matter, even in the face of the well-known and growing state effort that was being made in Germany. When an exception was made, as it was in the case of the School of Mines, the sums of money spent were niggardly by German standards, so that the early years of the Government's own foundation were scarcely less precarious than the short career of the privately founded Royal College of Chemistry. The scale of their provision may be indicated by the fact that when T. H. Huxley, his scientific reputation already firmly established, joined the staff of the School in 1854, he was paid £200 a year. As he had already bitterly remarked, 'A man who chooses a life of science chooses not a life of poverty, but, so far as I can see a life of *nothing*.'[21]

It would be quite wrong to suppose that in its attitude to higher technical and professional education the Government was seriously out of touch with public opinion. Many eminent men, as we have repeatedly seen, again and again pointed out the extreme national danger of neglect, and some at least of them realized quite clearly that the State alone had the resources to do what needed to be done. But they could make no headway against the indifference or hostility of most of their countrymen, secure in their assumption of British superiority to all foreigners, especially during the vital years between 1850 and 1870. After the United States had recovered from the Civil War, after the Germans had founded their Empire, they were both far more formidable competitors, far more difficult to overtake, than they had ever been before.

The attitude of industrial employers towards technological and scientific education seems to have been founded, on the one hand, on a distrust of 'theory' as against practical experience and, on the other, on an extreme unwillingness to reveal technical secrets. They were also, naturally, indisposed to pay for what they regarded as undesirable or unnecessary, and higher education was expensive. They were therefore unwilling to see the revenue from local rates or national taxation spent in this way, or to pay what seemed to them excessive salaries to junior scientists and technologists simply because the young men had got themselves degrees. Their German competitors made none of these mistakes, particularly not the last.[22]

The Royal School of Mines was nearly ruined by the attitude of the industry it was supposed to serve. In 1857 the *Mining Journal* said that the majority of Cornish miners at first 'believed that theory was to supersede practice, and the element of Germanism was to predominate.' It is unlikely that they were alone in some such views as these, and employers or potential students who were not hostile were presumably indifferent, for in the first nine years the annual average number of 'matriculated' students – that is, students who entered for all courses offered, and paid £30 in one instalment or £40 in two – was only twelve. The corresponding number of 'occasional' students was fifty-four. It was hardly surprising that a committee consisting of Lord Granville, Robert Lowe and Sir Charles Trevelyan – none of them in the least hostile to the idea of professional education – should have concluded that if 'matriculated' students had been the only ones, the maintenance of the school by public funds 'could hardly be justified.'[23]

Sir John Donnelly, when an official of the Department of Science and Art in 1871, came to the conclusion that the single greatest stumbling block to any effective system of technical education in England was the reluctance of business men to reveal anything that they considered a trade secret. This of course made it very difficult indeed to run useful courses on industrial processes since the people who could have given instruction preferred to refuse to do so.[24] When it was combined, as it often was, with a deep-rooted suspicion of the whole idea of organized teaching, it made the whole enterprise practically hopeless.

The members of the learned professions were hardly more sympathetic towards the idea of specialized academic training than the business men whom they greatly despised. The doctors accepted it, but the lawyers would have none of the scheme for a legal university. For the clergy, theological colleges were founded (in 1863 there were six, including Durham University and King's College London), but there was a distinct suggestion, which found expression in the Report of the Oxford University Commission, that they were cheap substitutes for Oxford and Cambridge. The number of students in them (295 in 1862) was nothing like so great as the number of undergraduates intending to take orders at the two universities. Bishops, by the sixties, were coming to expect some evidence of theological learning from candidates for ordination, but as late as the eighties men at Oxford who had 'even the faintest chance of obtaining a moderate class in Classics or Mathematics' were being advised to leave theology alone 'for the greater prestige and practical value of a class in Classics or Mathematics is well worth the slight extra work it will entail.'[25]

Nevertheless during the last thirty years of the century the movement for founding university colleges and similar institutions gathered speed. By 1898 twelve were sharing the Parliamentary grant of £25,000 for university colleges in Great Britain. Moreover in 1880 Owens College Manchester, Yorkshire Science College Leeds, and University College Liverpool were federated together as Victoria University, which in 1903–4 split to give birth to Manchester, Leeds, and Liverpool Universities. In 1900 another new university came into being, at Birmingham, formed by the union of Mason College and Queen's College, which already existed. It distinguished itself by appointing a Professor of Accountancy.[26]

These institutions, in conscious and sometimes aggressive contrast to Oxford and Cambridge, were explicitly secular and technological in tone. When Sir Josiah Mason (1795–1881), a self-made man, set about founding Mason College, he forbade the teaching of theology, saying that he wished 'to give all classes in Birmingham, in Kidderminster, and in the district generally, the means of carrying on their scientific studies as completely and thoroughly as . . . in the great science schools of the Continent.'[27] Most of the other founders would no doubt have agreed with him, though at some of the new university colleges the clergy of the establishment were represented, usually through the Bishop of the diocese, on the governing body. There was no question of religious tests, however.

The new university colleges were all private foundations, but in 1871 the Government again entered the field of technological education. They required engineers for the public service in India, and they founded a college to train them at Cooper's Hill near Staines.

This was an ambitious and expensive establishment. It offered a three-year course at £150 a year, 'including some months of practical training under a civil or mechanical engineer', and the obligatory subjects were mathematics pure and applied, with the mechanics of engineering; theory and practice of construction; elementary principles of architectural design; surveying; mechanical drawing and descriptive geometry, and natural science, besides certain subjects of purely Indian interest, and accounts.

There was an entrance examination, as well as periodical and final examinations, but students were not obliged to reside. So long as they spent at least eight months under a civil or mechanical engineer, and passed their examinations, they could carry on their studies where they liked. Although the college was intended for the Indian public services, particularly the Public Works Department, it was open to all comers. Anyone who could pass the entrance examination and pay the fees (official students were paid an allowance) could attend. It aroused considerable bad feeling in the Indian service and no great enthusiasm elsewhere, and it was closed in 1906 'because of the growth of engineering instruction in South Kensington and the provinces.'[28] Bessemer, Whitworth and Charles Manby founded a College of Engineering at Muswell Hill in 1881, but on the whole English engineers remained sturdily resistant to the idea of institutional training.[29]

There was one other important Government foundation: the Normal School of Science (1872) which, with a good deal of ill-feeling, was started by removing departments from the Royal School of Mines. It was presided over by T. H. Huxley and its main object, as he intended to indicate by his choice of title, was the training of science teachers. In 1890 it became the Royal College of Science and as such it was one of the fore-runners of the Imperial College of Science and Technology, formed in 1907 by the union of the Royal College of Science with the Royal School of Mines.[30]

So far as the State was concerned, the authority responsible for technical education was the Department of Science and Art, set up in 1853. Both Sir Henry Cole and Lyon Playfair were originally on its staff, but probably the man who had the greatest influence in it, as he certainly had the longest career, was John Fretchville Sykes Donnelly, an RE Officer, who joined the Department in 1859 and became its Secretary in 1884. In general the Department was concerned with education at a lower level than we are, but it was responsible both for the Royal School of Mines and the Royal College of Science. It had, moreover, a certain amount of money to spend, and the way in which it was spent had a strong influence on the teaching of science in state schools. Moreover in 1871 Donnelly, acting on behalf of the Department, persuaded the Royal Society of Arts to start a system of technological examinations.[31]

University colleges did not get any money from the State until a dozen of them were permitted to share £14,000 in 1889. By 1898 the figure had risen to £25,000. Even with the subsidy, some of them were not particularly cheap for full-time students to attend. Fees at King's College London might run to £50 a year: at Owens College, as high as £90. On the other hand at Durham College of Science Newcastle upon Tyne it was possible to do a degree course for £20 a year or even less, and at Nottingham, in 1898, it was reported that many of the students were very poor and paid about 12s. 6d. a week for board and lodging.[32]

Many of the students came to evening classes. Many were not studying for degrees. The colleges were essentially local institutions catering for local needs, often far below the level of a university or of the technical high schools of Germany and Switzerland. In 1872 Edward Frankland, Professor of Chemistry at the Royal School of Mines, referred longingly to the 'noble State laboratories' of those countries, while not long before, in his own School, the professor of physics had been trying to teach without any laboratory at all.[33] Things had no doubt improved by the nineties, but science teachers without laboratories were by no means unknown. No wonder some people said technical education was unpractical.

It is clearly absurd to think of the institutions we have been discussing, for the most part, as places of education for a professional class in the full meaning of that phrase, especially when it is considered what social overtones it carried in late Victorian England. The young Neville Chamberlain (1869–1940), it is true, went daily, during term, to Mason College Birmingham for a couple of years 'to learn something of science, metallurgy, and engineering' before he went into business. But he had been to Rugby School first. His brilliant half-brother Austen (1863–1937), intended for public life and the high places of politics, never went to Mason College, even though his father Joseph Chamberlain (1836–1914) was a strong supporter of it and later became the first Chancellor of Birmingham University. Austen went to Rugby first and then to Cambridge.[34]

Nothing could more clearly indicate the place of the new institutions in the educational system and in the minds of the upper middle class: the class, that is, from which the higher ranks of the professions were by convention, and to a large extent in practice, drawn. The new colleges in unfashionable provincial towns, the new institutions in London, had nothing of the grace and glamour of Oxford and Cambridge. Nor had they the intimate connection, on the one hand, with the public schools and, on the other, with the seats of political power and the possessors of national influence and wealth. Therefore they tended to be looked on as very much a second-best choice for university education. That was a pity. Their staffs had some very distinguished men and the subjects which they taught, such as chemistry and engineering, were what British industry stood gravely in need of.

Chapter 10

PROFESSIONAL MEN ESTABLISHED

BOLD upon the social landscape, in the late Victorian noon, stood the professional classes: self-conscious, self-confident, occasionally pompous, much less ready than their grandfathers to accept new ideas, at any rate in matters of education and training. Perhaps in other matters too. Dr Newman's chapter on medical education after the Act of 1858 is called 'The Safe General Practitioner'. In law, the Judicature Act of 1873 has been called by Sir Robert Ensor 'a piece of tidying up upon the largest scale', but neither he nor other critics, then and since, thought it had gone far enough. The Church, more and more out of touch with the mass of the nation, remained obstinately rural in an overwhelmingly townee society. In electrical engineering; in dyestuffs and organic chemistry generally; in the development of motive power with the internal combustion engine, great advances were made, but not in England, nor were they very eagerly taken up here.[1]

There is, in fact, every reason to suppose that by the last quarter of the century the professional classes, which may be taken to include most of the highly educated people of the nation, had moved a long way from the radicalism of forty or fifty years before. It was only natural, since they had achieved so much of what they had been campaigning for. The standing of the professions, especially the lower branches, had been much raised, qualifications greatly improved, aristocratic patronage almost abolished. Below the social heights, certainly, professional men remained, but not hopelessly so, and they were at last unquestionably at a comfortable sneering distance above 'trade'.

This seems to be the moment of the professional classes' final acceptance and establishment: the outsiders have become insiders.

What, in general terms, can we say of them? Who could claim to belong? How many? Which professions were growing, which stable, which shrinking? What was that elusive thing the 'professional outlook', with its associated precepts and prohibitions?

The first systematic attempt to count the members of the professions was made at the census of 1841. By way of definition the authorities took their stand on ancient usage. They admitted as 'professional persons' only clergy, lawyers of all kinds and both branches, and 'medical men'. These they found to number about 54,000 persons for England and Wales, 63,000 for Great Britain, which represented, they calculated, 0·3 per cent of the total population of the country or 0·8 per cent of everyone in 'occupations'. By 1851 the figure had risen to 72,265 for Great Britain (63,666 for England and Wales) and the report on the census of that year commented, 'their importance cannot be overrated, yet in point of numbers they would be out-voted by the tailors of the kingdom.'[2]

So strict an interpretation of the word 'profession' was already old-fashioned. The census authorities of 1841 themselves admitted it, in a sidelong way, by grouping people in a number of other occupations under the heading 'Other Educated Persons'. This list, as it was made up in 1841, included nearly all the civilian occupations later admitted to more or less unquestioned professional standing. Even when the list was compiled, many people would have been willing to recognize most of them, though in some cases with large reservations. If the 1841 list is studied, along with the dates of the censuses at which the various occupations were promoted by the census authorities to professional standing, it gives us a good base for discussing the later Victorian professional world. Leaving out some of the smaller, more picturesque groups, such as the twenty-six drill-masters, six ornithologists, five ventriloquists, four phrenologists, and one aeronaut, the 1841 list of 'educated persons', with the dates of achieving professional status in the census lists, is as follows[3]:

Schoolmasters, teachers, professors	69,745	1861
Actors	1,563	1861
Authors, editors, journalists	687	1861
Artists and Sculptors	4,643	1861
Musicians and Organists	3,992	1861

Architects	1,675	1881
Land Agents and Surveyors	5,416	1881
Civil Engineers, including 11 naval architects and 196 draftsmen	1,166	1861
Accountants	4,974	1921
Bank agents and Bankers	2,034	Never
Clerks	56,830	Never

(All figures are for Great Britain)

These occupations fall fairly readily into groups. There is the teaching group which was much the largest. Enough has perhaps been said (above p. 106) to indicate that at the mid-century none but a small minority would generally have been accorded anything like full professional standing, and then only if they were clergymen, not because they were schoolmasters.

The 'artistic' group gave social commentators grave trouble. It was evident that some actors, some artists, some authors, and some musicians were educated, cultured men (and women), and it was well known that they were welcomed, even sought after, in the best society. It was equally well known that the majority were not. It was difficult for a writer (which most of the social commentators were) to admit that people of his own kind, and akin to it, should not rank with doctors, lawyers, and clergymen. Yet for none of the 'artistic' group was there the kind of definite course of education required by the recognized professions. For none of them could you lay down exact qualifications: still less could you erect an examination ladder. And as for journalism, the *Contemporary Review* in 1859 remarked severely that it was 'not within the list of professions which give the conventional standing of a gentleman to their members.'[4]

'The conventional standing of a gentleman': that was very important. Too important, some people thought, including a writer in the *Saturday Review* in 1860, who thought that too many people were too proud. 'It is one of their fundamental precepts ... that their sons shall be brought up as "gentlemen"; which elastic word is further limited by the gloss that they shall serve no one except the Queen or the Church, or, if they are to receive payment for work done from anyone else ... it must be as barristers or doctors.' It would be better, he thought, if the idea of gentility could be divorced from professional occupations. 'England indeed is growing incalculably richer; but her wealth is due to manufacturers, and colonies, and commerce, and it is in these that they who would share in it must work. Very little of that wealth reaches the devout believer in gentlemanly professions.'[5]

From this kind of attitude arose the dubious standing of some of the occupations listed, particularly engineering, since accountancy scarcely emerged into the professional world until very late in the century, and architecture was widely regarded, not least by many of those who practised it, as one of the arts rather than anything approaching a science of construction. But engineering lay right at the heart of 'manufactures, and colonies, and commerce'. It will be observed that although the civil engineers were admitted to the professional group in the census of 1861, the closely allied architects and surveyors did not get in for another twenty years. The accountants, the closest of all of them to the commercial world, were not admitted until after the Great War.

Many observers tried to make sense of the hierarchy which was clearly emerging within the professional world. Although more occupations than formerly were allowed to be 'professions', it was obvious that some had a higher standing than others, but the reasons were by no means so obvious. Byerley Thomson, writing in 1857, was one writer who faced the problem. He was in no doubt about the social superiority of the professions as a whole – 'It is true that some merchants and manufacturers have been raised to the peerage, and that some professional men are not even gentlemen, but the former circumstance is as incapable of raising the general mercantile body in social position, as the latter is able to bring any general degradation upon the professional body' – but he had to account for the fact that not all professions were equally esteemed. His answer was that the higher professions were the 'privileged' ones, entrance to which, in the public interest, was regulated by law, and which were defended against unqualified competition. These, he said 'take a higher position than the others. They are more or less connected with the State; their importance is recognized by the law; they excel the others in numbers and wealth, receive a superior education, and are generally drawn from a superior class.'[6]

This analysis, which would probably have been very widely

accepted at the time Thomson was writing, gave him, as privileged professions, the Church, the law, and medicine; the Army and Navy; the mercantile marine; the public Civil Service. The mercantile marine was an obvious intruder – it had no social standing comparable with the rest – and he was bound to throw it out, but that only demonstrated the difficulty of the exercise he had set himself. A good many people, too, would have doubted the inclusion of the Civil Service, except at its highest levels. On the unprivileged professions he could have expected a greater measure of agreement. He listed 'painter, architect, sculptor, civil engineer, educator, parliamentary agent, actuary, average calculator, &c.' These, it will be observed, correspond closely with the 'other educated persons' of the census list.

Many writers, besides Thomson, picked on the degree of recognition by the State as a means of separating higher from lower. The *Contemporary Review*, in the article already referred to, cited the Church, the Bar, the Army and the Navy as higher professions. Medicine, solicitors, painting and civil engineering were 'lower' or 'outside', because they did not lead to the same ultimate reward: the peerage. The writer thought the House of Lords should always keep a connection with landed wealth, which he did not associate with these professions, and so he suggested that their members might be suitably honoured with life peerages 'unless the nation is to be burdened with endless pensions.'[7]

The doctors certainly felt aggrieved, throughout the century, at what they considered to be the neglect of their profession in the honours lists. They were greatly gratified when Lister was made a lord in 1897, only to have their satisfaction moderated when they noticed that Salisbury had recommended him not principally because he was a doctor but in recognition of his general scientific work.[8] It was often remarked that solicitors, unlike barristers, could hope for no official honours at all in their professional capacity. A. V. Dicey, one writer among many, said in 1867 'there is, perhaps, no other profession pursued by persons in the position of gentlemen which offers no public prizes as a reward for eminence.'[9] This neglect cut very deep. The prestige of the older professions was so evidently bound up with their position in the State, signalized by the grant of honours.

T. H. S. Escott, writing about 1880, took the same point and added others. 'Roughly', he wrote, 'it may be said professions in

England are valued according to their stability, their remu-
nerativeness, their influence, and their recognition by the State.'[10]
What this really amounted to was respectability. On that count the
arts were deeply suspect – 'The keen-scented, eminently decorous
British public perceives a certain aroma of social and moral laxity
in the atmosphere of the studio, a kind of blended perfume of
periodical impecuniosity and much tobacco-smoke.' Moreover
neither a painter nor an actor, in Escott's view, could be said to
have much influence on public opinion, though a writer, of course,
could.

On much the same criteria a merchant would be preferred to a
stockbroker (Escott, apparently, unlike Thomson some twenty-
three years earlier, was prepared to accept both as professional
men) because 'the life of the ideal stockbroker is one of display;
that of the ideal merchant, one of dignified grandeur or opulent
comfort.' There is in this passage, as in a good deal of Escott's
writing, a certain air of well-fed, middle-aged self-satisfaction which
is highly characteristic of his period – roughly the forty years before 1914 – and which deepens the impression that the English
professional classes, at this moment of their luxuriant flowering,
were not at the peak of their mental energy or enterprise.

Stability and money were very important ingredients of professional standing: there was no doubt about that. Yet one more
count in the indictment against journalism was that it could not be
relied on for a livelihood – 'there are certainly not twenty men in
London who are making even a thousand a year by the highest
kind of journalism.' This in 1859. But money was a tainted thing:
too close a connection with it – too much actual handling of the
sordid stuff, that is – and you might find yourself classed with
'trade'. This, in Escott's view, was why 'solicitors, general
practitioners, and even illustrious physicians in the daily intercourse of society labour under nearly the same disadvantages as
artists.' The trouble with them all was that having done their
work, they sent in a bill for it. 'But this is exactly what a tailor, a
wine merchant, a butcher, a grocer, or any other retail dealer
does.' On the other hand there were professional men – barristers,
clergy, authors – who did not receive money 'directly from those
with whom they consort nominally on a footing of social equality.' Thus it was that 'whatever the social disadvantage at which
artists, attorneys, and doctors may find themselves, it arises from

precisely the same cause as that which exists in the case of persons who derive their income from nothing that can be called a liberal or a learned trade.'

In making all these laboured distinctions writers of the period were chasing a mirage. The facts were there: some professions were more highly thought of, socially, than others. The reasons were a tissue of impalpability, shot through with a solid practical respect for wealth. These attitudes had more than a touch of absurdity, but in an age almost as obsessed as our own with the *minutiae* of class distinction and status symbols they were taken very seriously. And as a result the hierarchy of the professions was a real social fact, with real effects on the way the nation's work was done.

The rich complexity of the late Victorian professional classes is displayed in the census reports, which from 1861 onwards all follow broadly the same method of classification, though in detail they differ substantially. Let us take the report of 1881 as a statistical guide to the world of Escott, Sherlock Holmes, Dr Watson, *The Forsyte Saga*, and the upper middle classes generally.

The report divided the professional class into three main groups: The General or Local Government of the Country; The Defence of the Country; Professional Occupations. The total number of people given under these headings included many subordinate occupations which are not normally thought of as professions. All ranks of the Army and Navy were included: so were all government functionaries, national and local, from doorkeepers upwards. These have to be disregarded in order to arrive at a picture of 'the professional classes' conventionally so-called.

The core of the census's professional class is still the ancient three and the officers of the Army and Navy. The figures for England and Wales are as follows (rounded off):

Church of England clergy	21,700
Other clergy and theological students	23,100
Barristers and Solicitors (shown together)	17,400
Law students	1,600
Physicians, surgeons, GPs	15,100

Dentists	3,600
Medical Students, assistants	6,000
Midwives	2,600
Army and Navy officers at home	15,000

With the exception of the 614 'Peers, MPs and Privy Councillors (not otherwise described)', very few of the ninety-seven thousand people shown under National and Local Government, except for a few senior Civil Servants, would have been considered professional people in the usual sense. We are therefore left with the other sub-groups gathered under the head 'Professional Occupations', as follows:

Schoolmasters, teachers, &c.	168,800
Authors, editors, journalists, &c.	3,434
Artists, &c.	11,059
Actors, actresses	4,600
Musicians, Music Masters	25,500
Art Students	1,300
Architects	6,900
Engineers (Civil and Mining)	9,400
Surveyors	5,400
Persons engaged in Scientific Pursuits	1,200

Even with the drastic and rather arbitrary cuts which have been made in arriving at the groupings given above, it is clear that they would still include a great many people who would not rank among the professional classes, 'higher' or 'lower', 'privileged' or 'unprivileged', by any of the tests mentioned by the authors discussed above. Neither Escott nor Thomson would have admitted more than a small fraction of the teachers, and the low standing of teaching as an occupation, despite various efforts to improve it, was a matter of comment throughout the century.[11] It should be borne in mind, though, that teaching could provide a ladder to higher things. The son of the village schoolmaster might himself, if sufficiently able, hard-working, and lucky, achieve a position in one of the fully recognized professions.

The census figures were known to be fairly rough. The system of classification was less refined than later and there was often a good deal of doubt about how an individual should be described. Moreover the enumerators had to rely on what people said about themselves, giving ample scope for vagueness, misunderstanding, and deliberate misrepresentation, particularly in an upward direction. It appears, then, that the total of the figures given above (some 340,000) is a considerable overestimate of the numbers in the professional classes, if we confine ourselves to those whose occupations could reasonably be expected to bear the full weight of the implications which the word 'profession', in England, applies. Even the smaller figure given in Table 2 of Appendix 1 is probably also too large, but precision is quite impossible.

Tables based on all the censuses from 1841 to 1911 will be found in Appendix 1. It will be observed that the figures for individual occupations show wild fluctuations. Some can be explained by alterations of method: others, apparently, are not explainable at all. Nevertheless, considered broadly, the figures do show some sort of intelligible pattern, in so far as they suggest which professions were growing, which were declining, and which were standing still, both in relation to each other and in relation to the growth of population as a whole.

In only one census after 1851 did the number of Anglican clergy show an increase equal to the rate of increase in the population as a whole. It seems reasonable to think that this is likely to be among the more reliable census statistics, since an Anglican clergyman is fairly easy to define and not very readily impersonated. Moreover the decline is consistent with the general decline of religious faith in the nation as a whole.

The number of barristers increased very sharply between 1841 and 1851. About that time it was commonly said that the profession was over-crowded and there were more remarks than usual about the difficulty of making a living at the Bar. Shocking stories were told of young barristers slowly starving to death, from want of employment, in their chambers in the Temple, and the educated young were exhorted to seek other occupations.[12] The census of 1861 showed a slight fall in numbers, but for three censuses after that the number of barristers grew, if anything, slightly faster than the general population. By 1901, however, it was dropping sharply.

The solicitors, like the barristers, increased between 1841 and 1851, though not so fast: only about as fast, in fact, as the general population, while the barristers increased much faster. Then there seems to have been an actual drop followed by a slow rise, which only once (during the eighties) seems to have matched the proportionate rise in the population as a whole.

There seems to have been very little change in the number of doctors in the forties. During the fifties, apparently, the number dropped, but the census results of 1861 were probably affected by the Medical Act of 1858, which would have made it harder for unregistered practitioners to pass themselves off. This was certainly the reason advanced by the census authorities themselves for the negligible rise during the sixties. 'Medical men', said the 1871 report, 'remained nearly stationary: the qualification having been much raised.'[13] There was again practically no rise in numbers during the seventies, but the census of 1891 recorded a very sharp increase, which may have owed something to the Medical Act of 1886 which established the conjoint qualification. The census authorities suspected many so-called doctors of being unqualified. Then the rise slowed down again and after the turn of the century, once more, it failed to match the rise in population.

If census figures have any validity at all, therefore, it seems probable that the total numbers employed in the three ancient learned professions barely kept pace with the general rise in population during the fifty or sixty years before 1914. Certainly there is no evidence at all of a striking or steady increase, and where increases did occur, as among the doctors during the eighties and nineties, they may not have done much more than make good deficiencies.

Moving outwards from medicine we find that the dentists, whose technique, organization, and prestige improved a good deal from 1860 onwards (from very low levels before that), steadily increased in numbers a good deal faster than the general population. Striking rises were recorded, with one curious falter in 1891, at every census up to 1911. The vets were not admitted to the professional class until 1891, having previously been classed with farriers (in spite of a professional organization established by statute as long before as 1841). Their numbers fell steadily but slowly from census to census: no doubt they were among the first casualties of motor transport.

The 'creative' group of professions – actors, authors, artists, musicians – increased rapidly from 1841 until the end of the century. After that the numbers of actors and authors seem to have gone on up much faster than the general population until 1914, but the rise in the numbers of artists and musicians was checked or turned into a decline. Changing techniques in illustration no doubt affected the one group: the coming of canned music, perhaps, the other, but these are no more than guesses. The rise in the numbers in this group of professions as a whole almost certainly owed a great deal to better education and greater literacy fed by the cheap periodical press, and it is probably legitimate to couple it with the unbroken rise in the numbers of teachers recorded at every census throughout the period.

At every census from 1851 until the end of the century the number of civil engineers recorded rose sharply: usually faster than the general population, and the same may be said, in general, of the closely related architects and surveyors, though the surveyors show greater fluctuations, including a drop in 1851, than the other two. The figures for all three professions showed a sharp drop in 1911, caused by more exact methods of enumeration, and as regards the engineers the authorities seem to have been rather suspicious of the results for 1881. Nevertheless, unless there are quite monumental errors in the census figures persisting through several censuses, and almost all in the direction of exaggeration, the message is clear: the engineers and their relations were increasing a good deal faster than the general population. It may well be, also, that the accountants were, but the figures show such wide variations as to suggest that they gave even more trouble than most in matters of definition, and the results are probably even less reliable than the rest.

It seems reasonable to conclude, then, that during the latter part of the nineteenth century the 'new' professions, the 'lower' professions, the 'unprivileged' professions – however you liked to look at it – were growing faster than the ancient three. The impression is strengthened by evidence from the registers of public schools, though even less reliance can be placed on it than on evidence from the census figures, because the careers of a very high proportion of boys are unrecorded. However, the registers of Clifton, Marlborough, Mill Hill, Merchant Taylors', Sedbergh, and Winchester, analysed at various points (not the same for each school) between 1807 and 1911 do seem to show fewer boys leaving, as time goes on, to become parsons and more to become engineers and members of the newer professions generally, or Army officers. A summary of the figures from Winchester will illustrate the point:

Boys leaving to become:	*1836*	*1893*
Clergy	23	4
Schoolmasters	5	3
Dons	3	3
Barristers	5	9
Solicitors	2	6
Doctors	4	1
Accountants		3
Actors		1
Authors	2	
Engineers		6
Journalists		2
Army	10	25
Civil Service: home	2	
diplomatic	1	1
India	1	2
other overseas	1	5
Business	1	9
Others		3

This analysis of the structure and growth of the professional classes from 1841 onwards begs a good many questions, not all of which can be dealt with in this chapter, since they demand a rather fuller examination of the nature of late Victorian professional life (Chapter 12 below), and hence of the individual professions. But before we close the discussion of the professional classes as a whole, it may well be to raise once more the question: What were the full implications of 'professional status' as the late Victorians understood it?

Part of the answer has already been suggested in the discussion of 'higher' and 'lower' professions, but perhaps not the most important part. As well as matters of qualification, recognition by the State, the way you got your bills paid, and so on, there was also the claim to a particularly high standard of conduct, which was said to draw together all proper practitioners of the very varied range of occupations which we have been considering.

The claim arose from the underlying unity of the three learned professions, in their unregenerate state before the reformers got at them, in which it was assumed that all members would be gentlemen holding the same code of conduct and brought up on the same kind of liberal education. To feel like this about one's occupation – still more, to be sure that other people felt like this about it – was very gratifying: indeed, it was one of the main rewards of belonging to a profession. Hence the anxiety of the members of every emergent middle-class occupation – the sharp provincial attorneys, the rough Scotch surgeons, the engineers – to get their kind of work accepted as fit for liberally-educated gentlemen. Hence their triumph if they could get people to accept the kind of claim put forward by Sir George Stephen for the attorneys about 1840: 'Gradual elevation of our duties has naturally led to the introduction among us of many young men ... who, less than half a century ago, would have spurned the calling as derogatory to their birth.'[14] Hence the enduring strength of the traditional system of liberal education and the readiness with which the new professional men took to it, in spite of the fact that it was very ill-adapted to their bread-and-butter needs. But if the claim to be accepted as gentlemen – particularly as the word was understood by Dr Arnold and his followers – was to be taken seriously, then the professional man's outlook had to be developed beyond the simple feeling of social and cultural unity which had been enough for the eighteenth-century parson, physician, or barrister. For although the Victorian solicitor, surgeon, engineer, or accountant might become a gentleman he could not altogether cease to be a skilled tradesman with a thoroughly commercial outlook. Nor was it desirable that he should, seeing that much professional work lay among the growing commercial and industrial activity which was the source of England's wealth and power.

So the new professional man brought one scale of values – the gentleman's – to bear upon the other – the tradesman's – and produced a specialized variety of business morality which came to be known as 'professional ethics' or 'etiquette'. It is based upon the fact that what the professional man sells, generally, is expert advice, often upon confidential matters. Unless the client can rely on his adviser's honesty, exactness, and devotion to his (the client's) interest, the transaction falls to the ground. Therefore any professional man must cultivate and deserve a reputation for probity. He must cultivate it even more zealously than the ordinary business man, who deals with other business men who know what to expect. It is this sense of being obliged to observe exceptionally high standards which, more than anything else, gives some sense of unity to the professional classes as a whole, diverse though the occupations of their members may be.

There is also a perfectly reasonable desire to keep unqualified practitioners out of business and to keep competition between members of the same profession within comfortable limits. These desires, however, are common to skilled tradesmen on the one hand and to the general run of business men on the other. They are part, but not a peculiar part, of professional ethics, as the insistence on high standards of integrity is.

A. V. Dicey took the point in 1867. 'The chief difference between a profession and a trade or business', he said, 'is, that in the case of a profession its members sacrifice a certain amount of individual liberty in order to ensure certain professional objects. In a trade or business the conduct of each individual is avowedly regulated simply by the general rules of honesty and regard to his own interest.'[15] This was a charitable view of much of the business practice of his day. Honesty often weighed rather lightly in the scale against self-interest, not in acknowledged 'trade' only but also in aspiring professions, and the early campaigners for professional ethics were performing a genuine public service at the same time as they endeavoured to raise their own standing.

We have seen (above p. 125) what Sir John Rennie and others thought of some aspects of engineering. In medicine, we find that those who tried to stop doctors advertising were not simply trying to limit competition or to make a gesture to well-bred anti-commercial prejudice. They were trying to get rid of things like this, which appeared in *The Economist* – a respectable businessman's paper – in 1844:

> MANLY VIGOUR: a Popular Inquiry into the CAUSES of its PREMATURE DECLINE with instructions for its COMPLETE RESTORATION. Addressed to those suffering from the destructive consequences of excessive indulgence in solitary and elusive habits, youthful imprudence, or infection, terminating in mental and nervous debility, local or constitutional weakness, indigestion, insanity and consumption; including a comprehensive Dissertation on Marriage, with directions for the removal of disqualifications, and remarks on the treatment of gonorrhoea, gleet, stricture and syphilis. Illustrated with cases, etc. By C. J. LUCAS & Co. Consulting Surgeons, London ... Messrs Lucas & Co. are to be consulted from ten until two, and from five till eight in the evening, at their residence, No 60 Newman Street, Oxford Street, London, and country patients may be successfully treated on minutely describing their case, and enclosing the usual fee of £1 for advice.'
> 2s. 6d. – 3s. 6d. by post.

And this advertisement is by no means an isolated example of its kind. The instinct of the tradesman, to make money by any more or less legal means, was by no means quickly stifled by the professional conscience. And even as late as 1870 *The Lancet*, taking another point of professional ethics, observed: 'It is a curious discovery, which we are just beginning to make, that the largest amount of illegal practice is done under the protection of legal practitioners.' What that meant was that a qualified surgeon took on unqualified assistants, just as if he were a bricklayer needing a labourer's help.[16]

Some of the finer points of professional etiquette, especially among lawyers and doctors, looked to outsiders rather like restrictive practices and demarcation agreements, designed to protect the practitioner rather than his client. Bagehot was not alone in thinking it a scandal that the barrister was shielded from his client by the attorney, and that the attorney, in return, could always take refuge behind the opinion of counsel.[17] Nor could clients always quite understand how their interests were served by the rule of etiquette which required a QC never to appear without a junior, so that two barristers had to be paid for what appeared to be a reasonable amount of work for one. Then there was the custom known as 'going special', which absolutely required a barrister – etiquette again, my dear sir – to demand an extra fifty guineas if he were briefed to appear on a circuit not his own. In the medical world, patients sometimes found it hard to convince themselves that the complex rules which appeared to govern doctors' dealings with each other were framed and operated with nothing but the patients' health in mind. There seemed sometimes to be an element of self-interest about them, not to say a tenderness towards incompetence.

These things apart, there is no reason to doubt that many late Victorian professional men were perfectly sincere in their devotion to a standard of behaviour which was certainly higher than the standards accepted in ordinary business, and higher also than many professional men, particularly in the 'lower branches', had formerly considered necessary. One effect of the widespread striving after professional standing was that this regard for high standards of behaviour spread from one occupation to another. The result, inevitably, was an improvement of ethical standards over a wider and wider area of English business life.

Take, for instance, the profession of accountancy. At the beginning of the century it was usually practised as a sideline to some more lucrative occupation such as auctioneering, rent collecting, and stockbroking. It scarcely began to emerge as a profession in its own right until after the middle of the century, and until then, says N. A. H. Stacey, 'few who had the choice of practising other professions were attracted to it.'[18] Then, with the rise of large-scale business, and especially the railways, accountants moved from their almost total preoccupation with insolvency towards more general and less sordid matters. The movement was led from Scotland, where chartered professional institutions were set up in the fifties. In England professional associations were set up in Liverpool in 1870; in Manchester in 1871; in London in 1873; in Sheffield in 1877. In May 1880 all these societies were merged in the Institute of Chartered Accountants in England and Wales, which proceeded to apply itself to the usual objects of professional associations: proper qualifications, standards of conduct, lobbying in the profession's interest.

The movement for recognition which culminated in the grant

of the Charter had already forced the accountants to see that their conduct was up to the standard expected of a profession, rather than a mere trade. That in turn had made them careful of their clients' behaviour. A respectable firm like Deloitte's, for instance, would take great care about whom its name was associated with on the cover of a prospectus, and would refuse to be associated with directors whom the firm did not know or would not trust. Similarly, if a firm persisted in practices which a reputable accountant disapproved of, he would refuse to go on acting for them and professional solidarity – acting in this case unquestionably in the public interest – would see to it that the offending firm would find it difficult to get another accountant.[19] Respectable solicitors would act similarly.

It had long been impossible for a business of any size to carry on without fairly frequent legal advice. It later became impossible for such a business to get on without accountants' services also, especially after the passing of the Companies Act 1862, which one early twentieth-century historian of the profession called 'the accountants' friend.'[20] Once solicitors and accountants were accepted by a firm, they were often consulted on matters outside their own professional field. For the sake of their own reputation, if for no other reason, they were bound to bring something like professional standards to bear on these matters, and thus there were increasingly strong sanctions to ensure that the larger firms, at least, observed rather more than the minimum decencies of commercial conduct.

The improvement in commercial morality, therefore, was partly a function of the increasing scale of business activity. One man on his own, perhaps never very far from bankruptcy, would face temptations and would have opportunities for concealment which would never arise in a larger, more secure undertaking. Moreover while business was petty, professions were petty also, and the professional man was open to the same sort of temptation. Sir George Stephen, writing of attorneys' practice about the end of the eighteenth century, forty or fifty years before his own time, said 'the bulk of legal practice . . . was to be found in petty personal disputes or delinquencies – in small controversy between small people.' By 1840 this class of business had been overtaken in importance by business produced by the country's expanding commerce. 'There is scarcely any important transaction in which a merchant can engage that does not more or less require the counsel of his solicitor . . . The law of insurance, the law of principal and factor, of lien, or partnership, or bankruptcy, of bills of exchange, and many other heads that might be mentioned, enters into the daily affairs of the counting-house.'[21]

The railways brought really large opportunities for all kinds of professional men, especially engineers, lawyers and accountants. It can hardly be coincidental that the great period of railway building in England was the forties and that the number of civil engineers recorded at the census rose from 853 in 1841 to 3,009 ten years later. And the railways were a splendid source of legal work. Not only were there all the complicated negotiations over property, but there was a great flood of parliamentary work, which caused the number of parliamentary agents (a lawyer's job) to rise from 27 in 1841 to 141 in 1851. By 1861 the number had dropped back to 70, presumably because fewer lines were being built, but the railways were by then going concerns, some very large, which provided continuous professional work. Continuous, and sometimes very long-lasting. W. W. Deloitte became the Great Western Railway's accountant in 1849. His firm was still acting for the Western Region of British Railways in 1958.[22]

Businesses on the scale of the large railway companies were inherently less likely to offend against professional ethics than the small firms and one-man businesses. In a large undertaking the chance of being found out was much greater, and in fact Deloitte himself was employed to investigate frauds practised by Redpath, an official of the Great Northern Railway, in 1856. Isolated scandals like that there always have been and probably always will be, but it is difficult to operate a really large business for long on dishonest principles. The chance of an accountant being asked to connive at fraudulent tax returns, say, or of a solicitor being a party to continued breach of contract, was less in Lever Brothers in the nineties than in some small firm seeking to evade soap duty fifty years before.

An occupation's rise to professional standing can be pretty accurately charted by reference to the progress of its professional institute or association. In the early stages it is usually purely an unofficial body – in the eighteenth century, often a dining club – without any legal authority at all and dependent on itself for any authority it may acquire. The eighteenth-century Law Society was of this kind, and the civil engineers had a dining club (the Society of Civil Engineers) from 1771 onwards. The architects had the Architects' Club (for top architects *only*) and three other societies between 1791 and 1834. The doctors set up a great many societies of varying aims, reputation, and degrees of quarrelsomeness.[23]

The next stage in dignity is to form a body corporate. There are various ways of doing that in English law, but the one most favoured by the professions, as conferring the maximum prestige, is to get a Royal Charter, which may be said to confer official recognition by the State that the occupation concerned has achieved professional standing. It is not easy to get, and internal quarrelling within the profession, to which professions are very prone, is a certain bar. A Charter usually grants power to determine professional qualifications, by examination or otherwise, and it may give some measure of protection to a professional designation such as 'chartered accountant'.

The members of chartered associations usually hope to get some or all of their professional functions restricted by law to their own members. This is a privilege which Parliament is very chary of granting, and it was even charier in the nineteenth century than it is today. The doctors and the solicitors got themselves entrenched behind statutes (the barristers had no need), but except in cases where the safety of life and limb was at stake – in the case of mine managers, for example, and ships' officers – no other professional groups, chartered or not, were admitted to the privilege. And even then the law left large gaps, intentionally, in the doctors' defences.

The first of the new professional institutions, the Royal College of Surgeons, was chartered in 1800. The apothecaries got their Act, with its formidable disciplinary powers, in 1815. In 1818 the Institution of Civil Engineers was set up: in 1828 it was chartered. The Institute of British Architects, founded in 1835, was chartered in 1837 and entered on a long period of quarrelling with other architectural foundations, which delayed the grant of statutory privileges until 1931. The Law Society, founded in 1825, was chartered in 1831, but the charter was surrendered in 1847 in exchange for a new one. In 1844 the Pharmaceutical Society was chartered and in 1847 the Royal College of Veterinary Surgeons. Then at longish intervals throughout the century the grant of charters marked the advance of professional organization through Victorian society, as follows:

1854 Society of Accountants in Edinburgh
1855 Institute of Accountants and Actuaries in Glasgow
1867 Society of Accountants in Aberdeen
1880 Institute of Chartered Accountants, London
1881 Surveyors' Institution
1884 Institute of Chemistry
1891 Institute of Patent Agents
1898 Library Association
1902 Institute of Secretaries

Besides the chartered bodies there were many other professional societies, some incorporated, some not. They might represent important divisions within a profession, like the Institution of Mechanical Engineers (1847), the Institution of Electrical Engineers (1871: present name, 1888), and others in engineering and the growing number of specialized societies in medicine. They might represent divergent schools of thought, as they did in architecture and accountancy. They might, it was often suggested, represent lower and lower levels of qualification, as one substantial group after another found itself aggrieved by the standards set by some pre-existing organization.[24]

Whatever the nature and aims of a professional association, one thing was fairly certain: that it would set up a more or less elaborate hierarchy, starting with students, probationers and associates at the bottom and working up through licentiates or members (perhaps both) to fellows at the top, with honorary categories as required. Quite why such elaboration should be thought necessary is mysterious, but it evidently satisfied and still satisfies some deep need widely felt, for a glance at Geoffrey Millerson's list of qualifying associations at the present day will show that not one of them, with the sole and rather surprising exception of the Advertising Association (1926), is content with the single designation of Members.[25]

Professional associations multiplied to meet the growing complexity of Victorian industrial society and the advance of technology and science. Early in the century one broad classification could cover a wide variety of functions. In the thirties and forties the railway engineers had surveyed their own routes, built their own works and designed their own locomotives. Brunel built the largest steamship in the world as well. By the third quarter of the century those jobs would have been divided between civil engineers, mechanical engineers, surveyors and Naval architects, with no doubt a good deal of work for patent agents and electrical engineers as well. Again, in the early part of the century an energetic attorney could deal with all a firm's property problems and a good deal of its finance as well, but by the time Queen Victoria reached her Golden Jubilee the property might be in the hands of a chartered surveyor and the finance might be looked after by a chartered accountant.

Over the same period, in medicine, specialization ceased to be looked down on as an affair of quacks, as it had been in the thirties, and became highly respectable, besides becoming more profitable than general practice. As Morell Mackenzie wrote in 1885, 'the mere enumeration of such things as the stethoscope, the ophthalmoscope, the laryngoscope, the microscope, the pleximeter, the cardiograph, the sphygmograph, to say nothing of the various electrical instruments, is sufficient to strike dismay into the most resolute heart . . . but in cases which present any special difficulty the proper means of diagnosis must be employed or justice will not be done to the patient.'[26] And that meant more work for specialists, including Morell Mackenzie.

This multiplication of professional functions is no doubt an important reason why the old general-purpose professions did not expand very fast in the latter half of the nineteenth century. There was no longer the same compulsion to choose one of the ancient three or be without a profession. If, for instance, a young man was intending to teach at a public school, it was no longer absolutely necessary for him to become a clergyman to do so, which meant that one reason for the expansion of the clerical profession was very much diminished. On the face of things, with so many more occupations defined, it would seem that there were much greater opportunities of middle-class employment: certainly there was more variety. This, however, is a point much disputed, both at the time and since. Before we examine it we must glance at another development of the later years of the century: the emergence of the professional woman.

Chapter 11

PROFESSIONAL WOMEN

APART from teaching and prostitution, there were very few occupations by which an early Victorian middle-class woman could support herself – let alone any children she might have – if she were so unfortunate as to have to do so. She might keep a shop or run some other kind of business, if she had the capital for it. She might write, as Anthony Trollope's mother did, though whether that was quite proper was debatable, and female authors were apt to conceal their identity. She might go on the stage, though throughout a large range of middle-class society that would be considered quite definitely improper: more or less equivalent to prostitution, in fact. Domestic service was out of the question, though formerly its upper reaches had been quite an acceptable middle-class occupation. The kind of industrial work by which many working-class women earned money were certainly not likely to attract anyone who had the remotest opportunity of anything better. Altogether the openings for women of decent social standing were few, precarious, and apt to be tinged with social disapproval or contempt.

For the woman of decent social standing who had to support herself was an oddity, and oddities, like homosexuals today, are inclined to make society feel uncomfortable, censorious, and guilt-ridden, but not particularly constructive. So the general Victorian instinct was to leave the solution of the problem – for the existence of a problem was recognized – to private charity and to imply, only too often, that it was all the wretched women's own fault, anyway. The parallel with contemporary attitudes towards poverty (a closely related problem) is evident.

The orthodox assumption, enshrined in law and custom from

time immemorial, was that every woman belonged to some man, who in return for rights over her owed the duty of supporting her, just as she, in return for the right of support, owed a duty of obedience. It was only when the assumption broke down – as it was apt to do with spinsters and widows – that the question of self-support arose, and then there was a further assumption to hinder women in any efforts they might make towards independence. This was that they were by nature incapable of most of the occupations which men engaged in, particularly those (usually the more profitable) which needed a disciplined intelligence. If this were so, it would be foolish and even unkind to let them have a go; a conclusion that the male mind, with a surprising amount of support from the female, found extremely comforting: the more so since it ruled out the inconvenience of female competition. It also placed women in much the same position as oppressed subject races; a point which did not escape the notice of J. S. Mill and other contemporary observers.[1]

From all this it followed, by a not too shaky and (from the male standpoint) highly convenient process of logic, that the only occupation which women were indisputably and uniquely fitted for became the only female occupation which won unqualified social approval, always provided that it was exercised within the bonds of matrimony. Upon the dual character of wife and mother the Victorians, with their considerable capacity for sentimentality and self-delusion, poured out a flood of mingled idealism, good sense, and sheer squashiness. No one is likely to deny that they were right to emphasize the importance of good wives and mothers, but what was both unfair and foolish was their accompanying habit of blocking almost every other occupation for women, and of sneering at those which they did not actively try to prevent. As Mrs Fawcett (1847–1929), sister of Elizabeth Garrett Anderson, bitterly observed, 'the popular view of the duties of wives and mothers . . . assigns almost supreme importance to the animal rather than to the intellectual and moral functions of womanhood.'[2]

Mrs Fawcett was discussing women's education, which suffered severely from the traditional view of women's place in society. If a girl's chief hope – indeed, almost her only hope – of a decent livelihood was to become someone's wife, and someone's submissive wife at that; and if, in addition, her brain was rather inferior, then, it was a waste of time and money, and probably immoral into the bargain, to educate girls for anything but marriage, and even for that, because of prevalent notions of sexual morality, in a very inadequate way.

Some people might have said, and indeed Mrs Fawcett did say, that marriage itself would be made richer, stronger, and socially more beneficent if girls were given the same chance of developing their minds as boys, but this was not the accepted view. The Schools Enquiry Commission, in the late sixties, reported that the whole idea of anything like a liberal education for girls was novel and not very widespread.

'It leads', they said, 'to less immediate and tangible pecuniary result; there is a long-established and inveterate prejudice, though it may not often be distinctly expressed, that girls are less capable of mental cultivation, and less in need of it, than boys; that accomplishments, and what is showy and super-ficially attractive, are what is really essential for them; and in particular, that as regards their relations to the other sex and the probabilities of marriage, more solid attainments are actually disadvantageous.'[3]

In their account of the faults of conventional girls' schools the Commissioners came to much the same conclusions as Miss Beale and Miss Buss, those redoubtable pioneers, and in fact they relied heavily on the evidence which they took from them. The main complaint was that girls' education, in so far as it was any-thing more than a training in deportment and agreeable manners, was sloppy and unsystematic. Arithmetic and grammar were both taught 'in a manner merely empirical'; mathematics, if attempted at all, which was not often, were 'not taught *mathematically*.' The teaching both of astronomy (a fairly popular subject in girls' schools) and of physical science illustrated what the Commis-sioners called 'the common tendency to attempt the higher ranges in learning while the foundation has not been soundly laid.' Greek was hardly taught at all, and Latin very badly. The same difficulties in teaching French were reported from girls' schools as from boys' (above p. 105) and the results seem to have been even more disastrous.

Music, as a useful social accomplishment, was very much in demand, and all girls, regardless of natural ability, were subjected to it, almost always in the form of piano-playing, since that was what parents insisted upon. The Commissioners were very scathing. Music, they reported, 'is said to be seldom more than the acquisition of manual skill, to be taught without intelligence, and too much confined to instrumental music to the neglect of singing, in which boys are stated to be more accurate.'[4]

Many girls, particularly in wealthy families, got whatever education was considered suitable for them without going to school at all. 'The wealthiest class', said the Commissioners, 'very generally do not send their daughters to school; even in the middle class many more girls are wholly kept and educated at home than boys, and of those who do go to school the school education is brought to a close at the age of sixteen or seventeen in far more cases than with the male sex.' If the teaching was bad in girls' schools, it may fairly be assumed that the teaching at home was often worse, and there would be a total absence of the kind of mental friction engendered by work in class, which most commentators on boys' education considered highly desirable for proper intellectual stimulation.

The supreme irony, perhaps, of the whole situation was that this elaborate process of non-education could involve parents in just as much expense as the schooling of their sons. An expensive boarding school might run to more than £100 a year, which would put it well in the Rugby–Harrow class, though hardly as costly as Eton. At lower levels, fees for boarding-schools might run down to £25 to £30, and day school fees upwards from ten guineas or so. These figures were roughly equal to the charges for boys' schools of similar standing, but they were increased by the higher price of what the Commissioners called 'fancy articles' – that is, the much prized 'accomplishments' – which required, in small or smallish schools, the attendance of a good many specialist teachers who came a relatively long way to teach for a relatively short time.[5] And these heavy charges were undertaken by parents whose objection to the idea of soundly based education for girls, in part at least, was its cost. Successful business men though many of them were, they were very poor judges of value for money in matters of education, as the Commissioners (in discussing the education of boys) did not fail to point out.[6]

Education of this kind was firmly based on the assumption that women were inferior to men, and was designed to keep them so.

It was evident, therefore, to the early campaigners for women's rights, that education was a focal point in the struggle, just as it was in the newer professional men's struggle to raise their status, and for much the same reason – where tradition does not prescribe respect, education may compel it. About the middle of the century several important establishments were set up for the education of women – Queen's College, Harley Street (1848), Bedford College, London (1849), the North London Collegiate School (1850), and The Ladies' College, Cheltenham (1853). They were dedicated to the propositions, first, that girls were not to be educated solely with an eye to catching husbands, and secondly, the girls' education should be no less rigorous, intellectually, than boys'. If possible, it should be more so.

The early results of this dedication were somewhat alarming. The pioneers, like Miss Buss at the North London Collegiate, had mainly negative principles to go on, rather than a positive conception of how, if at all, the education of girls ought to differ from that of boys. Thus girls' education was no longer to be concentrated on 'accomplishments', was not to be unsystematic and scrappy, was not to be governed by the idea that the sole purpose of a good woman's life was to be attracting and pleasing a husband. All this rush of negative earnestness overwhelmed the fact that men have some part to play in most normal women's lives, married or not: that the majority even of educated women are likely to get married, and may even want to: that intellectual rigour is not entirely incompatible with freedom of thought, even with frivolity: that 'method' can fairly easily become repression. Miss Buss, according to one of her pupils in the eighties, fell into most of these traps, and in the absence of positive ideas of what women's education ought to be, harnessed it rather too firmly to the demands of outside examiners so that 'for better or worse, the education of girls became a feeble imitation of what the boys were doing, for the public examinations made no distinction of sex, and no woman's voice was heard at the examination boards.'[7] And, as the anonymous versifier put it:

> Miss Buss and Miss Beale
> Cupid's darts do not feel.
> Miss Beale and Miss Buss –
> They are not like us.

No doubt a girl from this kind of background all too easily grew up over-earnest, too conscious of her 'mission', resentful towards the entire male sex. Her plight, half-comic, half-pathetic, got very little sympathy either from other women or from men, because on the whole people were only too ready to believe that this, and this alone, was what 'liberal education' did for women. Nevertheless the campaigners for women's rights had firmly grasped one point: that unless women could make good their right to an education as good as a man's, they would gain equality with men in precious little else; certainly in nothing to which they attached importance, such as politics or the professions. And at the lowest bread-and-butter level most middle-class women would remain unable to earn a living except in what Sir George Stephen in 1840 called 'the slavery of teaching or companionship, the sad resource of every female whose infancy has been cherished in wealth, and whose maturity is gained in destitution.'[8]

The 1861 census found that 72.5 per cent of teachers were women. It was the only occupation to which the census awarded professional status, except midwifery, in which they outnumbered men, and in general usage the claim of teaching to be a profession, except at the very top of the scale, was not taken seriously, particularly in reference to women. How could it be, when the standards of performance were so low, when there was no attempt at serious training or qualification, when it was so miserably paid? There were continual complaints about the lack of professional training, and in 1846 Henry Stein Turrell and others made a serious attempt to put matters right by founding the College of Preceptors which, with a Royal Charter and a system of qualifying examinations, looked very much like a genuine professional institution, and which, from the start, made special provision for women. It was not very successful, though, and it hardly could be, as long as the conception of a teacher's job remained so low and there were so many women who, in the absence of other possibilities, were only too anxious to find some source of income, however small.[9]

There was a small handful of other professional occupations (taking the census authorities' own definition of 'professional') in which the 1865 census found a few women employed. (No previous census showed men and women separately in 'professional' occupations). On the stage there were 891 women to 1,311 men (the balance swung over to a majority of women in the seventies and has stayed that way since). In painting and sculpture there were 1,652 women (5,249 men), with a slight majority over men in sculpture. There were 145 female authors (1,528 men) and 1,618 musicians (7,848 men), many of whom, no doubt, might alternatively have returned themselves as teachers; 1,913 midwives were returned, but nursing was not shown as a profession until 1891, when midwives were absorbed under the same head.

In 1861 the women's assault on the real male strongholds among the professions, although preparing, had barely begun, and the census figures recorded things as they had been rather than indicating what they were to be. Everyone was used to schoolmistresses and governesses, poor things, and to women as midwives, as actresses, artists, and musicians, even as authors, so long as they kept reasonably quiet about it, but no one seriously pretended that they ranked level with doctors, clergymen, and lawyers. Most people would have been shocked by any woman who claimed such a standing, and shocked was what most people were about to be, for a few women, backed by a few prominent men, were preparing to break their way into the profession of medicine.

Already, as long ago as 1855, *The Lancet*, under the heading 'LADY DOCTORS', had reported that 'two ladies, of quiet, elegant deportment, attended Mr Fergusson's operations this week and are going out to assist Miss Nightingale', but no more seems to have been heard of these two ladies and it may be that they were nurses rather than doctors, for *The Lancet* went on, in the same paragraph, to say that 'the wife of one of the surgeons of the Smyrna staff is to have £300 a year as matron of the hospital.'[10] The juxtaposition – or confusion – is in any case significant, for *The Lancet* and many others were repeatedly to suggest, as time went on, that nursing was as near as any woman ought to be allowed to come to qualified medical practice.

The Lancet's two ladies of 1855 gave a faint hint of what was soon to come. Elizabeth Blackwell (1821–1910) gave a broader one. Having emigrated with her family to New York, and having, with two of her sisters, run a school for the support of the family after her father's death, she eventually took advantage of the fact that some American institutions were prepared to admit women to medical degrees. In 1849, after a stormy academic passage, she became MD of what Newman calls 'an obscure school at Geneva NY'.[11] Obscure the college might be, but its degree enabled her to assert a right to registration under the British Medical Act of 1858. The Act had been passed without a thought of women wanting to become doctors, so no clause had been put in to bar them, whereas there was a positive requirement to register practitioners who had been active before 1 October 1858. Of these Dr Blackwell, in spite of her sex, was incontrovertibly one.

Most of the English system of medical education and qualification was like that. Nothing specifically barred women, but that was simply because it had never entered anyone's head, much before the middle sixties, that any woman would present herself at a medical school or before an examining body. Nor was that in the least surprising when we consider the innocence which was part of the Victorian romantic myth about women, especially young unmarried ones, and the medical students' reputation for rowdiness, bawdiness, and general aggressive masculinity. It was hard enough for the mid-Victorian mind to conceive of a *lady* becoming a nurse, but that at least bore some relation to the duties expected of a woman in the home and could be dressed up, in flat contradiction to the true character of Florence Nightingale and a good many of her successors, with the attributes of sweetness, gentleness, and general harmlessness which orthodox Victorian folklore assigned to the female personality. To become a doctor was to invade a world hitherto exclusively masculine, where the crudest facts of life were not only not concealed, but had to be actively explored. To the mind of the average man or woman of the educated classes the notion was inexpressibly shocking.

At the same time we must bear in mind that although the Victorian conception of womanhood put great obstacles in the way of women becoming doctors, yet at the same time it opened the door to them. This was because considerate, and indeed deferential, behaviour towards women was required of that admired Victorian character, the Christian gentleman, in a way in which it had not been required of gentlemen (not yet specifically Christian) in earlier times. The general male instinct, hitherto faithfully reflected in English law and custom, is to take advantage of women rather than to protect them, and although in the eighteenth century women may have had greater freedom of action and expression, in some ways, than they had in the nineteenth, yet it is impossible to suppose that they would have been allowed to invade any important male privileges: still less so in earlier and even more barbarous ages. But once gentlemen had been taught that their proper attitude towards ladies should be respectful and protective, rather than simply domineering, it became difficult for them, in the last resort, to stand in the way of any claim, resolutely pressed, which was not manifestly barred by biological differences.

Moreover it is pertinent to remember that women cannot readily assert themselves outside their own homes unless they can go about in reasonable safety, unescorted, in the street and on the highway. Law and order was very precarious indeed, particularly in towns, until the police took hold, which was not until well into Victorian times, and there was sound reason behind the unwilling-ness to let women go about too venturesomely. Women have, perhaps, more to thank the policeman for than is generally recognized.

In 1865 Elizabeth Garrett (1836–1917), inspired by Dr Black-well's example, took the Licence of the Society of Apothecaries and became the first woman to gain a registrable English quali-fication. This she was only able to do because, as we have already observed, most English regulations, including the regulations of the Society of Apothecaries, simply did not contemplate the possibility of a woman complying with them. Once Miss Garrett could show that she had done so, the Apothecaries had no alter-native but to grant her their Licence, which they did most unwillingly. The operative wording in their rules spoke of 'persons', without distinction of sex, and the Apothecaries found themselves unable to deny that Elizabeth Garrett was a person.[12]

Once it became evident that women really meant to become doctors, the profession reacted fiercely, and in what many people might consider a curiously feminine way. They displayed alarm, a complete lack of logic, and a sense of propriety which would have done credit to a maiden aunt. And their tactics were often outrageously unfair. The women, on the other hand, were on the whole resolute, logical, fair-minded, and moderate: attributes which, on the whole, men are inclined to consider preponder-antly masculine.

The women's case was stated temperately, concisely and firmly by Sophia Jex-Blake (1840–1912) in a letter to *The Lancet* in June

1870. 'State clearly', she wrote, 'what attainments you consider necessary for a medical practitioner; fix your standard where you please, but define it plainly ... if ... in spite of all difficulties, we reach your standard, and fulfill all your requirements, the question of "mental equality" is practically settled, so far as it concerns our case; give us then the ordinary medical licence or diploma, and leave the question of our ultimate success or failure in practice to be decided by ourselves and the public.'[13]

But this plain, straightforward method of fair trial was precisely what the ruling bodies of the profession were determined not to grant, and one cannot help suspecting that they were afraid to grant it, because the case of Elizabeth Garrett had shown only too clearly what women were capable of. Certainly the Apothecaries were quick to see that nothing of the sort should ever happen again. They altered their regulations to forbid the grant of a licence to any students who had received any part of their medical education 'privately'. They knew that Elizabeth Garrett had had to study privately – under recognized teachers – because she had been shut out of the medical school of the Middlesex Hospital after an embarrassingly brilliant performance there, and they could count on all other public medical schools refusing to admit women students. Other examining bodies in London were more sweeping. They simply refused to admit women to their examinations, though with doubtful legal warrant.

The women thereupon (in 1869) descended on Edinburgh University, which after great heart-searching and five months' discussion decided to admit them, at the same time requiring them to attend separate classes from male medical students. This segregation was something which the orthodox members of the profession laid great stress upon, ostensibly on grounds of propriety. In the autumn of 1870 four students at Edinburgh were fined for demonstrating against the women and *The Lancet*, after a half-hearted and patently insincere condemnation of their offence, went on:

'We consider the system of mixed education for medical students to be more than a mistake ... no girl who has been brought up in the sphere in which persons of refinement are to be found, could dissect the different parts of a human body, or listen to anatomical and physiological lectures, in the presence of a number of young men, without outrage to the delicacy and sense of modesty of both sexes. If the male students feel this while the lady students do not, all we can say is that the former seem to us to manifest a far more delicate appreciation of what is modest and becoming than the latter.'[14]

There was, no doubt, a perfectly honest objection to mixed classes – Lister, for one, said he would refuse to lecture to them – which is understandable in the climate of opinion of the time. That would not have mattered very much if the segregated classes had run smoothly and the University had held to the natural consequences of its decision to admit women as students. In fact, after one peaceful session, agitation made certain professors refuse to run separate classes, and then on 28 October 1870 the General Council of the University rejected, by a majority of one, the proposal to admit women to the same classes and privileges as men as students of medicine. The proposal had been made, by Dr Crum Brown, because a woman had won a Hope scholarship in chemistry – a woman being awkwardly brilliant again – and the Professor concerned had decided she could not hold it under the regulations as they stood. The voting seems to have been greatly influenced by Dr Christison's announcement that 'he had the QUEEN's commands to make it known that, so far from approving, her Majesty looked with much disfavour on, proposals such as that introduced by Professor CRUM BROWN.'[15]

The women were thus effectively shut out from medical teaching, since the arrangements for segregated classes (which they had been required to agree to attend as a condition of being allowed into the University) had broken down and they were not to be allowed to go to mixed classes in case they offended the susceptibilities of male medical students – not, of all men, generally considered the most fastidious. The process of exclusion was crowned when the University changed its mind about admitting women at all, decided that it had behaved illegally in doing so, and went on to announce that it would not be legal to allow them to graduate. Litigation in 1872 and 1873 failed to get the women back into the University, there was no money for an appeal to the Lords, and the women and their backers transferred their efforts to getting an Act 'to remove Doubts as to the Powers of the Universities of Scotland to admit Women as

Students, and to grant Degrees to Women.' Sophia Jex-Blake herself finally qualified at Dublin.

The Lancet reported these struggles, and those which followed, with agitated attention. In common with the General Medical Council, it hated the whole idea of lady doctors, and it particularly hated their presumption in claiming admission to all branches of medical practice. 'If', it said in 1876, 'those women who are seeking, at an extravagant cost of time and money, to enter the medical profession, were content to work in the only department of medical practice which is properly open to them – namely, as midwives and nurses – no objections could be fairly raised, provided that they always practised under the supervision of qualified medical practitioners ... But this is a very different affair from what the female medical students in London are striving for. Their ambition is to be placed upon the Medical Register, and then to please themselves what branches of medical practice they shall engage in. But this is exactly the matter in dispute.'

Throughout this controversy individuals, bodies, and periodicals were very willing to tell women what was good for them, make up their minds for them, and generally to deny them what Sophia Jex-Blake had demanded – a fair trial and the right of independent action. But the idea of an independent woman – a 'strong-minded' woman, as she was disapprovingly referred to – was most unwelcome to most Victorian minds, and in this case she represented a threat to masculine livelihood, distant as yet, but perceptible. 'If', said *The Lancet*, 'sex is to be no hindrance to the pursuit of the medical profession, it can be to no other. In other words, the legislation which would admit women to medicine will mark a new era in social and political history, the effect of which may be more felt in other professions than in ours ... We are not afraid', the article concluded, although all the appearances are that they were, 'of being met in our profession by large numbers of competitors in the form of girl graduates.'[16]

After their rebuff in Edinburgh the women had turned back upon London where, in 1874, the London School of Medicine for Women was founded. There was an attempt to block it – the examining bodies at first refused to recognize it – but by this time resistance was weakening, largely because the men in control of the medical profession, when pushed to the uttermost, would not finally say that women ought to be shut out. 'The Medical Council', reported *The Lancet* in 1875, 'are of opinion that the study and practice of medicine and surgery, instead of affording a field of exertion well fitted for women, do, on the contrary, present special difficulties which cannot be safely disregarded; but the Council are not prepared to say that women ought to be excluded from the profession.'[17]

Such weak-kneed irresolution was useless against the determination of women like Elizabeth Garrett and Sophia Jex-Blake. With the help of the men who backed them, they finally got the right of properly-qualified women to be placed on the Register embodied in the statute law by Russell Gurney's 'Act to remove the Restrictions on the Granting of Qualifications on the Ground of Sex', 1876.

After that it was much more difficult for the teaching and examining bodies to put official obstacles in the way of women students, rather in the same way as it is difficult for public bodies to operate an official colour bar if the law of the land is against it. London University, in 1877, was brought to recognize that since it had been founded to admit 'subjects of every kind, without distinction', and 'all classes and denominations', it could not very well refuse to admit women, although the foundation clauses had been framed simply to rule out a colour bar or religious tests, and with no thought of female students.[18]

One by one others came in – Queen's Hospital at Birmingham, with the support of Joe Chamberlain, in 1876; the King's and Queen's Colleges of Physicians in Dublin, in 1876; even, at length (in 1886), the Colleges of Physicians and Surgeons of Edinburgh and Glasgow, at about the same time as Sophia Jex-Blake founded the Edinburgh School of Medicine for Women. In general, it may be said that the teaching institutions managed to preserve the principle of segregation, which in itself, given the contemporary climate of opinion, was no bad thing, but their manoeuvres to shut women out from any medical teaching at all, and from examinations, were gradually defeated. In 1882 the members of the Royal Commission on the Medical Acts, influenced, as they said, by the moderation of the representations made to them by Elizabeth Garrett Anderson, said they thought it 'only fair and reasonable that women should be admitted to the examinations on the same terms as men.'[19]

Official opposition might be dead but prejudice long survived.

The Lancet, commenting on the Royal Commission's recommendations, said:

> 'Certain *persons* have succeeded in passing the examinations thrown open to them, and others may do the same; but the common sense of the world and the good sense of the sex will no more permanently tolerate the unseemly invasion of an unsuitable province of labour than women, as a class, will ultimately show themselves fitted for the discharge of the duties they have rashly, and as we believe indecorously, undertaken.'[20]

There was another source of prejudice to be considered – the patients. One of the principal arguments the women had put forward for qualifying as doctors was that women, in particular, should have the opportunity to consult women if they wished, but this was not a view well received either within the profession or generally. Once again, it smacked of the 'independent woman': most offensive to masculine authority. There was consequently considerable hostility to the idea of women consulting women doctors, and Elizabeth Garrett Anderson, in her evidence to the Royal Commission of 1882, said:

> 'Fifteen years ago it required considerable courage on the part of a woman to consult a medical woman (except without the knowledge of her friends); now it has almost ceased to be thought anything exceptional to do so. Women are consulted, if they have a good reputation for skill and judgement, almost as naturally as men are. It has become increasingly evident, that to women of all ages, but especially to young and unmarried women, the opportunity of being able to get medical advice from a qualified woman is, in many cases, of real value.'[21]

That may well have been true. It is unlikely that all Victorian doctors were among the gentlest of men, or even all gentlemen, and they may not have put themselves out very much to soothe the embarrassment and discomfort of young women consulting them. But in her account of the dissipation of prejudice between the late sixties and 1882 one cannot help feeling that Dr Anderson was unduly optimistic. For a long time after 1882 a 'lady doctor' was regarded as something of a freak, highly suspect as to her professional competence, and it was not only the men who distrusted her.

The long struggle to get women into medicine seems to have engrossed the strength of the campaigners for professional status for women, leaving little to spare for any other battle. Certainly no other profession came under anything like such heavy pressure. There was nursing, of course, but that was not comparable with medicine because nurses, in the last resort, were not expected to exercise independent judgement and were, in fact, expressly restrained from doing so, which was one reason why so many people thought it such a suitable profession for women and so many women rejected it. Among the major professions, women invaded neither the law nor the church: nor have they done so, in any numbers, up to the present day, and the same may be said, with more or less minor reservations, of architecture, accountancy, engineering and, indeed, all the newer professional occupations which were developing so fast among the men in the latter part of the nineteenth century. Censuses up to 1911 record no women lawyers or engineers, and only a scattering elsewhere – half a dozen architects in 1901, for example, and nineteen accountants in 1911.

Towards the end of the century, nevertheless, a woman stood a considerably better chance of earning a living than fifty years earlier. Leaving the new, but non-professional, employments – particularly as telephonists and typists – on one side, there was a considerable increase in the number of women in teaching (especially after the Education Act of 1870), nursing (there were more than fifty thousand nurses when they first appeared separately in the census in 1891), and the arts, especially the stage and music, which by 1911 employed, together, some thirty-three thousand women (including teachers of music among the musicians).

Apart from direct pressure on the professions, there was a continuous campaign for more, better and higher education for women. Escott, as late as the mid-eighties, was still complaining of the superficiality of girls' education – and blaming the parents for it – in much the same terms as those used by the Schools Enquiry Commission twenty years before,[22] but in fact by that time a good deal had been done to improve matters, especially at the upper end. Girton (1869) and Newnham (1871) were both active at Cambridge. Oxford had its women too, and so had London and university colleges in the provinces. Women teachers were being trained at Cambridge and elsewhere.[23]

Nevertheless it cannot be said that women made any overwhelming rush even into medicine, when that was fully opened to them. Twenty-five women doctors were recorded in the 1881 census: 477 in 1911. This indicated a very large proportionate increase, but small absolute numbers – compare, for instance, the rise in women clerks from 5,989 in 1881 to 117,000 in 1911. Obviously not nearly so many women are fitted to become doctors as to become clerks, but still, after the tremendous fuss that had been made – and the agitation of the male doctors – the figures do look extremely small.

No doubt it all shows the force of centuries of social custom. Women never had gone into independent professional occupations on the same terms as men, and it took more than a mere fifty years or so of propaganda to get people used to the idea that they might do so. Nor is the notion by any means universally accepted yet. Moreover for a late Victorian girl of the comfortable classes, who alone could face the expense of professional training, life on the conventional pattern could be very agreeable. She had considerably more freedom than her mother or grandmother, and far greater opportunities of pleasure and entertainment were open to her. At the same time no one expected her to take any very crushing weight of responsibility for her own affairs. In due time she would be married, into the same sort of comfortable family as she was used to, and she would have a household of her own. Her freedom would be even greater. Ultimate authority would lie with her husband, but so would responsibility. Why should she give up all that for seven years' hard slog to a medical qualification, with an uncomfortable, isolated and responsible position at the end of it, in which few would applaud her successes and many would be delighted if she should fail?

Chapter 12

PROFESSIONAL LIFE: OPPORTUNITIES, OBSTACLES AND REWARDS

'Though the exigencies of modern life ... have multiplied professions in England', wrote Escott at the end of the seventies, 'they have not multiplied them in such numbers as to provide sufficient occupation for the sons of English parents.' He wrote off 'the opportunities of an empire established in each of the four quarters of the globe' as too few or not paying enough for boys with small capital. 'Success in the learned professions', he said, 'is denied to mediocrities. The navy requires strong interest and the army a competence.' He recognized the expansion of commerce, but said that there were more candidates than jobs, 'while the peculiar aptitudes which the occupation demands are not always forthcoming.' As to the Bar, he repeated the familiar assertion that it meant 'starvation and idleness' for most of those called. 'The Civil Service', he complained, 'is underpaid, and the meanest position in it is only to be won after success in an examination sufficiently difficult to act as a formidable barrier. The Church offers small inducement for the ambitious aspirant, and the profession of the schoolmaster is already overstocked.'[1]

Escott was a journalist and a good deal of a gossip. What he said reflected pretty faithfully what many people in upper-middle-class England felt, but not necessarily the underlying realities. This particular piece of gloom sounds rather like after-dinner chat in some comfortable Forsyte-type household in the middle of the Great Depression. Can it be statistically checked? The uncertainties of doing so have been sufficient to provoke sharp controversy between two recent writers on the subject[2], but the question is not one which we can afford to ignore.

Much depends on what you mean by 'a profession'. We have already observed (above p. 155) that any expansion there may have been in the ancient three was scarcely sufficient to keep pace with the rise in the general population. But Escott was thinking in much broader terms, just as we have been doing throughout this book. It seems justifiable, therefore, to base our discussion on the seventeen occupations which we have already looked at in Chapter 9, bearing in mind that these leave out of account the Civil Service, all occupations overseas, and the armed forces, so that they cover a considerably narrower field than Escott dealt with.

In Appendix 1, Table 2 shows the numbers recorded as being employed in these occupations at the censuses of 1841, 1881, and 1911. Three major observations may be made upon them:

(a) The totals rise from 125,000 in 1841 to 317,000 in 1881 and 474,000 in 1911. This is a very large absolute rise, and proportionately very much greater than the rise in the total population over the same period.

(b) Very much the largest figures are for teachers, many of whom, as we have repeatedly observed, would scarcely rate as professional people according to Escott's understanding of the term.

(c) The rise in the total from 1841 to 1881 is 154 per cent, but from 1881 to 1911 only 50 per cent.

It is now easier, perhaps, to suggest the realities of the situation which lay behind such complaints of lack of professional employment as Escott reported. First of all, opportunities in some of the highest employments, considered both socially and financially, were only increasing very slowly, if indeed they were increasing at all. If the census is to be believed, there were fewer doctors in practice in 1881 than in 1841, and, outside the range of the census, the number of vacancies offered in the ICS dropped from eighty or so in the early years of the competition to an average of about thirty-five, though against that fall must be set a very much larger rise in the number of Army officers required.

The corresponding rise in the opportunities of employment in the 'lower' professions was greatest in the one which, generally speaking, was beneath the notice of the established professional class entirely: that is, teaching. Other occupations, nevertheless, did attract boys whose choice of career might formerly have been restricted to divinity, physic, or law. Engineering appears more prominently among the occupations taken up by boys leaving public schools towards the end of the century, and Escott himself remarks: 'At the head of all the new professions must be placed that of the civil engineer' (it will be noticed that he says nothing of mechanical or electrical engineering).[3] It is easy to believe, however, that the idea of taking up anything so unfamiliar as engineering may not have occurred very readily to families accustomed to thinking in terms of the Church, the Bar, or medicine, and they may easily have come to the conclusion that the prospect before young men was narrower than in fact it was.

It does in any case appear that opportunities of professional employment, although still growing very fast in the latter part of the nineteenth century, were growing considerably more slowly than, say, between 1840 and 1870. This seems consistent with the general economic development of the country, with the effects of the Great Depression, and with the rise of foreign competition. It certainly seems sufficient to account for the sense of over-crowding in professional employment, which Escott so well conveys, and for his remark: 'Of the young men who have gone through an academic course, without discredit but without lustre, the great majority become curates, or schoolmasters, or emigrants. The mere university degree, even when accompanied by moderate honours, is becoming a drug in the market.'[4]

Nevertheless late Victorian England was not altogether a bad place to be an upper-middle-class boy in. The prospect before him may not have been expanding as fast as in his father's day, but it was certainly a great deal wider than in his grandfather's, and the possibilities of employment outside the three learned professions and the government service were becoming more widely recognized. The broadening of the professional classes' outlook can be conveniently examined by comparing two publications intended for Cambridge undergraduates, one dating from the sixties and the other from 1906.

The earlier one – *The Student's Guide to the University of Cambridge* – was edited by J. R. Seeley and came out in 1863, 1866, and 1874. Later it was replaced by *The Student's Handbook to the University and Colleges of Cambridge*, which became an annual and survives to the present day. The two manuals differ instructively both in what they say and in how they say it.

The *Guide* was evidently a product of progressive opinion within the university, intended to make it better known and more widely understood. It contains a great deal of general information and seems to be addressed to undergraduates who knew no one to tell them what they might expect; perhaps the sons of newly prosperous professional and business men without previous university connections. Certainly those who contributed to it were impressed by the prevailing demand for the university to do something about professional education for, as we have seen (above p. 130) they put forward the new regulations for the ordinary degree as a response to it.

Nevertheless the *Guide* was patronizing towards the ICS – a career very attractive to the professional classes – and one comes from it, as from Winstanley's *Later Victorian Cambridge*, feeling that Cambridge in the sixties had not really left the early nineteenth century behind. It still seems introverted; preoccupied with its own politics; inclined, as ever, to regard a classical scholar in holy orders as the only end-product it could unreservedly feel proud of. Certainly the contributors to the *Guide* assumed that many of their readers would go into the Church and they published the number of livings each college had in its gift (323 altogether in 1863), presumably as an aid to choosing a college. Altogether the *Guide* describes a university energetic and earnest according to its lights, but far from convinced that its mission lay much towards the education of the professional classes in an industrial country.

The *Handbook* of 1906 shows a Cambridge recognizably of the twentieth century. It had grown. There were over three thousand undergraduates (as well as three hundred women) against eighteen hundred in the sixties, though the number of fellows of colleges had hardly altered – 371 against 356 (1866), by no means all resident at either date. The range of subjects that could be taken for honours courses (triposes) included history; economics; law; mechanical, natural and moral sciences; various European and Oriental languages; and theology, as well as the traditional classics and mathematics. A Teachers' Training College had been set up in 1878. It was not part of the university, but Oscar Browning, a Fellow of King's College, was Secretary. Since 1896 graduates of other universities had been allowed to come to Cambridge for advanced studies and research. Besides the two women's colleges there was a new college for men (Selwyn 1882) and non-collegiate students (107 in 1906) had been let in. But the most striking change since the mid-sixties is represented in the much greater space given to careers in the 1906 *Handbook*, showing both a change of attitude in the university and a much wider range of possibilities for university men.

Already in 1874 the *Student's Guide*, referring to the recently founded Oriental Languages Tripos, had observed 'How useful ... is a knowledge of Hebrew, Chaldee or Syriac to the young theologian; and how invaluable is a knowledge of Arabic, Persian or Hindustani to the military or diplomatic cadet, whose profession is almost certain to take him sooner or later to the East, to say nothing of the large number of people whom business or pleasure continually calls to India or the Levant.'[5] This open recognition that an honours degree might be directly useful was novel, to say the least of it, and some people may have found it shocking.

Ten years later matters went farther. In 1884 a Scholastic Agency was set up, at first under Professor W. J. Lewis: later under Dr H. A. Morgan, Master of Jesus College. Its job, as described in the 1906 *Handbook*, was to find staff for 'the great public schools and ... many of the grammar schools' as well as 'a very large number of the best preparatory schools' and for schools in 'the Colonies' as well.[6] Schoolmastering in good schools was nothing new as a career for university men, but organized help in finding a job backed, however indirectly, by the official sanction of the university, was an innovation. What was also new was that by the eighties this kind of teaching was ceasing to be a parson's monopoly, though a writer in the *Saturday Review* in 1880 said 'even in smaller and inferior schools the change from a clerical to a lay headmaster almost always indicates a decline in the reputation and character of the school ... Parents, as a rule, prefer entrusting their children to clerical educators, and the really flourishing schools are accordingly conducted on this principle.'[7]

In 1899 the principle of the Scholastic Agency was carried farther and wider. An Appointments Board was set up to deal with a range of occupations that must have seemed bewildering to anyone with memories of Cambridge thirty or forty years before. The *Handbook* says the Board had 'mainly in view . . . the Army, Navy and Diplomatic Services; the Home, Indian, and Colonial Civil Services; other appointments in India and the Colonies; Law and Medicine; Journalism and Literary work; work on Railways in connection with both the administrative and engineering staff; Shipping and Shipbuilding; Commerce and Technical Industries; Agriculture, Mining, Surveying and Engineering; Lectureships in University Colleges, and Scholastic Work.'[8] In other words there was hardly a middle-class or upper-class calling which Cambridge men were not invited to consider.

Despite the fine, bold sweep of the Board's pronouncement, it was still unusual for university men to take up some of the occupations mentioned. The *Handbook* touched on them gingerly, rather in the tone of an anthropologist reporting on a strange, inferior culture. Of Railways it said 'a man has to be prepared at first to accept a "living wage", and his prospects of promotion will depend entirely on his showing himself more capable and conscientious than his fellow clerks.' Under Commerce there is a similar baffling reference to 'a living wage' (what more could a new man expect, university-educated or not? No profession would pay as much, and a premium would probably be demanded from the learner.) Still on the subject Commerce, the *Handbook* goes on 'there is no doubt that a University man of good manners and ability, who has half-a-dozen years' experience in the ways of a business-house, can often at twenty-eight or thirty years of age make his own terms.' Here is a hint of the rise of the professional manager. It sounds rather like the argument for hiring arts graduates sometimes heard forty or fifty years later: not that they have any technical training, but that with all that education they must be good, especially with social poise on top of it.

There was no mention of scientific careers in industry, although a few of the more progressive firms were already prepared to employ scientists trained in English universities rather than abroad. Engineering, however, was mentioned, since Cambridge was developing it as a subject. The *Handbook* said premiums formed 'a high tariff wall round employment under most firms' but they showed 'a strong tendency to give way in favour of the well-trained man. A short term of apprenticeship is, as a rule, substituted for the premium pupil system.'⁹ Even that cautious optimism may have been premature. As late as 1921 a writer on English secondary education remarked: 'American manufacturers discovered the use of university men in their works before England; but England is rapidly following suit. Engineering, mining, metallurgy, chemical industries, textiles, leather, dying, even brewing, look to the universities for researchers and managers.'¹⁰ The tone of the passage suggests that they had not long been doing so.

The Civil Service had a section of the *Handbook* to itself, and in dealing with it the authors give the appearance of being on more familiar ground than in their remarks on railways and commerce. The connection between the Civil Service Commissioners and the older universities had been gradually forged by men like Theodore Walrond (1824–87) an examiner in 1855 and a Commissioner in 1875, who had been a distinguished Oxford scholar and a Fellow of Balliol; like W. J. Courthope (1842–1917), First Commissioner in 1892 and Professor of Poetry at Oxford; like Stanley Leathes (1861–1938), Secretary in 1903, a Fellow of Trinity College Cambridge, Deputy Professor of History, and one of the editors of the Cambridge Modern History. The coolness of the sixties and seventies had gone, and the *Handbook* remarked: 'The advantages of a Civil Service career have long been recognized by Cambridge men; and the University has taken steps to satisfy all the requirements of those who desire to enter one or other of the State departments.'¹¹

A startling departure from earlier traditions, both academic and military, was represented by the section on the Army containing the remark: 'Of late years . . . the University has contributed more candidates than heretofore for commissions in the Army, and a system of Military Instruction has been organized in the University.'¹² It is true that as long ago as the forties Hodson of Hodson's Horse, a hero of the Indian Mutiny (1857), had done well at Cambridge before he was offered a cadetship in the East India Company's Army.¹³ But then the Company's Army was an unusual army and he was an unusual soldier. In his time, generally speaking, nothing was much further from the military mind or the mind of the university than the idea of a regular policy of commissioning university men. It was a product of the school of thought associated with Wolseley which assumed that an army officer ought to be a professional man – perhaps even an intellectual – rather than simply a gallant gentleman.

From the seventies onwards the authorities tried to get university men to try for Sandhurst. Between 1876 and 1882, 288 responded: 150 of them got in. The competition for Sandhurst was fairly hot, as Winston Churchill found in the nineties when he twice failed. Between 1876 and 1882 there were about four candidates for every vacancy (six thousand for fifteen hundred, roughly) in the open competition, which was separate from the university competition. Over the same period, at Woolwich, the proportion of candidates (2,473) to vacancies was only 1.73 to 1: perhaps yet another example of the stubborn English resistance to formal technological education.[14]

The careers reviewed in the 1906 Cambridge *Handbook* understate the breadth of opportunity open to young men of the public-school and university class, partly because most professional training was still a matter of apprenticeship, which hardly came within the notice of the Appointments Board: partly because non-professional openings were increasingly attracting young men of the upper middle classes. From the mid-century onwards, in the public school registers examined (see Appendix 2), there is a steady trickle of boys going to farm overseas, particularly in South Africa, Australia and Canada. A little later a boy here and there is recorded as joining the South African or Australian police; a little later again, and the administrative services of the newly organized colonies such as Nigeria begin to appear in the lists – these, on the whole, were not in their early days recruited from the universities; more often from the services. And in the thirty years or so before 1914 there is a marked growth in the number of boys shown as having gone into business of one sort or another, either at home or abroad.

Although professional opportunities were widening, the obstacles to a professional career remained formidable. The first was money.

We have already discussed the costs of professional training and it has been shown that they were high (Chapters 8 and 9). But they were by no means the end of the matter. There was also the cost of getting established, which applied to virtually every occupation of a professional nature except the reformed, competitive Civil Service and the less fashionable branches of the

Army. In most of the Army, as we have seen, it was generally expected that a junior officer would have something besides his pay: if he had not, life was very difficult and India the best solution. In the Church, unless there was a living to step straight into, or one of the better-paid teaching posts, life would be very thin on a curate's unaugmented wage. In the 'open professions' – that is, those outside the public service and the Church – there appeared the hungry, expensive gap between formal qualification and establishment in profitable practice.

What was required, in fact, for the young doctor, or lawyer, or architect, or any other professional man starting on his own, was some source of income to provide a couple of hundred pounds a year or so. Below that level, even in mid-Victorian England, it was difficult to keep up sufficient appearance of gentility to attract clients, though determined men did contrive to do so. The best source of funds, naturally, was a reasonably prosperous father or private means, and indeed most Victorian writers on the professions make it clear that without one or the other it would be almost impossible to lay the foundations of a career.

This was one reason, perhaps the main one, why competition for Fellowships was so hot at Oxford and Cambridge, particularly for those which did not require the holder to take orders. Apart from the academic prestige which a fellowship conferred, it also brought an assured income, even if a small one, which gave a man time to launch himself on his career. Residence was not enforced nor, generally, any other academic duty, so that if the fellow did not feel drawn towards university teaching, or the very lucrative practice of private coaching, he could devote himself, if a clergyman, to seeking preferment: if a layman, to the Bar, to politics, or to journalism – perhaps to all three simultaneously.

The representative figure, however, of the young professional man trying to get started is the doctor in general practice. We have the picture of Conan Doyle and a long line of other writers slipping sideways into authorship while they waited for patients to come in. For most, however, it was a matter of keeping up appearances, perhaps on the meagre earnings of a parish surgeon or some other minor public appointment, and ingratiating himself with local society. 'The great struggle', says Thomson, 'is for a connection, and every art is necessary to extend it, as far as it can be done without ... compromising the integrity of the mind.'[15]

He recommended getting married – 'a wife is almost a necessary part of a physician's professional equipment' – but of course that would add to the expense. *The Lancet*, a little later, referred to the ferocity of medical competition, fair and unfair. After some years as an assistant, the young doctor would find himself 'launched on the great ocean of the world ... surrounded by vessels all competing in the race; some with true colours; some mere pirates ... quacks, hydropaths, homeopaths, mesmerists, and a host of other knaves ...'[16]

The cost of all this waiting, manoeuvring and in-fighting, which could be paralleled amongst lawyers, architects, and other professional men, is not very easy to arrive at and obviously could vary a great deal. There are, however, indications. In 1883 *The Lancet* discussed the finances of general practice in provincial towns. If a young doctor bought a half-share in a practice of £1,200 or £2,000 gross receipts a year, then somewhere between one-third and one-half would go in working expenses; the lower figure if there were little or no rural practice, the higher if there were a good deal, for then the doctor would need enough horses to get over his work without undue effort, and probably an assistant for emergencies. 'Then his social position has to be attended to' – a constant cry among the professional classes – and 'a considerable proportion of his assets is represented by deferred payments.' One doctor in the nineties said that his bad debts ran as high as 40 per cent of the total (presumably by number, not by value). A new doctor would find it difficult to attract patients until he was known, and altogether he would be unlikely to receive, net, more than a very small income.[17]

'If a man can tide over the first three or four years', *The Lancet* rather ominously concludes, 'he will find his income improved by the gradual payment of book debts and ultimately secure a position both socially and financially good.' But even for established men, the general run of rewards did not rule very high. The average income of late Victorian medical men has been put at £200 a year. That no doubt covers those just starting, those retired, the misfits and the failures and may to some extent be misleading as a guide to the income of the ordinary competent man, well established. Nevertheless, in country practice in East Anglia about 1905, £600 was looked upon as a good income: it may have been enough for comfort, but hardly for affluence. To make anything like a decent living, most doctors had to rely on getting posts carrying something in the way of an assured income, as well as private practice. The great paymasters were the friendly societies (the 'clubs') and the Poor Law. Competition amongst doctors was fierce and collective bargaining practically unknown, so that these authorities could and did drive very hard bargains. That partly accounts for the doctors' hostility to Lloyd George's National Health Insurance Bill of 1912, which proposed to rely heavily on the friendly societies. In the event, far from ruining the medical profession, it turned out to be their salvation.[18]

All these rigours could be much relieved, if not avoided altogether, by family interest or salaried employment, which came to much the same thing. The professional classes, having got rid of aristocratic patronage in the public service, had no intention of doing the same for their own affairs. Openings in family businesses or practices, like family livings, were family property, only to go to outsiders under the most unusual circumstances, and even where a business grew too large for this principle to be applied exclusively, as the railways did, and some shipping lines, and such companies as Lever Brothers, it nevertheless remained a great advantage to have the interest of a Director, whether by direct family connection or otherwise. The principle of open competitive entry stopped short at the boundary between the 'public sector' and the 'private sector'.

For the boy without money or family connections, therefore, the road to a professional career was almost impossibly hard. His best chance was probably in the public service. It is instructive to compare the social background of army officers, amongst whom, even after competitive entry was long established, older traditions lingered, with the background of Civil Servants, also recruited by competition but without the same requirement for private means or family influence. The comparison can be made from figures published in the 45th Report of the Civil Service Commissioners, 1900. They refer to successful candidates for Woolwich and Sandhurst, on the one hand, and for Class I Clerkships in the Home Civil Service, for the ICS, and for Eastern cadetships, on the other. They cover the years 1896 to 1900.

These figures show 15–20 per cent of the Army entrants whose fathers are classed as titled or 'landowners and others of no profession', against 7 per cent in the Civil Service group (the three titled fathers were all bishops). About one-third of the Army officers had fathers who had also been Army officers, but only 11 per cent of the other group were the sons of Civil Servants. In each group, as might be expected, there was a strong contingent – a quarter or rather less – whose fathers had been professional men: that is, clergy, lawyers, or doctors, and the clergy were the largest group, especially among the Civil Servants. Thirteen to fourteen per cent of the Army officers' fathers had been in business, against 20 per cent of the fathers of Civil Servants. There were very few engineers amongst the fathers of either group, there were no 'tradesmen' among the fathers of Army officers (5 per cent among the Civil Servants), and the only working-class origins revealed were amongst the Civil Servants (four 'artificers', one engine-driver and a coachman).

The preponderance of aristocratic influence in the Army is evident, and there is a strong suggestion of family influence generally. Neither are so apparent among the Civil Servants. On the other hand what is equally evident is that the system of open competition had by no means removed the barriers against boys from the lower end of the social scale, even if it had made them slightly less formidable, at least in the Civil Service. The middle classes had very successfully captured the gateway into Whitehall and the ICS, but they had not opened it very wide to anyone beneath their own standing.

This is by no means a surprising conclusion when one considers the English educational system as it set hard in the seventies, eighties, and nineties, after the failure of the attempts to get it radically overhauled. In the centre of this system, the all but indispensable foundation for a professional career (except for Scotch incomers, who had their own way of doing things), were the public schools. After the proposals of the Schools Enquiry Commission (1868) for a national system of secondary education had been turned down, they had no competitors, and by the end of the century the number of secondary school pupils in the country was not, at the outside, more than 2·5 per thousand of the population.[19]

This was a finding of a Royal Commission under Lord Bryce which, as a result of growing uneasiness about secondary education in England compared with secondary education in competing countries, investigated secondary schools (apart from the public schools) in the early nineties. In 1895 it reported what it had found. For a great industrial nation it really was not very much.

The only direct effort by the State was represented by 'higher grade elementary schools' set up by School Boards under the Education Act of 1870. There were only sixty of them outside London, mostly in the North, and twenty-three counties had none. Their pupils left at the age of fifteen, except a few who tried for scholarships to more advanced schools or who took 'matric', and the law forbade government grants to be used in support of 'higher grade' teaching, except indirectly through the Science and Art Department, and so it had to be financed by fees. Within these crippling limitations the 'higher grade' elementary schools did what they could to teach history, grammar, French, mathematics, and the elements of physical science. It is a revealing comment on the lower depths of late Victorian professional life to find Charles Booth calculating that 10 per cent of the pupils of these schools, in London, were sons of clergy, doctors, accountants, and schoolmasters.[20]

There were many private schools, mostly patronized by parents who could not stomach the Board schools and could not afford the public schools. They ran from establishments where educational developments of great value and wide influence were pioneered to ill-run commercial swindles which had long been the despair and disgrace of the teaching profession. Lord Bryce's Commission did not think there were quite so many of the worst type as thirty years before.

Then there were the endowed schools – the old grammar schools – which the Schools Enquiry Commission of the sixties had paid close attention to. They were not State schools but the State had accepted some responsibility for them, in so far as the Endowed Schools Acts of 1869 and 1874 had made reform much easier. The Acts covered 1,448 endowments and by 1894, 902 schemes of reform had gone through. Reform often created very good schools for boys who looked no further, generally speaking, than shopkeeping or other small business in the towns where they were born, farming in country districts, or perhaps a job in a bank. The country's total provision for secondary education was not greatly increased, nor were matters made easier for boys of limited means. Reform, indeed, was inclined to make things rather harder for them. It was a cardinal principle among the reformers, who had some awful warnings among the unreformed grammar schools, that free education, formerly the rule under the old endowments, was nearly always bad education, or certainly unvalued. It therefore became that much harder for the working-class boy, or the middle-class boy in straitened circumstances, to thrust himself towards higher things, as occasional very bright ones had sometimes been known to do in the past, before the free grammar schools fell into the decline which attracted the attention of the reformers.

In the absence of State secondary education, until the passing of the Education Act of 1902, and with the grammar schools inadequate, the public schools dominated late Victorian secondary education. Like the ancient universities with which they were closely connected, they stood at the peak of their prestige. The folklore and myth in which they entwined themselves had never been stronger nor more widely accepted, though a great deal of it was of very recent origin. 'The English public school system', said Escott, 'has become as much a national institution as household suffrage or vote by ballot' (both, as he was well aware, very recent innovations).[21] During the eighties and nineties, and later, the public schools were romanticized and glamourized in the heroics of Newbolt, the curious cross-grained tributes of Kipling, and the fiction of numerous boys' writers from Talbot Baines Reed to Frank Richards – who wrote, very largely, for an audience never likely to see so much as the outside wall of a public school, let alone to get into one.

This is not the place to go in detail into the development of the late Victorian public school, which has been very ably and fully dealt with elsewhere.[22] In general it seems clear that the name of Arnold was held in high reverence, but he would not very readily have acknowledged the paternity of the institutions which revered him. Most authorities agree that the late nineteenth century saw the worship of physical prowess develop inordinately, largely through compulsory games (surely a contradiction in terms, but they never thought of that). Correspondingly such respect as had existed for intellectual achievements fell even lower, and any kind of independent thought, if it tended towards criticism of conventional articles of belief, was firmly discouraged. The 'public school man', predictable in all his enthusiasms, loyalties, absurdities and sublimities, emerged as the standard pattern of an Englishman, not least in foreign eyes. Such was the remarkable influence of a group of schools to which not more than about one Englishman in twenty – if so many – could put forward any claim to have belonged.

If these schools provided the high road to a professional career – and increasingly they did, for the old customs of local education or private education were fast dying – they also helped to put up its cost. You could get a year's education at Hurstpierpoint, in the mid-sixties, for £37, but Rossall would cost £50 and Haileybury £77. At the higher end of the scale, fees at Rugby would run about £90: at Eton, twice that.[23] It is unlikely that fees went down as the century went on, and any lingering remnants of the idea that foundations such as Harrow, Rugby and Shrewsbury (to say nothing of Eton) were intended for the benefit of the poor of the neighbourhood, or even the trading middle classes, were firmly discouraged and suppressed.

On top of the public school education it became increasingly the fashion among the prosperous classes, as the century went on, to add three or four years at Oxford or Cambridge, not for any direct professional training but rather as a highly desirable finishing school, valued as much for social reasons as for any intellectual polish it might confer. 'A young man', said Vinogradoff in 1885, 'goes to Oxford, not to learn anything definitely bound up with his future line of work, but to get up a certain amount of general knowledge, to develop as far as possible his literary tastes and abilities, and, more than anything else, to try life on a larger scale than he has known it at the public school.'[24] This was fair comment, which would not have been disagreed with either by critics or supporters of the ancient universities.

It was an attitude of affluence. There had always been young men at the universities who could afford it, but in earlier times they had come almost entirely from the wealthier landed families, because no one else could contemplate such heavy expenditure as was required for such imponderable advantages. The fact that increasing numbers of professional and business families, towards the end of the nineteenth century, could afford to take such a lordly view of their sons' education is a measure of the wealth and social standing of the late Victorian upper middle class. Exactly what the cost would be is very difficult to estimate, but the Cambridge *Handbook* of 1906 suggested figures running upwards from about £110 a year to about £127, which it quotes as the actual expenditure of a student 'not a candidate for honours. He is a keen boating man, and may serve as a specimen of a large class. Owing to a failure in one examination he had a private tutor for two terms, and his kitchen account is high.' Right at the top of the scale was 'an extravagant person with wealthy parents and a large set of rooms. He entertains a great deal and his kitchen account is high.' His bill for a year was nearly £170.[25]

It was possible to go to Cambridge for much less. The *Handbook* quotes figures as low as £1 6s. 10d., but those were for a scholar holding an award worth £70 a year and living at the least possible expense. But it seems doubtful whether a really poor boy – a working-class boy or a boy from the lower middle classes – would have had any real chance of getting such a scholarship, in the conditions of late Victorian England.

The obstacles in his path had probably been increased by the very reforms that were intended to open the education system up. In the old days of the unreformed grammar schools a poor boy would have been able to get such teaching as they gave, for what it was worth, free, provided he was within an area served by such a school – and they were fairly widespread. Then he might have been able to get a scholarship limited to those who lived in the locality, either provided by the school's endowments or from the endowments of some Oxford or Cambridge college with local connections.

The reformers, with the best of intentions, had altered all that. They had got rid of free schooling, so far as they could. They had industriously opened closed scholarships to wider competition. This meant, admittedly, that far more talent was admitted to try for them, but it also meant that local schools were at a great disadvantage against the wealthy public schools in the matter of teaching. Moreover, the closed scholarships which survived or were founded later were mostly attached to public schools or schools aspiring to that standing. Thus it was not very likely, in the closing years of the nineteenth century, that anyone would repeat the achievements of Lord Tenterden (Chapter 1) and other grammar schoolboys of the eighteenth century. Such careers had never been common, naturally, but in late Victorian England they were probably more difficult to achieve than at any time before or since. Somewhat later the State began to subsidize promising boys, but in the years we are immediately concerned with – the thirty or so before 1914 – it is probably not unfair to say that the two ancient English universities were more closely allied with wealth and social privilege than at any other period.

And yet, when all the money was spent, when all the barriers were thrown down, people did not in general expect to get very rich by going into a profession, except perhaps at the Bar. The professional man, that is to say, did not generally expect to get so rich as the great business man: nor, to be fair to him, was he probably greatly ambitious for great wealth. It was important to him to live like a gentleman, and to launch his children. Beyond that many might not have considered it proper to go. One of the numerous things which a traditional liberal education did not teach was an excessive desire for wealth for its own sake.

The archetype of the professional man, as he was in fact the father of many, was still the country clergyman. It is instructive to consider briefly what kind of figure he was. His social position was unassailable and carried considerable authority. His parson's free-hold gave him security in his living. He had therefore great independence of thought and action – something which many people might consider a necessary condition for the satisfactory practice of a learned profession. But it was unlikely that his professional earnings would be large.

In 1836 the Ecclesiastical Commissioners published an analysis of the incomes of benefices in England and Wales which probably gives a reasonably good indication of the size and distribution of clerical incomes during the century as a whole. Out of 10,478 benefices they found 184 worth more than £1,000 a year, including 18 over £2,000: 1,291 benefices (including those just mentioned) had incomes over £400. The incomes of the majority (6,261) lay between £100 and £400, with 1,978 between £200 and £300. 1,926 were worth less than £100.[26]

Benefices could be held in plurality and there were other sources of clerical income such as prebendal stalls, canonries, chaplaincies, and grammar school headmasterships which were not incompatible with holding a living. Even so, and even allowing for the legendary cheapness of living in the Victorian countryside, it cannot be said that the majority of parsons were highly paid. That was why so many took pupils: a practice tolerated because it was known to be necessary and because it supplied a useful service, especially before the hey-day of the public schools. But it was not universally approved of, for it could easily get in the way of pastoral duties.

Let us look at another central figure of Victorian professional life: the doctor. About the middle of the century Johnston thought a physician – presumably in London – 'who is becoming popular' might get as much as £6,000[27] but Thomson, in 1857, explicitly leaving the very top men out of consideration, thought 'a successful physician in London' might make between £800 and £3,000 – very wide limits, which probably indicate the difficulty of getting at the facts – and a physician of equivalent standing in the provinces, £500 to £1,500. As to general practitioners, he thought that many in the great towns were making £2,000 and 'not a few' even £3,000 or £4,000. But he put the ordinary range of GPs' earnings between £300 and £1,200, with an average of £500.[28]

Escott, about 1880, thought 'the average medical man in London can make ... £1,000 to £2,000 a year; the more distinguished, from £5,000 to £12,000. Incomes above this are very rare, for the simple reason that there is literally not the time in which to do the extra work.'[29] Escott's idea of the 'average' was almost certainly exalted. Without going as low as the doctors discovered by Booth who were sending their children to higher-grade elementary schools, or even those who did their rounds by public transport because they could afford no other, it seems likely that a great many Victorian doctors in established practice would scarcely have come within the limits Escott suggests. *The Lancet*'s survey of the finances of general practice in 1883 suggests net incomes on the low side of £1,000 to be shared between two partners, and in rural East Anglia about 1905 'there were plenty of practices with an income of £400 a year; £600 was looked upon as a good income.'[30]

In the profession of the law almost anything was possible, from beggary upwards. The leaders of the Bar probably made more money than any other professional men: at any rate common opinion credited them with doing so. Thomson said that in 1850 there were said to be eight barristers making £8,000, perhaps two dozen £5,000, and five £11,000. The law, too, was the one profession in which permanent officials – judges, the Lord Chancellor, the Law Officers – were paid really large salaries (£5,000 for a puisne judge: £8,000 for the Chief Justice of the Queen's Bench), which in itself shows that great incomes could be made by independent practice. At a slightly lower level, Thomson thought very few QCs made £3,000, 'and the majority not half that sum.' Junior barristers would be doing well and working very hard at £2,000 and 'from £500 to £1,200 a year is the ordinary income.'[31] The trouble, as was so frequently pointed out, was that it was very difficult to make an income at all: many barristers never contrived to do so, and drifted off, if they could, into other occupations.

Solicitors may have found it more difficult to make as much money as the leaders of the Bar, although their opportunities, at the top of their own branch of the profession, must have been nearly as great. It was much easier for them to make a comfortable living. Thomson suggested £2,000 a year as the upper limit for a solicitor 'not going beyond the pure practice of his profession', but the whole point was that many did. They were deep in the expanding business world of Victorian England, close to opportunities of profitable investment, conveniently near at hand when directorships were being created. The solicitor, like his predecessor the attorney, was very much the 'man of business', and although he missed the public honours of the law he was by no means ill-placed to reap material rewards.[32]

Enough has perhaps been said to indicate the level of income which a Victorian professional man might expect. About £1,000 a year, or a little on either side, evidently represented modest prosperity. There were plenty below and a reasonable chance of getting fairly well above though naturally the very high incomes – say, from £5,000 up – were rare. Taking like with like – the country parson with the country doctor and the small-town lawyer, or, slightly higher up the scale, the Church dignitary (below the bishops but above the parish parsons) with the physician in a good way of practice and the rising barrister – it would appear that the rewards were roughly comparable, or certainly not disproportionately different between one profession and another. There was consequently a solid economic basis for the general unity of the professional classes, in addition to anything there may have been in the way of similarities of thought and attitude. The doctor could meet the parson, the parson could meet the lawyer, the lawyer could meet the architect, and so on, without any very oppressive feeling of great differences in wealth, income, or standard of living.

And professional incomes were much better than the general run of middle-class incomes. It was open to a successful business-man from any level of society, of course, to make a great deal of money, but the general run of tradesmen's profits or of clerks' salaries only overlapped with professional incomes at the lower levels. A clerk was well paid on £200 a year. A salaried factory manager, right up to the end of the century, would be doing very well indeed to get £500 or £600. The First Commissioner of the Civil Service Commission in the sixties and two of his examiners were paid £1,500, £700, and £600 respectively. The First Com-missioner today (1965), according to *Whitaker's Almanack*, gets £5,885.

At any time before 1914, £1,000 a year represented considerable worldly success, though not great wealth, and placed a man, economically speaking, well towards the top of the middle classes. On an income of £500 a year, soon after 1900, the editors of *Mrs Beeton's Every Day Cookery* allowed 'two women servants only' for a family of four, 'but a family living in the country ... would probably require a gardener or useful man.'[33] A professional man, with decent luck and ability, might expect an income comfort-ably above the middle-class average: perhaps a long away above it. The letters after his name, apart from any social prestige they might confer, had a hard cash value too.

But it cannot have been easy for the majority to find the money to launch sons into professional life. How did the parsons do it in such numbers? Some parsons were rich and many public schools made allowances for the sons of those who were not. One major school – Marlborough – was founded for their benefit. Similarly there were awards at Oxford and Cambridge colleges reserved for them. But in many clerical families the strain must have been heavy: as, also, in the families of officers without private means, though for them, too, allowances were made at some schools and one major one – Wellington – was intended especially for them. In general, as a late Victorian ICS man remarked: 'Money for younger sons was scarce, and it was not easy to be independent.'[34]

This is one more reason for surprise that the mid-Victorian movement for the reform of secondary and higher education petered out. Why was no system established, like the system in

Germany, for providing excellent professional and technical education at a very low cost to those who wanted it? Why was the very expensive system of late Victorian England not only acquiesced in, but actively connived at, by the professional classes? They were the very people who had forced through drastic schemes of qualifying and competitive examinations, requiring a curriculum totally different from that of the traditional 'liberal education' which in the public schools they had to pay so heavily for. They more than most people, it might have been thought, would appreciate the danger to England from persistent neglect of professional education and education in science and technology. And yet nothing was done: nothing, after at one time it had seemed that everything was possible.

Perhaps the explanation lies in the dual character of the professional man's ambition, which was pointed out in the opening paragraphs of this book. On the one hand he cared deeply about purely professional matters. He took a pride in his work; he wanted to see skill developed by education and recognized by a regular process of qualification. And he certainly took seriously the obligation to observe at least a minimum standard of ethical behaviour, which even at its minimum was above the standard commonly expected and observed in contemporary 'trade'. And by caring for these matters the professional man, as he progressively asserted himself during the early and middle years of the century, permanently enriched and purified the life of the nation.

But there was another thing the professional man cared deeply about, and that was his social standing. Sir Astley Cooper, early in the century, considered that the only true basis for a professional man's social standing was his scientific understanding of his profession, but then Sir Astley in his young days had been a radical and a democrat. By Escott's time not many professional men were like that. Their idea of social standing was to get as close as they could to the pattern set by the landed gentry, or what they imagined the pattern to be.

In this they followed the example set by successful Englishmen in every age before them. Nor is their aim to be wondered at, considering how extremely attractive the life of the landed gentry could be, with their unassailable social position, their independence, their authority, their influence, and their wealth. It was unfortunate, though, that the leaders of an industrial nation threatened by foreign competition should have chosen to emulate a class whose whole cast of mind and scale of values was anti-commercial. It hardened yet one more division – the division between 'professions' and 'trade' – in an already deeply divided society. It put a formidable obstacle in the way of those who could feel the foundations of England's prosperity cracking under their feet, and wanted to repair them.

It was doubly unfortunate that, as the competitive situation grew worse, English attention was distracted by the heady vision of Empire. The early Victorians had paid very little attention to their possessions overseas, except periodically to wonder whether they would not certainly lose them, and whether things might not be better if they did. They had got on with their own affairs with conspicuous success, and England's strength in the forties and fifties was firmly based on her own industrial supremacy.

The later Victorians, on the other hand, increasingly found it easy – and comforting – to believe that England, beset by industrial competitors, drew strength from her empire, and their belief was widely shared, not least in Germany and America. How much reality there was in it may be questioned. The 'white dominions' were no doubt profitable enough, with food supplies moving one way and manufactured goods the other. Even then, it may be supposed that the trade would have gone on without the existence of any British connection except the British fleet and that, after all, protected America as well. It is much more doubtful whether India and the African and Asian dependencies were ever really worth their keep, when the expense of administration and defence is taken into account, especially when it is considered that in some parts of the empire, notably West Africa, the ruling power, acting, as was sincerely believed, in the interests of the ruled, prevented the exploitation of agricultural resources by forbidding the alienation of land to Europeans.

Whatever may be the economic truth of the matter, and it is certainly highly debatable, it nevertheless seems incontestable that expanding imperial glory, in the last twenty years or so of the nineteenth century and during the first part of the twentieth, drew attention away from England's competitive position in the world and tempted people to underestimate the seriousness of it. Empire-building and empire-holding were congenial activities:

much more congenial, to the mind of the ruling classes, than running an industrial economy. Imperialism, late in the day, was grafted on to the public school tradition and took its place among the public school boy's set of neatly packaged received ideas.

British rule did a great deal of good for most of those who came under it: that need not be doubted. Nor need it be doubted that the pursuit of empire gave British public life a spaciousness and a sense of purpose which it subsequently lost and has not yet found again. And there was much that was good in the public school boy's outlook, especially when it was illuminated by intelligence and culture. The public school boy was brought up to a sense of duty. He was expected to sacrifice himself unquestioningly for what was regarded as his country's good. He had a strong sense of personal loyalty, not least to those – of any race – who came under his authority. These excellent qualities make it all the sadder that the fundamental antipathy induced by public school education to everything commercial made it fatally easy for men from public schools to miss the central fact of England's power – that without her own industrial strength, let her empire be never so large, she was nothing more than an over-populated island off the coast of north-west Europe. Late Victorian and post-Victorian imperialism, seen from this point of view, looks like nothing so much as a large and gaudy Union Jack hiding the facts of life from the British ruling class.

It would not be true to suggest that the danger was entirely ignored, especially after the Boer War in which, in Kipling's inelegant words, 'We have had no end of a lesson. It will do us no end of good.'[35] Once again, as in the sixties, foreign technical education was anxiously inspected and reported on: once again the air was astir with good intentions.

Between 1903 and 1905, for instance, the *Architectural Review* published the results of an elaborate comparative survey of foreign and English methods of training architects. The German Technical High Schools were reported on, with their four-year full-time courses, their severe entrance requirements and qualifying examinations, and their State subsidies. The social mixture in them was duly noted – at Berlin 'the students are drawn, to a far larger extent than ... in England or France, from all classes.' They were uncomfortably compared with 'the old-fashioned system of articles' – 'relics of a medieval system of training stripped of its severe sanctions.' The courses of instruction, most of them part-time, provided by various authorities, including the Architectural Association, Liverpool University, and the London County Council, were anxiously examined. It was plain that they did not look very well against the elaborate long-established German system.[36]

There were stirrings in the provincial universities. Imperial College of Science and Technology came into massive existence in 1907. A few public school boys began to go to the 'new' universities. But there was nothing like a radical change of attitude. So far as the really prosperous classes were concerned, these developments were for other people's children. The public schools, increasingly criticized, went on their way practically unaffected, and the central citadels of English education, with all their authority, wealth and social prestige, remained divorced from the growing realities of power in the modern world. The waves of change beat all around them: they could not break in. And they were more than ever the accepted nursery of the professional class. Even the *Architectural Review*, the organ of a profession generally considered artistic and therefore eccentric, assumed as a matter of course that a young man looking for architectural training would have come from a public school.[37]

Thus, as the professional men had a hand in the rise of Victorian England, so they must bear some responsibility for its decline. Look at Sir Astley Cooper, especially in his early days. Look at those quarrelsome doctors who fought for the due recognition of good qualifications and high professional standards. Listen to the attorneys of the fifties, insisting that it was the business of a barrister to know the law and never mind his social standing. Surely they had a firm grip on the essentials of professional life, and indeed on the practical essentials of life generally. It is impossible to feel so confident of those who were perfectly well aware that Germany was putting all her formidable strength and organizing powers into first-rate technical and professional training, and yet were content to muddle along, reserving all their real enthusiasm for a system of education openly contemptuous of anything with a practical bent to it, and biased very heavily towards the social and sporting side of life. Their awakening, from 1914 on, was slow, and bitter, and perhaps it is not quite completed even yet.

Appendix 1

THE CENSUS AND THE PROFESSIONAL
CLASSES

EVERY census since 1841 has tried to record and classify the occupation of every individual in the nation, and there is no other source of information covering so wide a field. The difficulties and the possibilities of error, however, are very large and have always been recognized, so that every census has seen refinements in the methods employed. This has no doubt made for greater and greater accuracy, but it has multiplied the uncertainties of comparisons between censuses. All attempts at comparison must in any case be interrupted at 1921, for in the census of that year such great changes were made in the methods of classifying occupations that the Report said 'little comparison can be made between the numbers returned under occupational headings in 1921 and at previous censuses.' (Census of England and Wales 1921 – *Occupations*.)

For the purposes of this book, an attempt was made to trace the variations in the numbers recorded, from census to census, in every occupation that could be regarded as a profession and, for purposes of comparison, in certain other middle-class occupations also. Army and Navy officers were left out, since the census only records those at home, which would give quite a serious underestimate of the totals. Table 1 sets out the figures for seventeen occupations for which something like a reliable series could be constructed from 1841 to 1911. Table 2 is an attempt to indicate what may have been the proportionate growth in professional employment over the latter part of the period covered by this book.

TABLE I. Percentage Increase or Decrease (−) between Censuses in Numbers recorded in 17 Professional Occupations, and as Commercial Clerks 1841–1911 (* denotes cases in which figures were not separately published).

Census	Teachers	Surveyors	Solicitors	Priests (R C)	Physicians and Surgeons	Musicians	Ministers of Religion	Midwives	Engineers (Civil)	Dentists	Commercial Clerks	Clergy (C of E)	Barristers	Authors	Artists	Architects	Actors	Accountants	Population of England and Wales
1841				*															
1851	61	−29	13	..	0	17	63	66	183	124	24	21	49	214	36	100	60	50	13
1861	32	63	−14	11	−18	125	−19	−34	11	34	−7	9	−1	219	1	29	8	−6	12
1871	15	2	8	33	2	97	18	16	57	50	63	8	17	44	11	48	63	58	13
1881	33	18	9	29	3	37	5	20	36	52	99	5	12	43	31	21	27	18	14
1891	15	18	13	20	26	51	3	*	35	39	36	12	22	68	53	14	60	−31	12
1901	36	10	6	13	19	12	15	14	15	7	47	4	−14	92	14	37	71	13	12
1911	9	−21	8	16	3	9	4	119	−35	63	31	−1	−2	25	−17	−17	46	5	11

208

From Census of:

1841 Occupation Abstract Part I Preface pp. 56–67
1851 Population Tables II pp. lxxvi–lxxxviii; Table 25
1861 Population Tables II Table XIX
1871 Population Abstracts III Table 17
1881 Census of England and Wales III Table 5
1891 Census of England and Wales III Table 5
1901 Census of England and Wales Summary Tables Cd 1523 of 1903

Changes of Definition and General Notes:

ACCOUNTANTS 1891 Institute of Chartered Accountants founded 1880

ARTISTS 1841–81 Painters

1891–1901 Painters, Engravers, Sculptors. The inclusion of engravers and sculptors accounts for the large increase shown at 1891. The Census Report gives an increase of 11·1%, arrived at by adding engravers and sculptors to the 1881 figure of painters

AUTHORS 1861 Author, Editor, Writer

1871–1911 Authors, Editors, Journalists (also Shorthand Writers in 1901)

BARRISTERS 1881–1901 Solicitors included: number of barristers estimated

DENTISTS 1841 Cuppers and dentists

1891 Dentists, dental apparatus makers – 'Many lads and girls ... merely employed in the manufacture of false teeth and dental apparatus.' 4,168 names on Dental Register against 4,628 shown in Census

CIVIL ENGINEERS 1881 'It is by no means certain that the persons who returned themselves as Civil Engineers in 1881 precisely corresponded to those who did so in 1871.' Report 1881 p. 32

1891–1911 Civil and Mining Engineers

1911 'These numbers are considerably below those shown for 1901, but comparison cannot fairly be made owing to the number of cases in which the additional information now given for the first time ... has enabled many of the mining engineers to be more properly classified ... to the headings for "Mine and Quarry Owners, Agents, Managers". Better information has also shown a number of "Surveyors" to be "Auctioneers, House-Agents and Surveyors." '
Report 1911 X p. xxiii

MIDWIVES	1891	included under Nurses. Comparison is with 1881
MUSICIANS	1841–51	Musician and Organist
	1861	Musician (not Teacher)
	1871–91	Musician, Music master
	1891–1911	Musician, Music master, Singer
PHYSICIANS AND SURGEONS	1841–1861	Physicians and Surgeons shown in separate columns of census tables
	1871	Physicians and Surgeons taken together
	1881–1911	Physicians, Surgeons, General Practitioners
	1891	Report suspected many to be unqualified
	1911	Report shows increase of 10·4%: basis of calculation not specified
SOLICITORS	1881–1901	included with Barristers: numbers estimated
SURVEYORS	1851	'See also Architects' (Report)
	1861–71	Land Surveyor; Land, Estate Agent
	1881–1911	Land, House, Ship Surveyor
	1911	see Civil Engineers
TEACHERS		Changes of definition at nearly every census. Figures quoted for 1881, 1891 agree with figures quoted in census reports

General Note

The census reports occasionally quoted figures directly comparable with those in this table. Except in the cases noted above (Artists 1891 and Physicians and Surgeons 1911), and in the case of Barristers 1891 (14·9%) the official figures agree closely with our calculations.

All figures are for England and Wales.

TABLE 2: Increase of 17 Professional Occupations 1841–81–1911 and of Commercial Clerks

	1841	1881	1911
ACCOUNTANTS	4,416	11,606	9,499
ACTORS	1,357	4,565	18,247
ARCHITECTS	1,486	6,898	8,921
ARTISTS	4,272	11,059	11,619
AUTHORS	167	3,434	13,786
BARRISTERS	2,088	4,019	4,121
CLERGY	14,527	21,663	24,859
DENTISTS	522	3,583	8,674
ENGINEERS (CIVIL)	853	7,124	7,208
MIDWIVES	734	2,646	6,602
MINISTERS	5,923	9,734	11,984
MUSICIANS	3,600	25,546	47,116
PHYSICIANS AND SURGEONS	17,500	15,116	23,469
PRIESTS (RC)	*	2,089	3,302
SOLICITORS	11,684	13,376	17,259
SURVEYORS	4,086	5,394	5,063
TEACHERS	51,851	168,920	251,968
Total	125,066	317,222	473,697
Increase %		154	50
Total less Teachers	73,215	148,302	221,729
Increase %		103	50
Commercial Clerks	48,689	181,457	477,535
Increase %		273	163
Population of England and Wales	15,914,000	25,974,000	36,070,000
Increase %		63	39

Sources of Figures and Notes as for Table 1.

Appendix 2

PUBLIC SCHOOLBOYS' OCCUPATIONS
1807-1911

In order to get an idea of the occupations followed by public school boys during the period covered by this book, the registers of six schools were examined. The occupations recorded for all boys who left in certain years between 1807 and 1911, arbitrarily chosen, were collated and analysed, with results summarized in Tables A to F below. The principal occupations recorded in the registers, on which the classifications in the tables are founded, are listed after the tables.

Each Table, below the year numbers, shows the number of boys who left in each year. The remaining lines* show the *percentage* recorded for each occupation, and the percentage (usually large) for whom the register shows no occupation. The percentages usually come to more than 100, since many boys went to a university and then into one or more occupation, and some boys who did not go to a university engaged in more than one occupation, so that one entry in the line 'boys leaving' can give rise to two or three entries in the lines below.

TABLE A.: CLIFTON COLLEGE
A Victorian foundation (1862) with a bias towards the Army.

	1867	1887	1907
Number of boys leaving:	112	152	144

Percentage entering:

	1867	1887	1907
Universities	24	31	39
Professions	33	37	22
Armed Forces	8	19	18
Business	9	16	25
Other Occupations	8	11	16
No known Occupation	41	22	35

Source: *Clifton College Register 1862 to 1947*, ed. A. O. Muirhead, Bristol 1948.
* With the exception of Table E.

APPENDIX 2

TABLE B: MARLBOROUGH COLLEGE

Founded 1843 to provide a full classical education more cheaply than at the ancient public schools. Special provision for the sons of clergymen.

	1846	1866	1886	1906
No. of boys leaving:	162	133	164	177
Percentage entering:				
Universities	41	37	42	32
Professions	39	47	38	23
Armed Forces	23	11	13	14
Business	6	17	23	23
Other Occupations	15	15	17	14
No known Occupation	15	15	15	32

Source: *Marlborough College Register 1843–1933*, 8th Edn., ed. A. H. and Mrs D. E. Wall, Marlborough 1936

TABLE C: MERCHANT TAYLORS' SCHOOL

Founded 1561. A London school with a large number of day boys. One of the nine schools of the Clarendon Commission.

	1851	1871	1891	1911
No. of boys leaving:	49	61	134	102
Percentage entering:				
Universities	24	2	20	13
Professions	28	59	42	22
Armed Forces	10	5	4	11
Business	6	13	42	25
Other Occupations	10	7	11	20
No known Occupation	44	19	10	28

Source: *Merchant Tailors' School Register 1851–1920*, ed. E. P. Hart. Published at the School 1923

TABLE D: MILL HILL SCHOOL

A non-conformist foundation (1807) just outside London: now within it.

	1807	1827	1837	1857	1877	1897	1907
No. of boys leaving:	17	38	24	20	61	63	95
Percentage entering:							
Universities	1*	16	12·5	10	20	25	25
Professions	24	42	33·3	20	34	37	26
Armed Forces	0	0	2*	2*	2*	0	1*
Business	24	18	33·3	35	31	30	32
Other Occupations	0	2*	0	0	6	10	11
None known	41	34	29	35	26	26	31

Source: *The Register of Mill Hill School 1807–1926*, ed. E. Hampden-Cook, Mill Hill 1926

* Absolute figure.

213

TABLE E: SEDBERGH SCHOOL

An ancient (1525) Yorkshire Grammar School closely connected with St John's College, Cambridge

All figures are absolute: no percentages.

	1822	1835	1852	1884
No. of boys leaving:	20	19	22	48

No. entering:

Universities	8	10	9	7
Professions	7	13	14	18
Armed Forces	0	0	1	2
Business	7	0	0	12
Other occupations	1	0	0	7
No known occupation	4	6	7	11

Source: *The Sedbergh School Register 1846–1895*, ed. B. Wilson, Leeds 1895

TABLE F: WINCHESTER COLLEGE

An ancient (1394) and famous foundation: fully classical. One of the nine schools of the Clarendon Commission.

	1836	1893
No. of boys leaving:	60	100

Percentage entering:

Universities	64	49
Professions	63	38
Armed Forces	17	23
Business	1*	12
Other Occupations	17	11
No known occupation	12	20

Source: *Winchester College 1836–1906, A Register*, ed. J. B. Wainwright, Winchester 1907

* Absolute figure.

Occupations covered by Tables A to F:

PROFESSIONS:

Clergy	Church of England; Free Churches; Roman Catholic
Law	Barristers; Solicitors; Attorneys
Medicine	Physicians, Surgeons, Dental Surgeons; Veterinary Surgeons
Others	Accountants, Actors, Actuaries, Architects, Artists, Authors/Journalists, Chemists (not pharmacists), Engineers (all kinds), Merchant Service Officers, Musicians, Naval Architects, Surveyors

ARMED FORCES:
  Royal Navy/Royal Marines
  Army, Indian Army
BUSINESS:
  Various, or vaguely stated
OTHER OCCUPATIONS:
  Civil Service:
  Home – Administrative Grade (or earlier equivalent); Diplomatic
         Service, Consular Service; other official appointments
  India – HEICS, ICS; Public Works Department; Posts and Tele-
           graphs; Political Service; Forestry Service; other official
           appointments.
  Ceylon
  Colonial Service, Sudan Political Service, Egyptian Service
  Police – Home, Overseas (eg: Australian Police, British South
           African Police).
  Farming, planting, at home and overseas

NOTES

ABBREVIATIONS

ABBREVIATIONS used in the list of references, with their meanings (where these are not self-evident), are as follows:

CR   *Contemporary Review.*
CSC Annual Reports of the Civil Service Commissioners.
CSI Civil Service Inquiry Commission (Playfair Commission).
CUC Cambridge University Commission, 1852.
DNB Dictionary of National Biography.
DUC Durham University Commission, 1863.
FR   *Fortnightly Review.*
ICC Inns of Court Commission, 1854–55.
Northcote-Trevelyan: *Report on the Organisation of the Permanent Civil Service,* 1854 (the 'Northcote-Trevelyan Report').
OUC Oxford University Commission. 1852.
Papers on the Re-Organization: *Papers relating to the Re-Organisation of the Civil Service,* 1855 (a collection of supporting papers to the Northcote-Trevelyan Report).
PSC Public Schools Commission, 1864 (the Clarendon Commission).
Purchase Report: Report on the Purchase System 1857.
SCME Select Committee on Medical Education, 1834.
SEC Schools Enquiry Commission, 1868 (the Taunton Commission).
Selection and Training: *The Selection and Training of Candidates for the India Civil Service,* C1446/1875.
SR   *Saturday Review.*

When a work is first cited, the author's name (if applicable) and the title are given in full. In subsequent references the author's name, a short title or an abbreviation is used.

CHAPTER ONE

1 Thomson, H. Byerley: *The Choice of a Profession*, London, 1857, p. 5.
2 Cobden, Richard: *Speeches on Questions of Public Policy*, ed. Bright and Rogers, London, 1878, p. 548.
3 Mingay, G. E.: *English Landed Society in the Eighteenth Century*, London, 1963; Thompson, F. M. L.: *English Landed Society in the Nineteenth Century*, London, 1963; Wilson, Charles: *England's Apprenticeship 1603–1763*, London, 1965, Chapter 12.
4 *Papers relating to the Re-Organisation of the Civil Service*, 1855, p. 79.
5 Edgeworth, R. L.: *Essays on Professional Education*, London, 1812, pp. 307–312.
6 *Augustus Hervey's Journal*, ed. David Erskine, London, 1953, pp. 76, 143, xix.
7 Parkinson, C. N.: *Trade in the Eastern Seas 1793–1813*, Cambridge 1937, pp. 71, 319.
8 Whewell, William: *Of a Liberal Education in General*, London, 1850, esp. Sec. 1. Also Report and Evidence of Public Schools Commission 1864; Thring, Edward, *Education and School*, London, 1864.
9 *A Century of English Essays* (Everyman 1933 Ed.) p. 93.
10 Reeks, Margaret: *Register of the Associates and Old Students of the Royal School of Mines and History of the Royal School of Mines*, London, 1920, p. 83.
11 Edgeworth, p. 64.
12 Edgeworth, Thomson, Davenant, F.: *What Should my Son be?* London, 1870.
13 Cooper, Bransby Blake, *The Life of Sir Astley Cooper, Bart.* 2 vols, London, 1843, I, p. 5.
14 Woodforde, James: *The Diary of a Country Parson 1758–1802*, ed. John Beresford, *World's Classics* No. 514, pp. 100, 102.
15 Edgeworth, p. 64.
16 Edgeworth, Thomson, Davenant; writers in periodicals. Marshall, Dorothy: *English People in the Eighteenth Century*, London, 1956, pp. 97, 101–2
17 Thomson, p. 78.
18 Thomson, p. 29; Bax, B. Anthony: *The English Parsonage*, London, 1964, p. 101.
19 Eliot, George: *Middlemarch*; *Scenes from Clerical Life*.
20 Newman, Charles: *The Evolution of Medical Education in the Nineteenth Century*, London, 1957, p. 5.
21 Peacock, George: *Life of Thomas Young MD FRS*, London, 1855, p. 216.

22 Munk, William: *The Life of Sir Henry Halford, Bart.*, London, 1895, p. 39.
23 Peacock, pp. 23, 41.
24 *The Lancet,* 1855 I p. 201.
25 *Lancet,* 1883 I p. 254.
26 Peacock, p. 221.
27 *Dictionary of National Biography.*

CHAPTER TWO

1 Boswell, James: *Life of Dr Johnson*, Everyman edn, I p. 393.
2 36 and 37 Vict. cap. 66 sec. 87.
3 Robson, R.: *The Attorney in Eighteenth-Century England*, Cambridge, 1959, p. 34 and generally.
4 Cope, Sir Zachary: *The Royal College of Surgeons of England, a History:* London, 1959, p. 34.
5 Freshfield, Edwin: *The Records of the Society of the Gentlemen Practisers in the Courts of Law and Equity called the Law Society*, London, 1897, pp. ix, 20, 306.
6 Robson, Chap. IV.
7 Freshfield, p. 305.
8 Freshfield, pp. 20, 30, 51.
9 Freshfield, pp.99–102.
10 Freshfield, pp. 114, 132.
11 *Report of the Select Committee on Medical Education with Minutes of Evidence and Appendix*, 1834, in three parts – Part I Royal College of Physicians, London; Part II, Royal College of Surgeons, London; Part III, Society of Apothecaries, London. Part II Q5574, Part I A295.
12 Carr-Saunders, Sir A. and Wilson, P. A.: *The Professions*, Oxford, 1933, pp. 74–5.
13 *Lancet,* 1855 I p. 228.
14 *Lancet,* 1860 I p. 130.
15 *Lancet,* 1860 I (7 i 60).
16 Cooper, I.
17 Cope, p. 15.
18 Cope, pp. 17, 43.
19 SCME, II Q5400.
20 SCME, II Q4833.
21 Cooper, I p. 290, II p. 193.
22 Cooper, I pp. 272–3, II pp. 157–62.
23 Cooper, I p. 358.
24 Cooper, I pp. 411–13.

25 Cooper, I p. 358.
26 Quoted Cooper, I p. 406.
27 Cooper, I p. 408.
28 SCME, I A2126.
29 SCME, I A239.
30 SCME, III A663.
31 Cope, p. 146.
32 SCME, II Q4897-8.
33 SCME, III Q12; App. to Part I pp. 13-14; Part III A280.

CHAPTER THREE

1 SCME, I Qq2017-27; App. to Part I p. 13.
2 SCME, I A143; App. p. 13.
3 Book of Common Prayer, 1856, Preface to *The Ordering of Deacons.* Hart, A. Tindal and Carpenter, Edward: *The 19th Century Country Parson*, Shrewsbury, 1954, p. 24.
4 SCME, I App. pp. 13-14.
5 Johnston, W.: *England as it is ... in the middle of the nineteenth century*, 2 vols, London, 1851, 2 p. 148.
6 Prayer Book, 1856; SCME, I A113.
7 DNB.
8 SCME, II App. p. 1; Report of the Inns of Court Commission – Parl. Papers, 1854-55 XVIII p. 345, A1531.
9 Cooper, I Chap. 12.
10 SCME, III A36.
11 SCME, III App. p. 101; SCME, II App. p. 8.
12 Carr-Saunders and Wilson, p. 47.
13 ICC, A1537.
14 ICC, A1527.
15 ICC, Q1531.
16 ICC, evidence of Cookson.
17 ICC, Qq 18, 344, 521, 524.
18 ICC, Q339.
19 ICC, Qq 1110, 1505, 1617.
20 ICC, Report p. 15.
21 ICC, Q1556.

CHAPTER FOUR

1 Cope, p. 33.
2 SCME, II Q5400 et seq.
3 Cooper, II pp. 36-7; SCME I Qq 433, 5750.

4 SCME, I Aa1404, 232, 239, 855.
5 SCME, I Q1640 et seq.; DNB.
6 Cope, p. 44.
7 *Lancet*, 1869 I p. 480; 1870 II p. 169; 1883 I p. 83; 1870 II p. 420; 1860 I p. 130.
8 Cope, pp. 68–70.
9 Vaughan, Paul: *Doctors' Commons*, London, 1959, Chapter 1, p. 14.
10 SCME, III A101; Vaughan p. 33.
11 *Lancet*, 1855 II p. 59.
12 Vaughan, Chapter 4.
13 *Lancet*, 1860 I p. 176.
14 *Lancet*, 1860 I p. 20.
15 *Lancet*, 1870 II pp. 409, 486.
16 Newman, p. 241; Report of the Royal Commission on the Medical Acts C3259 of 1882.
17 Newman; Carr-Saunders and Wilson.
18 Carr-Saunders and Wilson, p. 133.
19 Carr-Saunders and Wilson, p. 127; Cooper, I pp. 186–90.
20 Johnston, 2 pp. 169–72; Trollope, Anthony: *Dr Thorne*, Chapter XXXIV.
21 Duckham, B. F. (1965): 'John Smeaton, the Father of English Civil Engineering.' *History To-day* XV 3; Nock, O. S.: *The Railway Engineers*, London, 1955, p. 54; Wilson C. H. and Reader, W. J.: *Men and Machines*, London, 1958, p. 11; Smiles, S.: *Industrial Biography*, 1897 Ed. (London), p. 199; Rolt, L. T. C.: *George and Robert Stephenson*, London, 1960, p. 13.
22 Thomson, p. 301.

CHAPTER FIVE

1 Cobden, *Speeches* p. 172.
2 Report on the Purchase System. Parl. Papers, 1857 (sess. 2) XVIII.
3 Thomson, p. 189.
4 Trevelyan, Sir Charles: *The Purchase System in the British Army*, London, 1867, p. 15; Woodham-Smith, C.: *The Reason Why*, Penguin Ed. p. 36.
5 Trevelyan, *Purchase System* pp. 42–3.
6 Purchase Report; Trevelyan, *Purchase System* p. 4.
7 Purchase Report, Qq 1892, 1894.
8 *Saturday Review*, 5 i 56 p. 167.
9 Purchase Report, Q1423.
10 Purchase Report, Q4607.
11 SR, 8 iii 56.

12 Army Medical Department – Statistical Sanitary and Medical Reports – Vol. VI 1864 (pub. 1866).

13 Thomson, p. 192; First Report of the Council of Military Education, Parl. Papers 1857 (sess. 2) XXVII.

14 Lewis, Michael: *The Navy in Transition*, London, 1965, Chapter VI; Davenant, pp. 60–1.

15 Thomson, p. 211.

16 Lewis, Chapter V.

17 Report on the Organization of the Permanent Civil Service, 1854, p. 4.

18 Papers on the Re-Organization, p. 75.

19 Zinkin, Taya and Maurice: *Britain and India: Requiem for Empire*, London, 1964 pp. 55–6.

20 Papers on the Re-Organization, p. 156.

21 Papers on the Re-Organization, p. 77.

22 Civil Service Inquiry Commission, 1875, 2nd Report, App. F.

23 Hodder, Edwin: *The Life of Samuel Morley*, London, 1887, p. 126.

24 *Lancet*, 1855, I p. 250.

CHAPTER SIX

1 DNB.

2 Public Schools Commission, 1864 App. F.

3 CSI, 2nd Report 1875 App. F.

4 *Fortnightly Review*, II (1865); *Economist* 5 iv 62; CSI 1st Report (C1113/1875) p. 361 App. F.

5 SR, 5 i 56; Third Report on the Education of Officers by the Director-General of Military Education, Parl. Papers, 1883 XV, App. 3.

6 Report of the Schools Enquiry Commission, 1868 I pp. 322–3; L. H. Griffin in FR XVII (New Series) p. 522; Regulations for entry into ICS, Woolwich &c.

7 Trollope, FR II (1865); Pelly FR II (1865).

8 Northcote-Trevelyan, p. 24.

9 Report of a Committee on the Education of Artillery Officers, C 258/1871, p. ix.

10 SR, 41 (1876), 24 vi 76.

11 The Selection and Training of Candidates for the India Civil Service, C1446/1876 p. 36; Report of the Civil Service Commissioners for 1900, pp. xvi–xviii.

12 9th Report of CSC.

13 CSC Reports.

14 Brodrick, Hon George C.: *Political Studies*, London 1879, p. 126.
15 4th Report of CSC, p. xxxix.
16 SR, 18 Sept. 58 p. 269.
17 FR, XVII (New Series) p. 522.
18 8th, 6th Reports of CSC.
19 Selection and Training, C 1446/1876, p. 5.
20 Selection and Training, App. E p. 35.
21 4th Report of CSC, p. xxiii.
22 *Economist*, 26 viii 1862.
23 CSC Reports, esp. 26th (1882).
24 Smyth, Sir John, VC: *Sandhurst*, London, 1961.
25 Burn, W. L.: *The Age of Equipose*, London, 1964, p. 224.
26 Trevelyan, *Purchase System*, pp. 24–5.

CHAPTER SEVEN

1 Selection and Training, C 1446/1876, pp. 24–30.
2 CSC Reports; Griffin in FR XVII (New Series) p. 522.
3 Thomson, p. 200.
4 CSC, 5th and 6th Reports; Thomson, p. 297; PSC, pp. 23–7.
5 Rennie, Sir John: *Autobiography*, London, 1875, p. 430.
6 Newsome, David: *Godliness and Good Learning*, London, 1961; PSC.
7 Taine, H.: *Notes on England*, ed. Edward Hyams, London, 1957, p. 104.
8 Johnston, 2 pp. 99–100.
9 SR, IV 8 viii 57 p. 127.
10 PSC, p. 223.
11 PSC, p. 253, pp. 81–2.
12 PSC, p. 23; App. F; Trollope in FR II p. 476.
13 *Contemporary Review* I Jan–Apr 1866, p. 86.
14 SR, IV 1 viii 57.
15 PSC, App. F; Answers p. 312.
16 PSC, Answers.
17 Thring, p. 103.
18 Thring, p. 101.
19 Selection and Training, C1446/1876, p. 10.
20 Armstrong, Rev. B. J.: *Armstrong's Norfolk Diary*, London, 1963, 28 viii 77.
21 Churchill, Sir Winston: *My Early Life*, Reprint Society Ed. p. 37.
22 Selection and Training, C1446/76, p. 10.
23 FR, XVII (New Series) p. 522.
24 FR, III (New Series) pp. 239–40, 242.
25 PSC, App. pp. 549, 534, 513.

NOTES

26 Fairbairn, Sir W.: *Useful Information for Engineers*, London, 1864 (4th Ed.), p. 11.
27 SEC, I.
28 SEC, VI pp. 626–7.
29 SEC, I pp. 82–3.
30 SEC, I pp. 16–18.
31 SEC, I pp. 80–1.
32 CR, I Jan–Apr 66 p. 89.

CHAPTER EIGHT

1 SCME.
2 Newman, pp. 224–6.
3 Thomson, p. 290.
4 Wilson and Reader, p. 4; Bentley, W. O.: *W O.*, London, 1958, p. 22; DNB.
5 Ferriday, Peter (Ed.): *Victorian Architecture*, London, 1963, p. 237.
6 Thomson, pp. 290, 301–2; Davenant, p. 140.
7 SR, IV 5 xii 57 p. 507.
8 ICC, Qq 1531, 1565, 1569.
9 Thomson, pp. 287–90; Davenant, p. 144.
10 Thomson, pp. 301–2.
11 Rennie, p. 430.
12 Census of England and Wales, 1911 X p. xxiii.
13 Lord Weir's papers.
14 DNB; Day-Lewis, Sean: *Bulleid, last Giant of Steam.*
15 SEC, VI p. 629.
16 Argles, Michael: *South Kensington to Robbins*, London, 1964, p. 24.
17 Rennie, p. 430.
18 Prebble, John: *The High Girders*, London, 1956.

CHAPTER NINE

1 Report of the Cambridge University Commission 1852, pp. 29, 25, 97, 92.
2 Report of the Oxford University Commission, 1852; CUC.
3 FR, XXXVII (New Series) p. 863; SEC, VI p. 633.
4 Newman, p. 129.
5 Seeley, J. R. (Ed.): *The Student's Guide to the University of Cambridge,* 2nd Ed. 1866, pp. 284–8.
6 Stedman, A. M. M.: *Oxford: its Life and Schools*, London, 1887, p. 306.
7 SEC, VI p. 633.

223

8 FR, III (New Series) 1 iii 68.
9 FR, XVII (New Series), p. 844.
✓ 10 Playfair, Lyon: *The Universities and Professional Education* in *Subjects of Social Welfare*, London, 1889.
11 FR, XXXVII (New Series) p. 864.
12 Thomson, p. 65.
13 Report of Dublin University Commission, Parl. Papers 1852–3 XLV, generally and p. 92.
14 SR, VI 18 ix 58.
15 Newman, p. 299.
16 FR, XXV (New Series) p. 47.
17 FR, XXV (New Series) p. 47 ff.
18 Report of Durham University Commission, Parl. Papers 1863, XVI p. 1.
19 DUC; Whiting, C. E.: *The University of Durham 1832–1932*, London, 1932, p. 104.
20 Reeks, p. 49.
21 Reeks, pp. 94–5.
22 Beer, J. J.: *The Emergence of the German Dye Industry*, Urbana, Ill., 1959, p. 59.
23 Reeks, p. 98; pp. 99–100.
24 Armytage, W. H. G.: *A Social History of Engineering*, London, 1961, pp. 234–7; Argles, pp. 22–5.
25 Stedman, p. 334. Ward, W. R.: *Victorian Oxford*, London, 1965, p. 249.
26 Brown, Richard: *A History of Accounting and Accountants*, Edinburgh, 1905, p. 328.
27 Reports from University Colleges, C 8984/1898.
28 17th Report CSC (1872), p. xxvi. Armytage, pp. 166, 235.
29 Armytage, pp. 234–7.
30 Reeks; Argles.
31 Armytage, pp. 234–7.
32 Reports from University Colleges.
33 Reeks, pp. 111–12, 123.
34 Feiling, Keith: *The Life of Neville Chamberlain*, London, 1946, pp. 11–12.

CHAPTER TEN

1 Newman, Chapter V; Ensor, R. C. K.: *England 1870–1914*, Oxford, 1936, pp. 16–19.
2 Census Report 1851, Population Tables II, p. lxxxvii.
3 Census of 1841 – Occupation Abstract.
4 *Contemporary Review*, VII, l xii 59, p. 9.

5 SR, X, 21 vii 60.
6 Thomson, pp. 16, 4.
7 CR, VII, p. 9.
8 Godlee Sir R. J.: *Lord Lister*, 3rd Edn., Oxford, 1924, p. 541.
9 FR, II (New Series), p. 169.
10 Escott, T. H. S.: *England: its People, Polity, and Pursuits*, New Edn., Oxford, 1885, p. 332.
11 Report of the Royal Commission on Secondary Education, 1895, pp. 14–15.
12 Johnston, 2 p. 148; Thomson, p. 96; SR, IV (1857) p. 507.
13 1871 Census, Report p. xli.
14 Anon (Sir George Stephen): *Adventures of an Attorney in search of Practice*, 2nd Edn., London, 1840, pp. 198–203.
15 FR II (New Series) p. 177n.
16 *Lancet*, 1870 II p. 229.
17 FR, II (New Series), p. 689.
18 Stacey, Nicholas A. H.: *English Accountancy 1800–1954*, London, 1954, p. 50
19 Brown; Anon. (Sir Russell Kettle): *Deloitte & Co. 1845–1956*, Oxford, 1958.
20 Brown, p. 318.
21 Anon.: *Adventures of an Attorney*, pp. 198–203.
22 *Deloitte & Co.*, pp. 17–22.
23 Carr-Saunders and Wilson, pp. 157, 177.
24 Carr-Saunders and Wilson; Millerson, Geoffrey: *The Qualifying Associations*, London, 1964.
25 Millerson, p. 223.
26 FR, XXXVII (New Series) p. 782.

CHAPTER ELEVEN

1 Mill, J. S.: *The Subjection of Women*, 2nd Edn., London, 1869, p. 17; Fawcett , M. G., in FR IV (New Series), p. 554.
2 FR, IV (New Series) p. 568.
3 SEC, I pp. 546–7.
4 SEC, I pp. 550–52.
5 SEC, I pp. 568, 569.
6 SEC, I pp. 299–302, 306–7.
7 Hughes, M. V.: *A London Family 1870–1900*, London, 1946, p. 179.
8 Anon.: *Adventures of an Attorney*, pp. 344–5.
9 FR, IV (New Series), pp. 554–68.
10 *Lancet*, 1855 I p. 251.
11 Newman, p. 300.

12 Manton, Jo: *Elizabeth Garrett Anderson*, London, 1965, Chapter Ten.
13 *Lancet*, 1870 II p. 63.
14 *Lancet*, 1870 II p. 828.
15 *Lancet*, 1870 II pp. 641–42.
16 *Lancet*, 1875 II p. 213.
17 *Lancet*, 1877 II p. 213.
18 Newman, p. 303.
19 Newman, p. 304; RC on Medical Acts 1882, para 67.
20 *Lancet*, 1882 I p. 998.
21 RC on Medical Acts, p. 402.
22 Escott, *England*, p. 299.
23 Hughes, Chapter VI, p. 235.

CHAPTER TWELVE

1 Escott, *England*, p. 555.
2 *Economic History Review*, Ser. 2 XII p. 98; XIV p. 122.
3 Escott, *England*, p. 554.
4 Escott, *England*, p. 558.
5 Seeley, *Student's Guide*, 3rd Edn., 1874, pp. 402–3.
6 *The Student's Handbook to the University and Colleges of Cambridge*, 5th Edn., Cambridge, 1906, p. 539.
7 SR, 17 vii 80 p. 70.
8 *Student's Handbook*, 1906, p. 534.
9 *Student's Handbook*, 1906, pp. 535–6.
10 Archer, R. L.: *Secondary Education in the Nineteenth Century*, Cambridge, 1921, pp. 268–9.
11 *Student's Handbook*, 1906, p. 465.
12 *Student's Handbook*, 1906, p. 465.
13 Trotter, L. J.: *A Leader of Light Horse: Hodson of Hodson's Horse*, London, 1901, Chapter II.
14 Churchill, *Early Life*, p. 43; 3rd Report on the Education of Officers, 1883.
15 Thomson, pp. 161–2.
16 *Lancet*, 1860 I p. 404.
17 *Lancet*, 1883 I p. 205; *The Practitioner*, Jan 1966 p. 155.
18 *The Practitioner*, May 1965 p. 687; Jan 1966 pp. 154–8.
19 Archer, p. 310.
20 Booth, C. E. (Ed.): *Life and Labour of the People in London* – 1st Series (Poverty) 3 Pt II, p. 260.
21 Escott, *England*, p. 298.

22 Mack, Edward C.: *Public Schools and British Opinion since 1860*, New York, 1941; Ogilvie, Vivian: *The English Public School*, London, 1957; Newsome, David: *Godliness and Good Learning*, London, 1961.

23 SEC, I App III; PSC, pp. 100, 260.

24 FR, XXXVII (New Series), p. 864.

25 *Student's Handbook*, 1906, p. 69.

26 Quoted, Johnston 2 p. 148.

27 Johnston, 1 p. 228.

28 Thomson, p. 169.

29 Escott, *England* p. 560.

30 *Lancet*, 1883 I p. 205; *Practitioner*, May 1965, p. 687.

31 Thomson, p. 98.

32 Thomson, p. 134.

33 Beeton, Mrs: *Mrs Beeton's Every Day Cookery and Housekeeping Book*, New Edn., London, n.d., p. xxxvi.

34 Various Authors: *Fifty Years*, London, 1932, p. 161.

35 *The Lesson* in *The Five Nations*.

36 *Architectural Review*, Vols. 13–16; Vol. 11 (1902).

37 *Architectural Review*, 13 p. 217.

BIBLIOGRAPHY

AUTHORITIES

ANON. (F. Davenant): *What should my Son be?* London, 1870.

ANON. (Sir Russell Kettle): *Deloitte & Co. 1845–1956.* Oxford University Press (privately printed), 1958.

ANON. (Sir George Stephen): *Adventures of an Attorney in Search of Practice or, a Delineation of Professional Life.* 2nd Edition, Saunders & Otley, London, 1840.

ARCHER, R. L. *Secondary Education in the Nineteenth Century.* Cambridge University Press, 1921.

ARGLES, MICHAEL. *South Kensington to Robbins,* an account of English technical and scientific education since 1851. Longmans, Green & Co., London, 1964.

ARMSTRONG, Rev. B. J. *Armstrong's Norfolk Diary.* Harrap, London, 1964.

ARMYTAGE, W. H. G. *A Social History of Engineering.* Faber & Faber, London, 1961.

ARNOLD, MATTHEW. *Report to the Schools Enquiry Commission* – Schools Enquiry Commission VI – *General Reports of Assistant Commissioners* pp. 449–712. H. M. Stationery Office, London, 1868.

ARNOLD, MATTHEW. *Culture and Anarchy.* Smith, Elder & Co., London, 1869.

BANKS, J. A. *Prosperity and Parenthood*: A Study of Family Planning among the Victorian Middle Classes. Routledge & Kegan Paul, London, 1954.

BAX, B. ANTHONY. *The English Parsonage.* John Murray, London, 1964.

BEER, J. J. *The Emergence of the German Dye Industry.* Urbana Ill., 1959.

BEETON, Mrs *Mrs Beeton's Every Day Cookery and Housekeeping Book.* New Edition, Ward, Lock & Co., London.

BENTLEY, W. O. *W. O.* The Autobiography of W. O. Bentley. London, 1958.

BESANT, Sir WALTER. *Fifty Years Ago.* Chatto & Windus, London, 1888.

BOOTH, C. E. (Ed.) *Life and Labour of the People in London*. Second Series: Industry, Vol. 4 – the Public Service and the Professional Classes. Macmillan & Co., London 1903–4.

BRODRICK, Hon. GEORGE C. *Political Studies*. London, 1879, containing *Promotion by Merit in Relation to Government and Education*, 1858.

BROWN, RICHARD. *A History of Accounting and Accountants*. Jack & Co. Edinburgh, 1905.

BURN, W. L. *The Age of Equipoise*. George Allen & Unwin, London, 1964.

BURSTALL, F. W. and BURTON, C. G. *Souvenir History . . . of the Mason Science College and of the University of Birmingham*. James Cond Ltd. Birmingham, 1930.

CARR-SAUNDERS, Sir A. and WILSON, P. A. *The Professions*. Oxford University Press, 1933.

CHADWICK, OWEN. *Victorian Miniature*. Hodder & Stoughton, London, 1960.

CHECKLAND, S. G. *The Rise of Industrial Society in England 1815–1885*. Longmans, Green & Co., London, 1964.

CHRISTIAN, E. B. V. *A Short History of Solicitors*. London, 1896.

CHURCHILL, Sir W. L. S. *My Early Life*. Macmillan & Co., London, 1930. The Reprint Society, 1944.

CLAPHAM, Sir JOHN. *Economic History of Modern Britain*. 3 vols. Cambridge University Press, 1932–8.

CLARK, G. KITSON. *The Making of Victorian England*. Methuen, London, 1962.

COBDEN, RICHARD. *Speeches on Questions of Public Policy*. Ed. John Bright and James E. Thorold Rogers. Macmillan & Co., London, 1878.

COOPER, BRANSBY BLAKE, FRS. *The Life of Sir Astley W. Cooper, Bart.* 2 vols., John W. Parker, London, 1843.

COPE, Sir ZACHARY. *The Royal College of Surgeons of England: a History*. Anthony Blond, London, 1959.

DAVENANT, F. *What Should my Son be?* London, 1870.

DAY-LEWIS, SEAN. *Bulleid, last Giant of Steam*. George Allen & Unwin, London, 1964.

DEVEY, JOSEPH. *The Life of Joseph Locke*. Richard Bentley, London, 1862.

DICTIONARY OF NATIONAL BIOGRAPHY.

DUCKHAM, B. F. *John Smeaton, the Father of English Civil Engineering*. History To-day XV3 (March, 1965).

EDGEWORTH, R. L. *Essays on Professional Education*. 2nd Edition, J. Johnston & Co., London, 1812.

ELIOT, GEORGE. *Scenes from Clerical Life* (1858), *The Mill on the Floss* (1860), *Middlemarch* (1871–2.)

ENSOR, Sir ROBERT: *England 1870–1914.* Oxford University Press, 1936.

ERICKSON, CHARLOTTE. *British Industrialists – Steel and Hosiery 1850–1950.* Cambridge University Press, 1959.

ERSKINE, D. (Ed.) *Augustus Hervey's Journal.* William Kimber, London, 1953.

ESCOTT, T. H. S. *England: its People, Polity and Pursuits.* New and revised Edition, Chapman & Hall, London, 1885.

ESCOTT, T. H. S. *Social Transformations of the Victorian Age.* Seeley & Co. Ltd, London, 1897.

FAIRBAIRN, WILLIAM. *Useful Information for Engineers.* 4th Edn. Longmans, Green & Co., London, 1864 (1st Edn., 1855).

FEILING, K. *The Life of Neville Chamberlain.* Macmillan & Co., London, 1946.

FERRIDAY, PETER (Ed.) *Victorian Architecture.* Jonathan Cape, London, 1963.

FRESHFIELD, EWIN (Ed.) *The Records of . . . the Law Society.* Incorporated Law Society, London, 1897.

GODLEE, Sir RICKMAN JOHN. *Lord Lister.* 3rd Edn. Revised. Oxford University Press, 1924.

HABER, L. F. *The Chemical Industry during the Nineteenth Century.* Oxford University Press, 1958.

HALDANE, J. W. C. *Civil and Mechanical Engineering popularly and socially considered.* E. F. & N. Spon, London, 1887.

HART, A. TINDAL, and CARPENTER, EDWARD. *The Nineteenth Century Country Parson* (circa 1832–1900). Shrewsbury, 1954.

HERVEY, AUGUSTUS. *Augustus Hervey's Journal.* Ed. David Erskine, William Kimber, London, 1953.

HODDER, EDWIN. *The Life of Samuel Morley.* Hodder & Stoughton, London, 1887.

HUGHES, M. VIVIAN. *A London Family 1870–1900.* Oxford University Press, 1946.

HYAMS, EDWARD (Ed.) *Taine's Notes on England.* Thames & Hudson, London, 1957.

JOHNSTON, W. *England as it is . . . in the middle of the Nineteenth Century.* 2 vols. John Murray, London, 1851.

KAYE, BARRINGTON. *The Development of the Architectural Profession in Britain.* Allen & Unwin, London, 1960.

KELSALL, R. K. *Higher Civil Servants in Britain: from 1870 to the Present Day.* Routledge and Kegan Paul, London, 1955.

KETTLE, Sir RUSSELL: *Deloitte & Co. 1845–1956.* Oxford University Press (privately printed), 1958.

KILVERT, REV. FRANCIS. *Kilvert's Diary 1870–79*. Ed. William Plomer. Jonathan Cape Paperback, JCP 22, London, 1964.

LATHAM, R. G. *A Dictionary of the English Language* founded on that of Dr Samuel Johnson, London, 1870.

LEWIS, MICHAEL. *The Navy in Transition*. A Social History 1814–64. Hodder & Stoughton, London, 1965.

LEWIS, ROY, and MAUDE, ANGUS. *Professional People*. Phoenix House, London, 1952.

MACK, EDWARD C. *Public Schools and British Opinion Since 1860*. New York, 1941.

MANTON, JO. *Elizabeth Garrett Anderson*. Methuen & Co., London, 1965.

MARSHALL, DOROTHY. *English People in the Eighteenth Century*. Longmans, Green & Co., London, 1956.

MEREDITH, GEORGE: *The Ordeal of Richard Feverel* (1859.)

MILL, J. S. *The Subjection of Women*. Longmans, Green & Co. London, 1869.

MILLERSON, GEOFFREY. *The Qualifying Associations*. Routledge & Kegan Paul, London, 1964.

MINGAY, G. E. *English Landed Society in the Eighteenth Century*. Routledge & Kegan Paul, London, 1963.

MOSES, ROBERT. *The Civil Service of Great Britain*. New York, 1914.

MUNK, WILLIAM. *The Life of Sir Henry Halford, Bart*. Longmans, Green & Co., London, 1895.

MUSGROVE, FRANK. *The Migratory Elite*. Heinemann, London, 1963.

MUSGROVE, FRANK. *Middle-class Education and Employment in the Nineteenth Century*. Economic History Review XII, p. 98.

NEWMAN, C. *The Evolution of Medical Education in the Nineteenth Century*. Oxford University Press, 1957.

NEWSOME, DAVID. *Godliness and Good Learning*. John Murray, London, 1961.

NOCK, O. S. *The Railway Engineers*. B. T. Batsford Ltd, London, 1955.

O'BRIEN, EDWARD. *The Lawyer*: His Character and Rule of Holy Life after the Manner of George Herbert's Country Parson. William Pickering, London, 1842.

OGILVIE, VIVIAN. *The English Public School*. B. T. Batsford Ltd, London, 1957.

PARKINSON, C. N. *Trade in the Eastern Seas 1793–1813*. Cambridge University Press, 1937.

PARLIAMENTARY PAPERS, &c:

Census Reports:

1841: Abstract of the Answers and Returns – Occupation Abstract MDCCCXLI. HMSO, London, 1844.

1851: Population Tables II. HMSO, 1854.

1861: Population Tables II.

1871: Population Abstracts.

1881: Census of England and Wales III.

1891: Census of England and Wales III.

1901: Census of England and Wales Summary Tables Cd 1523/ 1903.

1911: Census of England and Wales Summary Tables Cd 7929/ 1915.

Report of the Select Committee on Medical Education 1834.

Report of the Cambridge University Commission 1852.

Report of the Oxford University Commission 1852

Report of the Commission on the University of Dublin and Trinity College. Parl. Papers 1852–3 XLV.

Report on the Organization of the Permanent Civil Service 1854.

Papers relating to the Re-Organization of the Civil Service 1855.

Report of the Inns of Court Commission. Parl. Papers 1854–5 XVIII.

Report on the Purchase System. Parl. Papers 1857 (sess. 2) XVIII.

Reports of the Civil Service Commissioners, yearly from 1856.

First Report of the Council of Military Education. Parl. Papers 1857 (sess. 2) XXVII.

Report of Durham University Commission. Parl. Papers 1863 XVI.

Report of Scotch Universities Commission. Parl. Papers 1863 XVI.

Report of the Public Schools Commission. Parl. Papers 1864 XX (Vol. 1).

Army Medical Department – Statistical Sanitary and Medical Reports – Vol. VI 1864. HMSO, London, 1866.

Report of the Schools Enquiry Commission 1868.

Report of the R. C. on Military Education. Parl. Papers 1868–9 XXII.

Report of a Committee on the Education of Artillery Officers. C258/1871.

Report of the Committee on Civil Employment of R.E. Officers. C276/1871.

Civil Service Enquiry Commission (Playfair Commission):
First Report C1113/1875.
Second Report.

The Selection and Training of Candidates for the India Civil Service. C1446/1876.

Report of the R. C. on the Medical Acts C3259/1882.

Third Report on the Education of Officers. Parl. Papers 1883 XV.

Report of the R. C. on Secondary Education (Bryce Commission) 1895.

Reports from University Colleges. C8984/1898.

PEACOCK, GEORGE. *Life of Thomas Young MD, FRS*. London, 1855.

PERIODICALS:

The Architectural Review.

Contemporary Review.

The Economic History Review.

The Economist Newspaper.

Fortnightly Review.

The Lancet.

The Practitioner.

The Saturday Review.

PLAYFAIR, LYON: *Subjects of Social Welfare*, Cassell & Co., London, 1889, for *Universities in their Relation to Professional Education*.

PLOMER, WILLIAM (Ed.) *Kilvert's Diary*. Jonathan Cape Paperback JCP 22, London, 1964.

PREBBLE, JOHN. *The High Girders*. Secker & Warburg, London, 1956.

REEKS, MARGARET. *Register . . . and History of the Royal School of Mines*. Royal School of Mines (Old Students' Association), 1920.

RENNIE, Sir JOHN. *Autobiography*. E. & F. N. Spon, London, 1875.

ROBSON, R. *The Attorney in Eighteenth-Century England*. Cambridge University Press, 1959.

ROLT, L. T. C. *Isambard Kingdom Brunel*. London, 1957.

ROLT, L. T. C. *George and Robert Stephenson*. London, 1960.

SCHOOL REGISTERS:

Clifton College Register 1862 to 1947 ed. J. A. O. Muirhead, Bristol, 1948.

Marlborough College Register 1843–1933. 8th Edn. Ed. A. H. & Mrs D. E. Wall. Marlborough, 1936.

Merchant Tailors' School Register 1851–1920. Ed. E. P. Hart. At the School, 1923.

The Register of Mill Hill School 1807–1926. Ed. E. Hampden-Cook. Mill Hill, 1926.

Register of the Royal Grammar School, Newcastle-upon-Tyne 1545–1954. Ed. B. D. Stevens, LLB. Gateshead, 1955.

Sedbergh School Register, 1846–95. Ed. B. Wilson, Leeds, 1895.

Winchester College 1836–1906: A Register. Ed. J. B. Wainwright, Winchester, 1907.

SEELEY, J. R. (Ed.) *The Student's Guide to the University of Cambridge*. Cambridge University Press 1863, 1866, 1874.

SMILES, SAMUEL. *Lives of the Engineers*. 5 vols. John Murray, London, 1874–9.

SMILES, SAMUEL. (Ed.) *James Nasmyth, Engineer: an Autobiography*. John Murray, London, 1883: cheap reprint, 1912.

SMILES, SAMUEL. *Industrial Biography*. John Murray, London, 1863: Popular Edition, 1897.

SMITH, G. BARNETT. *The Life and Speeches of the Rt Hon John Bright MP*. 2 vols. Hodder & Stoughton, London, 1881.

SMYTH, Sir JOHN, VC. *Sandhurst*. The History of the RMA Woolwich and the RMC Sandhurst, 1741–1961. Weidenfeld & Nicolson, London, 1961.

STACEY, NICHOLAS A. H. *English Accountancy 1800–1954*. Gee, London, 1954.

STEDMAN, A. M. M. (Ed.) *Oxford: its Life and Schools*. Bell, London, 1887.

STEPHEN, Sir GEORGE. *Adventures of an Attorney in Search of Practice*. 2nd Edn. Saunders and Otley, London, 1840. (Published anonymously.)

TAINE, H. *Taine's Notes on England*. Ed. Edward Hyams. Thames & Hudson, London, 1957.

THOMAS, HUGH. *The Story of Sandhurst*. Hutchinson, London, 1961.

THOMPSON, F. M. L. *English Landed Society in the Nineteenth Century*. Routledge & Kegan Paul, London, 1963.

THOMSON, H. BYERLEY. *The Choice of a Profession*. Chapman & Hall, London, 1857.

THRING, EDWARD. *Education and School*. Macmillan & Co., London, 1864.

TRAILL, H. D. (Ed.) *Social England*. 6 vols. Cassell & Co., London, 1898.

TREVELYAN, Sir CHARLES: *The Purchase System in the British Army*. Longmans, Green & Co., London, 1867.

TREVELYAN, G. M. *English Social History*. Longmans, Green & Co., London, 1942.

TROLLOPE, ANTHONY. *An Autobiography*. Fontana Library (Collins), London, 1962.

TROLLOPE, ANTHONY. *Doctor Thorne* (1858) and other Barchester novels: *The Three Clerks* (1858).

TROTTER, L. J. *A Leader of Light Horse*. William Blackwood & Sons, London, 1901.

VARIOUS AUTHORS:

Great Public Schools. London, 1893.

The Student's Handbook to the University and Colleges of Cambridge. Cambridge University Press, annually.

Fifty Years. A Composite Picture of the Period 1882–1932 by 27 contributors to *The Times*. Thornton Butterworth, London, 1932.

VAUGHAN, PAUL. *Doctors' Commons*, Heinemann, London, 1959.

WARD, W. R. *Victorian Oxford*, Frank Cass, London, 1965.

WHEWELL, WILLIAM, DD. *Of a Liberal Education in General.* John W˙ Parker, London 2nd edn., 1850.

WHITING, C. E. *The University of Durham 1832–1932.* Sheldon Press, London, 1932.

WILLEY, BASIL. *Nineteenth-Century Studies.* Penguin Books, 1964.

WILSON, C. H. *England's Apprenticeship, 1603–1763.* Longmans, Green & Co., 1965.

WILSON, C. H. and READER, W. J. *Men and Machines*: a history of D. Napier & Sons, 1808–1958. Weidenfeld & Nicolson, London, 1958.

WINSTANLEY, D. A. *Later Victorian Cambridge.* Cambridge University Press, 1947.

WOODFORDE, JAMES. *The Diary of a Country Parson 1758–1802.* Ed. John Beresford. The World's Classics, 514. Oxford University Press, 1949.

WOODWARD, Sir LLEWELLYN. *The Age of Reform 1815–1870.* 2nd Edn. Oxford University Press, 1962.

ZINKIN, TAYA and MAURICE. *Britain and India: Requiem for Empire.* Chatto & Windus, London, 1964.

INDEX

Whitehurst, C. H. Q.C., 56
Whitworth, Joseph, engineer, 119,
125, 143
Wilde, Edward Archer, solicitor, 26
Williams (body-snatcher), 38
Wilson, B., 214
J. A., physician, 20
James, surgeon, 62
Winchester College, 156–7, 214
Winstanley, D. A., 186
Wolseley, F-M Lord, 98, 189
Wood, Sir Matthew, 3, 48
Woodforde, James, 13–14
Woodham-Smith, Mrs, 75
Woolwich, Royal Military Academy,
97–9, 102–3, 136, 190, 193
World War I, 9
Women accountants, 181
architects, 181
artists, 173, 181
Schools and colleges for, 171, 181
doctors, 173–6, 178–82
education of, 168–72
Edinburgh School of Medicine for,
179

engineers, 181
lawyers, 181
London School of Medicine for,
178
ministers of religion, 181
musicians, 173, 181
Women's rights campaign, 172
status, 3, 167–8, 170, 174–5, 182
Women medical students, 176–9
teachers, 167, 172, 181–2
writers, 167, 173
Wreathocke, William, 27
Writers, census figures of, 147, 153,
156, 208–10
clerical, 12
female, 167, 173
medical, 191
status of, 150–1

Yelloly, John, physician, 18
Yeomanry cavalry, 78
York, Duke of, 77
Yorkshire Law Society, 28
Science College, Leeds, 142
Young, Thomas, physician, 20